Microsoft®
PROJECT 4
For Windows™
Step by Step

Catapult

MicrosoftPress®

PUBLISHED BY
Microsoft Press
A Division of Microsoft Corporation
One Microsoft Way
Redmond, Washington 98052-6399

Library of Congress Cataloging-in-Publication Data
Microsoft project 4 for Windows step by step / Catapult, Inc.
     p.   cm.
   Includes index.
   ISBN 1-55615-595-6
   1. Microsoft Project for Windows.   2. Industrial project
management--Computer programs.   I. Catapult, Inc.
HD69.P75M5334   1994
658.4'04'02855369--dc20   94-14971
                                               CIP

Printed and bound in the United States of America.

6 7 8 9 10   MLML   9 8 7 6

Distributed to the book trade in Canada by Macmillan of Canada, a division of Canada
Publishing Corporation.

A CIP catalogue record for this book is available from the British Library.

Microsoft Press books are available through booksellers and distributors worldwide. For further
information about international editions, contact your local Microsoft Corporation office. Or
contact Microsoft Press International directly at fax (206) 936-7329.

LaserWriter is a registered trademark of Apple Computer, Inc. Genigraphics is a registered
trademark of Genigraphics Corporation. LaserJet is a registered trademark of Hewlett-Packard
Company. Microsoft Access and Visual Basic are registered trademarks and Windows is a
trademark of Microsoft Corporation.

For Catapult, Inc.
Managing Editor: Donald Elman
Writer: Marie L. Swanson
Project Editor: Ann T. Rosenthal
Production/Layout Editor: Jeanne K. Hunt

For Microsoft Press
Acquisitions Editor: Casey D. Doyle
Project Editor: Kerry A. Lehto

Catapult, Inc. & Microsoft Press

Microsoft Project 4 for Windows Step by Step has been created by the professional trainers and writers at Catapult, Inc., to the exacting standards you've come to expect from Microsoft Press. Together, we are pleased to present this self-paced training guide, which you can use individually or as part of a class.

Catapult, Inc. is a software training company with years of experience in PC and Macintosh instruction. Catapult's exclusive Performance-Based Training system is available in Catapult training centers across North America and at customer sites. Based on the principles of adult learning, Performance-Based Training ensures that students leave the classroom with confidence and the ability to apply skills to real-world scenarios. *Microsoft Project 4 for Windows Step by Step* incorporates Catapult's training expertise to ensure that you'll receive the maximum return on your training time. You'll focus on the skills that increase productivity the most while working at your own pace and convenience.

Microsoft Press is the independent—and independent-minded—book publishing division of Microsoft Corporation. The leading publisher of information on Microsoft software, Microsoft Press is dedicated to providing the highest quality end-user training, reference, and technical books that make using Microsoft software easier, more enjoyable, and more productive.

After you've used this *Step by Step* book, please fill out the feedback form in the back of the book and let us know what you think! Incorporating feedback from readers is a key component in continuously improving the books in the *Step by Step* series, and your help ensures that our materials remain as useful to you as possible.

WE'VE CHOSEN THIS SPECIAL LAY-FLAT BINDING

to make it easier for you to work through the step-by-step lessons while you're at your computer.

With little effort, you can make this book lie flat when you open it to any page. Simply press down on the inside (where the paper meets the binding) of any left-hand page, and the book will stay open to that page. You can open the book this way every time. The lay-flat binding will not weaken or crack over time.

It's tough, flexible, sturdy—and designed to last.

Contents

Part 1   Learning the Basics

Lesson 12   **Printing Views and Reports   167**

Part 3   Review & Practice   185

Part 4   Controlling the Project

Lesson 13   **Adjusting Project Costs   191**

Lesson 14   **Scheduling Task Constraints   201**

Lesson 15   Tracking Project Progress   211

Lesson 16   Working with the Critical Path   227

Part 4   Review & Practice   237

Part 5   Customizing Microsoft Project 4

Lesson 17   Customizing Tables, Views, and Reports   243

About This Book

Microsoft Project is a powerful project management application that you can use for planning, scheduling, and charting project information for project management, as well as for presenting project information to others. You can use *Microsoft Project Step by Step* as a tutorial to learn Microsoft Project to increase your productivity at your own pace and at your own convenience. You can also it use in a classroom setting.

By completing the lessons in this book, you will learn how to organize and create project plans using Microsoft Project. This book also shows you how to use the features in this powerful program to manage projects and communicate results.

You also get hands-on practice using the files on the accompanying disk. Instructions for copying the practice files to your computer hard disk are in "Getting Ready," the next section in this book.

Each lesson is estimated to take approximately 45 minutes or less and ends with a short exercise called "One Step Further."

Finding the Best Starting Point for You

This book is designed for new users learning Microsoft Project for the first time, and for experienced users who want to learn and use the new features in Microsoft Project version 4.0. Even if you are a novice user, *Microsoft Project Step by Step* will help you get the most out of Microsoft Project.

The modular design of this book offers you considerable flexibility in customizing your learning. To help you decide whether you need to work through a particular lesson, review the Lesson Summary at the end of the lesson. You can work through the lessons in any order, skip lessons, and repeat lessons later to brush up on certain skills. Each lesson builds on concepts presented in previous lessons, so you might want to back up if you find that you don't understand some concepts or terminology.

This book is divided into five major parts, each containing several related lessons. At the end of each part, you will find a Review & Practice section that gives you the opportunity to practice the skills you learned in that part. In this less-structured activity, you can test your knowledge and prepare for your own projects.

You start most lessons by opening a practice file from the PRACTICE directory in the Project home directory—the directory in which Microsoft Project is installed on your hard disk. You then save the practice file with a new name so that the original file remains unchanged while you work on your own version. This allows you, or another learner, to reuse the original files.

Use the following table to determine your best first step.

If you are	Follow these steps
New to a computer or graphical environment, such as Microsoft Windows	Read "Getting Ready," the next section in this book. Next, work through Lessons 1 and 2. Work through the other lessons in any order.
New to the mouse	Read "If You Are New to Using the Mouse" in "Getting Ready," the next section in this book. Follow the instructions for installing the practice files in "Getting Ready," the next section in this book. Next, work through Lessons 1 and 2. Work through the other lessons in any order.
Familiar with a graphical computer environment, but new to project management and Microsoft Project	Follow the instructions for installing the practice files in "Getting Ready," the next section in this book. Next, work through Lessons 1 and 2. Work through the other lessons in any order.
Familiar with a graphical computer environment and project management, but new to Microsoft Project	Follow the instructions for installing the practice files in "Getting Ready," the next section in this book. Next, work through Lesson 2. Work through the other lessons in any order.
An experienced Microsoft Project user	Read "Getting Ready," the next section in this book, for installing the practice files and for information about new features and techniques you can try. Read "New Features in Project 4.0," to learn where these new features are covered in this book. Read the summaries at the end of Lessons 2, 3, and 4 in Part 1. Note the new toolbar and buttons. Work through the other lessons in any order.

Using This Book as a Classroom Aid

If you're an instructor, you can use *Microsoft Project Step by Step* for teaching Microsoft Project to novice users and for teaching the new features of Microsoft Project version 4.0 to experienced users. You might want to select certain lessons that meet your students' needs and incorporate your own demonstrations into the lessons.

If you plan to teach the entire contents of this book, you should probably set aside two full days of classroom time to allow for discussion, questions, and any customized practice you might create.

Conventions Used in This Book

Before you start any of the lessons, it's important that you understand the terms and conventions used in this book.

Notational Conventions

- Characters you are to type appear in **bold**.
- Important terms and titles of books appear in *italic*.

Procedural Conventions

- Procedures you are to follow are given in numbered lists (1, 2, and so on). A triangular bullet (▶) indicates a procedure with only one step.
- The word *choose* is used for carrying out a command from either a menu or a command button.
- The word *select* is used for highlighting fields, text, and menu or command names, and for selecting options in a dialog box.

Mouse Conventions

- If you have a multiple-button mouse, Microsoft Project assumes that you have configured the left mouse button as the primary mouse button. Any procedure that requires you to click the secondary button will refer to it as the right mouse button.
- *Click* means to point to an object and then press and release the mouse button. For example, "Click the Cut button on the Standard toolbar."
- *Drag* means to press and hold the mouse button while you move the mouse. For example, "Drag from task 1 through task 8."
- *Double-click* means to rapidly press and release the mouse button twice. For example, "Double-click the Microsoft Project application icon to start Microsoft Project."

  You can adjust the mouse tracking speed and double-click speed in Control Panel. For more information, see your system documentation.

Keyboard Conventions

- Names of keys are in small capital letters—for example, TAB and SHIFT.
- You can choose commands with the keyboard. Press the ALT key to activate the menu bar, then press the keys for the underlined letters in the menu name and the command name. For some commands, you can press the key combination listed in the menu.
- A plus sign (+) between two key names means that you must press those keys at the same time. For example, "Press SHIFT+SPACEBAR" means that you hold down the SHIFT key while you press the SPACEBAR.

Other Features of This Book

Cut

Text in the left margin, like this, gives tips, useful information, or keyboard alternatives.

- You can perform many commands by clicking a button on a toolbar. When a procedure instructs you to click a button, a picture of the button appears in the left margin, as the Cut button does here.

- The "One Step Further" exercises at the end of the lesson are less structured, and present additional options or features related to the skills you learned in the lesson.

- At the end of each major part of the book, there is a Review & Practice section where you can practice the skills you learned in that part.

Cross-References to Microsoft Project Documentation

Microsoft Project Step by Step will help you learn about your Microsoft Project documentation. At the end of each lesson, you'll find references to the documentation that come with Microsoft Project. If you work through a lesson that teaches skills you use frequently and want to know more about the skills, check the chapter or online lesson referenced at the end of the lesson. You'll find cross-references to the following Microsoft Project documentation and features:

- *Microsoft Project User's Guide* provides comprehensive information and detailed instructions for using all of the functions and options in Microsoft Project. Use it whenever you want more information about a particular topic covered in a lesson.

- *Microsoft Project Help* provides online information about Microsoft Project features and gives instructions for performing specific tasks. You will learn more about Help in "Getting Ready," the next section in this book.

- The *Microsoft Project Quick Preview* is an online demonstration of many features in Microsoft Project, and it provides an animated overview for each of the main parts of the application. You will learn how to run Quick Preview in the "One Step Further" section of Lesson 1, "Understanding Project Management Basics."

Getting Ready

This section of the book prepares you for your first steps into the Microsoft Project environment. You will learn how to install the practice files on your computer hard disk and how to start both Microsoft Windows and Microsoft Project. You will also review some useful Microsoft Windows techniques, as well as terms and concepts that are important to understand as you learn to manage projects with Microsoft Project.

You will learn how to:

- Install the practice files onto your computer hard disk.
- Start Microsoft Windows.
- Start Microsoft Project.
- Use basic Windows features such as windows, menus, and dialog boxes in the Microsoft Project environment.
- Use Microsoft Project Help and Cue Cards.

Installing the Step by Step Practice Files

The disk attached to the inside back cover of this book contains practice project files that you'll use to perform the tasks you learn in each lesson in the book. For example, the lesson that teaches you how to enter project tasks instructs you to open one of the practice files—a partially completed project file—and add tasks to the project. Because the practice files simulate projects you'll encounter in a typical business setting, you can easily transfer what you learn from this book to your own work.

Copy the practice files onto your hard disk

You must have Microsoft Windows version 3.1 or later installed on your computer, in addition to Project 4, to use the practice files. Follow these steps to copy the practice files to you computer hard disk so that you can use them with the lessons.

1 If your computer isn't already on, turn it on now.

- If Microsoft Windows starts automatically when you turn on your computer, go to step 2.
- If MS-DOS starts (the blinking cursor on your screen appears immediately after C:\> or similar characters when you turn on your computer), type **win** and press ENTER to start Microsoft Windows.
- If a menu appears and Windows is one of the choices, select and start Windows.

2   Remove the disk from the package on the inside back cover of this book, and put the disk into drive A or drive B of your computer.

3   In the Program Manager window, select the File menu and then choose Run.

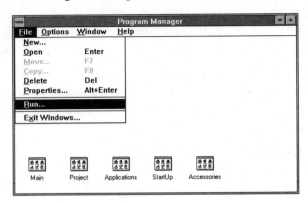

4   In the dialog box that appears, type **a:\install** (or **b:\install** if you put the disk in drive B), and choose the OK button.

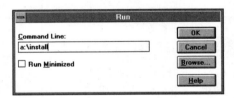

Do not type a space between the drive letter and the slash.

5   After the installation program begins, a new window appears, asking some questions. Simply follow the directions onscreen.

For best results in using the practice files with this book, accept the recommendations made by the installation program until it finishes.

6   Remove the disk from your computer and replace it in the package on the inside back cover of the book.

Because the practice files are now on your computer hard disk, you won't need the Practice Files disk again as you work through the lessons, unless you want to reinstall some or all of the practice files later.

The installation program copies the practice files from the floppy disk onto the hard disk in a subdirectory called PRACTICE of the Microsoft Project home directory (called WINPROJ or whatever it is named on your system). You'll need to remember the name of the drive and directory where the practice files are stored so that you can open a file for each lesson.

Using the Practice Files

The text in each lesson in this book explains when and how to use the practice file for that lesson. The installation doesn't create any icons—when it's time to use a practice file in a lesson, the book will list instructions for how to open the file from within Microsoft Project. Be sure to follow the directions for saving the files and giving them new names. Renaming the practice files allows you to use the renamed copy of a file to complete a lesson while leaving the original file intact. That way, if you want to start a lesson over or repeat a lesson later, you can reuse the original file.

At the beginning of each lesson in this book, you will open a new practice file, whose name corresponds to the lesson number. Be sure to close your current project file and open the correct one before you begin a new lesson. Using a practice file from another lesson might not give you the results you expect.

Lesson Background

For the lessons in this book, imagine that you are the operations manager for Victory Sports, Inc., a sporting goods manufacturer and distributor. The lease is up for your office and warehouse, and your company wants to move to a larger facility. You need to organize the move of 100 workers and a completely full warehouse. Throughout these lessons, you will use Microsoft Project to assist you in managing the project.

Types of Lesson Files

At the beginning of most lessons in this book, you will open a practice file whose name *begins* with a lesson number. Then you will save the project file with a different filename so that the original file remains unchanged. When you save or create a practice file, the filename *ends* with the lesson number. The following table describes the types of project filenames used in this book.

This type of filename	Is used in this way
*nn*LESSN.MPP	The form for filenames you open in each lesson, where the characters *nn* represent the two-digit number or code that corresponds to the lesson or appendix number. For example, 03LESSN.MPP is the practice file for Lesson 3, or XALESSN.MPP is the practice file for Appendix A. The extension MPP is used by Microsoft Project for all project files. If additional files are used in a lesson, the lesson number (*nn*) is followed by different letters, such as, 17MOVE.MPP.
LESSN*nn*.MPP	The form for filenames that you save in each lesson. For example, LESSN03.MPP is the filename you will use to save 03LESSN.MPP.
P*n*REVIEW.MPP	The form for filenames you open in each Review & Practice section. In this case, *n* is a single digit that represents the Review & Practice part number. For example, P3REVIEW.MPP is the practice file for Part 3 Review & Practice.
REVIEWP*n*.MPP	The form for filenames you save in each Review & Practice section. For example, REVIEWP3.MPP is the filename you will use to save P3REVIEW.MPP.

Starting Microsoft Windows and Microsoft Project

You start Microsoft Project from within Microsoft Windows. If Microsoft Windows is not already running, you need to start Windows first.

Start Microsoft Windows from the MS-DOS command prompt

1   At the command prompt, type **win**

2   Press ENTER.

After the initial startup, you will see the Program Manager window. You can start all of your applications, including Microsoft Project, from Program Manager.

When Windows is active, everything on your screen is displayed in a *window*. You can adjust each window to the size you want and you can move windows anywhere you want on the desktop. You can have multiple windows open at the same time to compare and share information easily.

Start Microsoft Project from Program Manager

Double-clicking the Microsoft Project group icon opens the Microsoft Project program group window. This window contains the icons for Microsoft Project and its related applications.

Microsoft Office

1   Double-click the Microsoft Office group icon.

The Microsoft Office program group opens.

Microsoft Project

2   Double-click the Microsoft Project application icon.

The Microsoft Project application window opens and the Welcome dialog box appears. From this dialog box, you have several options about what you can do next.

Note   If this is the first time you are running Microsoft Project, you see a Planning Wizard message. Choose the OK button to continue.

---

3   In the Welcome dialog box, choose the OK button.

The dialog box closes.

4   If you see the Tip Of The Day dialog box, read the tip and then choose the OK button.

The dialog box closes, and you see a blank project window.

5   If the project window is not already maximized, click the maximize button in the upper right-hand corner of the title bar.

Note   You can customize what appears when you open Microsoft Project. If you do not see the Welcome dialog box, it means someone has disabled this feature. If you want to see this dialog box each time you open Microsoft Project, you can choose Options from the Tools menu. Click the General tab and select the Show Welcome Dialog On Startup check box. Then choose the OK button to close the Options dialog box. The next time you open Microsoft Project, the Welcome dialog box will appear.

If You Are New to Microsoft Windows

Microsoft Windows is an easy-to-use work environment that helps you handle virtually all of the daily work that you perform with your computer. Microsoft Windows also provides a common basis among many applications—both in the way they share data and in the way you use them.

Using Windows-Based Applications

Once you become familiar with the basic operation of Microsoft Windows, you can apply these skills to learn and use Microsoft Project, as well as many other types of Windows-based applications.

The project window in Microsoft Project looks like the following illustration.

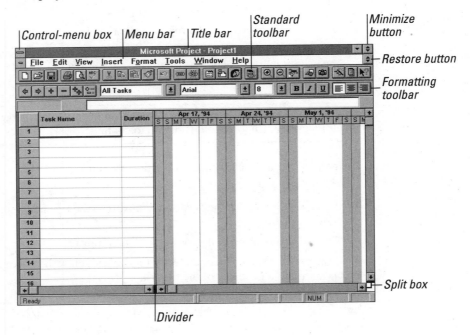

You can scroll, move, split, and close a window by using the mouse.

To	Do this
Scroll through a window (to see another part of the project)	Click the scroll bars and arrows or drag the scroll box.
Change the size of a window	Drag any of the window edges or corners.
Enlarge a window to fill the screen	Double-click the title bar or click the Maximize button.
Restore a window to its previous size	Click the Restore button.
Move a window	Drag the title bar.

To	Do this
Split a window	Drag the split box on the scroll bar to where you want the split. You can also double-click the split box to automatically split the window in half.
Close a window	Double-click the Control-menu box.

If You are New to Using the Mouse

Toolbars, shortcut menus, and many other features of Microsoft Project were designed for working with the mouse. Although you can use the keyboard for most actions in Microsoft Project, many of these actions are easier to do with the mouse.

Mouse Pointers

The mouse controls a pointer on the screen. You move the pointer by sliding the mouse over a flat surface in the direction you want the pointer to move. If you run out of room to move the mouse, lift it up and put it down again. The pointer moves only when the mouse is touching the flat surface.

Moving the mouse pointer across the screen does not affect the information in the project; the pointer simply indicates a location on the screen. When you press the mouse button, something happens at the location of the pointer.

When the mouse pointer passes over different parts of the Microsoft Project window, it changes shape, indicating what it will do at that point. The following mouse pointers are examples of those you will see as you work in this book.

This pointer	Appears when you
$\k$	Point to the menu bar, toolbars, buttons, the title bar, the scroll bars, and the graphical areas of a chart.
$\Leftrightarrow$	Point to a column heading boundary or the divider between different parts of a view.
$\Updownarrow$	Point to a split box on the scroll bar to split a window horizontally.
$\k?$	Point to an item in the window after clicking the Help button on the Standard toolbar.
I	Point in a text box, or any area where you can enter characters from the keyboard.
$\oplus$	Position the pointer in the task list area.

Using the Mouse

You will use four basic mouse actions throughout the lessons in this book.

Pointing. Moving the mouse to place the pointer on an item is called *pointing*.

Clicking. Pointing to an item on your screen and then quickly pressing and releasing the mouse button is called *clicking*. You select items on the screen and move around in a document by clicking. Occasionally there are operations you perform with the right mouse button, but unless you are instructed otherwise, click with the left mouse button.

Double-clicking. Pointing to an item and then quickly pressing and releasing the mouse button twice is called *double-clicking*. This is a convenient shortcut for many tasks in Microsoft Project. Whenever you are unsure of the command to use for an operation, try double-clicking the item you want to affect. This often displays a dialog box in which you can make changes to the item you double-clicked.

Dragging. Holding down the mouse button as you move the pointer is called *dragging*. You can use this technique to select data and drag to move and copy text.

Try the mouse

Take a moment to test drive the mouse. You can slide the mouse so that the pointer moves around the Microsoft Project application window.

1   Slide the mouse until the pointer is over the menus and tools at the top of the screen.

   The pointer is a left-pointing arrow.

2   Slide the mouse pointer around the document window, the large open area in the center of the screen.

   The document window is the area in which you work with the text on a project. The pointer looks like a large plus sign.

3   Slide the mouse pointer over the entry bar, above the project.

   The pointer looks like an I-beam.

4   Position the pointer anywhere in the Task Name column and click the right mouse button.

You can explore other shortcut menus by clicking the right mouse button on different parts of the application window.

   A shortcut menu of commands appears, as shown in the following illustration.

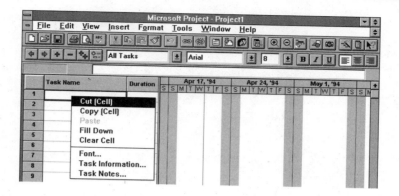

Clicking the right mouse button displays a shortcut menu of commands that are available in the area you clicked. The list of commands on a shortcut menu depends on the position of the pointer when you clicked the right mouse button.

5 Click the left mouse button anywhere outside of the menu.

Clicking outside of a menu closes it. You can also press ESC to close a menu.

Working with Microsoft Project

When you start Microsoft Project, it opens a new project file called Project1. The next project you create is called Project2, and so on. You can rename a project when you save it. Each project is displayed in a separate window.

Menu names appear in the *menu bar*, across the top of the screen. A list of related commands appears when you click on a menu name in the menu bar. The rows of buttons below the menu bar are called *toolbars*. Clicking buttons on a toolbar is a fast way to perform the commands you are likely to use most often. You will learn more about toolbars later in this section.

Using Menus

To choose a command, you click the menu name and then you click the command on the list. Some commands have a *shortcut key* combination shown to the right of the command name. Once you are familiar with the menus and commands, you might prefer to use these shortcut keys to save time if your hands are already at the keyboard.

When a command name appears dimmed, it doesn't apply to your current situation, or it is unavailable. For example, the Paste command on the Edit menu appears dimmed if the Copy or Cut command has not been used first.

To close a menu without choosing a command, click the menu name again or click anywhere outside of the menu. You can also press ESC to close a menu.

Open the Edit menu

1 Click <u>E</u>dit in the menu bar.

The list of commands looks like the following illustration.

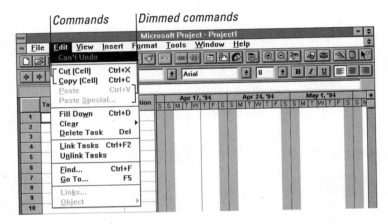

If you prefer to use the keyboard to make menu selections, press ALT and type the underlined character in the menu item and then in the command. The characters you type are also underlined in these instructions for your convenience.

2 Click the menu name to close the menu.

The menu closes.

Change the active view

When a command name displays a mark to its left, the command is already in effect. For example, when you open the View menu, a mark appears next to the name of the active view. With Microsoft Project, you can look at the same information in a variety of views.

1 Click <u>V</u>iew in the menu bar.

The list of commands looks like the following illustration. Notice the mark in front of the Gantt Chart command. This mark identifies the active view.

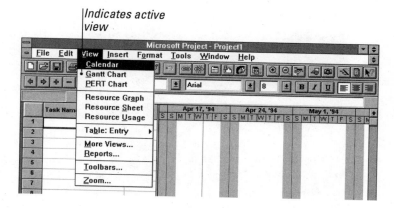

Indicates active view

2 Choose Calendar.

The view changes to the Calendar view. You will learn more about views in Lesson 2, "Learning Microsoft Project Basics." Notice the mark in front of the Calendar command, reflecting the new active view.

Note Changing views can also determine which commands are available on some menus. For example, in the Gantt Chart view, the Edit menu contains the Delete Task command. In the Resource Sheet view, the Edit menu contains the Delete Resource command.

---

3 From the View menu, choose Gantt Chart.

You return to the default Gantt Chart view. From this point forward in this book, the instructions for clicking a menu and choosing a command will be combined into a single step. This convention allows you to work through the steps more quickly.

Using Dialog Boxes

When you choose a command name that is followed by an ellipsis (...), Microsoft Project displays a dialog box in which you can provide more information about how the command should be carried out. Dialog boxes also appear when you double-click parts of the application window.

Dialog boxes consist of a number of standard features identified in the following illustration.

List boxes   *Tabs*

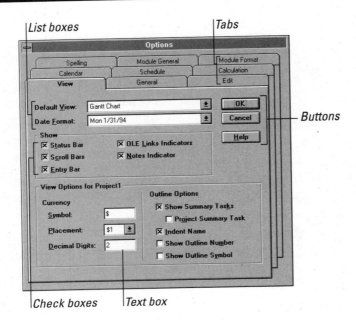

Buttons

Check boxes   *Text box*

To move around in a dialog box, click the item you want. You can also hold down ALT as you press the underlined letter. Or, you can press TAB to move between items.

After you enter information or make selections in the dialog box, choose the OK button or press ENTER to carry out the command. Click the Cancel button or press ESC to close a dialog box and cancel an entry.

Display the Options dialog box with a command

Some dialog boxes provide several categories of options displayed on separate tabs. Click the top of an obscured tab to bring it forward and display additional options in the dialog box.

1   From the Tools menu, choose Options.

The Options dialog box appears. In this dialog box you can specify the options and features you want for many categories of Microsoft Project commands.

2   Click the General tab (if it is not already displayed in the dialog box).

The options for general use of Microsoft Project appear.

3   Select the Show Tips At Startup check box to place an x in the box.

With the Show Tips At Startup option enabled you will see a Tip Of The Day dialog box the next time you start Microsoft Project. The Tip Of The Day dialog box displays useful tips and shortcuts for using Microsoft Project.

If the check box is already disabled, skip step 4.

4 Click the Show Welcome Dialog On Startup box to remove the x.

With the Show Welcome Dialog On Startup option disabled, you will not see the Welcome dialog box the next time you start Microsoft Project.

5 Choose the OK button to close the dialog box.

The dialog box closes and you return to the application window.

Open and close the Bar Styles dialog box

Although you can open dialog boxes by choosing commands from a menu, double-clicking offers an excellent shortcut. For example, if you want to change the appearance of a Gantt Chart (the right half of the project window), and you cannot recall the command you need, double-click the Gantt Chart to display the Bar Styles dialog box.

1 Double-click anywhere on the Gantt Chart.

Microsoft Project displays the Bar Styles dialog box. In this dialog box, you can adjust the appearance of bars and text in a Gantt Chart.

2 Choose the Cancel button to close the dialog box.

The dialog box closes and you return to the application window.

Using Toolbars

The first row of buttons below the menu bar is the *Standard toolbar*. It contains buttons that represent the commands for performing basic operations for working with a project plan, such as opening, closing, and printing. The following illustration identifies the buttons on the Standard toolbar.

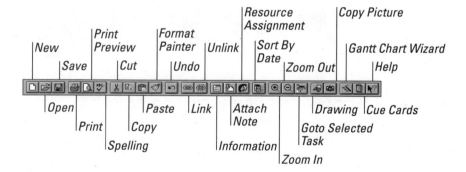

The second row of buttons is the Formatting toolbar. It contains buttons that represent the commands that affect the appearance of the project. The following illustration identifies the buttons on the Formatting toolbar.

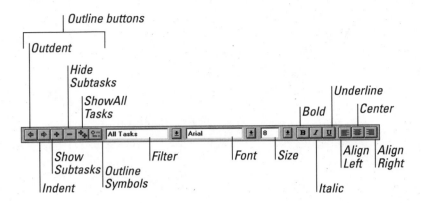

It is generally much faster to click a button on the toolbar. When you click a button on a toolbar, Microsoft Project carries out the corresponding command using the command's default options. Use the command from the menu if you want to specify different options for carrying out the command. The instructions in this book emphasize using the toolbar for almost all Microsoft Project operations.

Take a quick guided tour of the Standard toolbar

Take a moment to get acquainted with the buttons on the Standard toolbar. If you accidentally click a button, you can press the ESC key or click the Undo button on the Standard toolbar.

▶ Move the pointer over a button, and wait.

After a moment, the name of the button appears.

If you do not see the button name, from the View menu, choose Toolbars. Click the Show Tool Tips check box.

Displaying Alternative Toolbars

There are other toolbars you can display in addition to the Standard and Formatting toolbars. For example, you can display the Tracking toolbar when you are working extensively with project tracking-related commands.

Display and hide the Tracking toolbar

You can control the display of alternative toolbars from the Toolbars dialog box. You can also hide toolbars you no longer want displayed, giving you more space in the application window for your project.

You can also click the right mouse button while pointing to a toolbar. This displays a shortcut menu of toolbars you can display or hide.

1 From the <u>V</u>iew menu, choose <u>T</u>oolbars.

The Toolbars dialog box appears as shown in the following illustration.

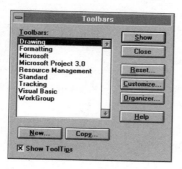

2 In the Toolbars list, select Tracking.

This selection displays the toolbar containing the buttons for tracking-related commands.

3 Click Show and then click Close.

The dialog box closes and the Tracking toolbar appears in the application window.

Tip   If the toolbar appears to "float" above the application window, you can move the toolbar by dragging its title bar and change the toolbar size by dragging its border. You can also double-click a toolbar title bar to "dock" the toolbar under the other toolbars. By double-clicking a toolbar that is already docked, you can display a floating toolbar.

---

4 Click any toolbar with the right mouse button.

The Toolbars shortcut menu appears.

5 Choose Tracking.

The Tracking toolbar is no longer displayed.

Using Wizards

Wizards (a new feature in Microsoft Project version 4.0) are intelligent assistants that monitor how you use Microsoft Project and keep track of the decisions you make. Various wizards will be used or described in appropriate lessons of this book. The PlanningWizard, for example, helps you complete tasks by asking questions at key points in the project. It also makes suggestions for shortcuts to help you work more effectively. Another wizard, called the GanttChartWizard, helps you focus on key information in a Gantt Chart by adjusting the formatting of the Gantt Chart based on your answers to questions posed by the wizard.

Locating Information in Help

With online Help in Microsoft Project, there are several ways you can get more information about using a feature. When you want general information, you can choose Contents from the Help menu. This Help window works like a table of contents to give you access to the entire online help system. When you want to look up information about a specific topic, you can use the Search command. In addition, when you are in a dialog box, you can press the F1 key to see information about the currently open dialog box. Another way to get help in Microsoft Project is with Cue Cards. Cue Cards provide step-by-step instructions that appear alongside your project as you learn a new technique or procedure.

Search for a topic in Help

You can quickly search the online Help topics for the information that you need. Once you display a topic, you can click phrases that have solid underlines to jump to related topics. You can click a button to retrace your path through Help, backtracking through the topics.

1 Press the F1 key.

Pressing F1 (when you are not in a dialog box) displays the Help window. This is the same as choosing Contents from the Help menu.

You can click any of the underlined topics and browse for information, but it's often faster to have Microsoft Project search for what you need.

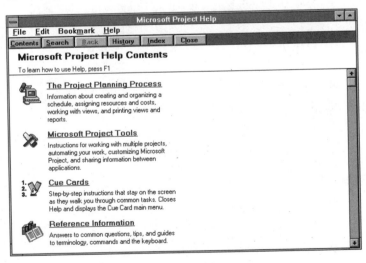

2   Click the Search button at the top of the Help window.

Clicking the Search button is the same as choosing Search from the Help menu. This help window works like an index in which you enter a word or phrase, and then you select from a list of related topics that you want to see.

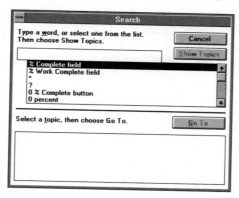

3   Type **schedules** but do not press ENTER.

As you type, Microsoft Project searches for terms containing the word "schedule," and displays those terms in the middle box as shown in the following illustration.

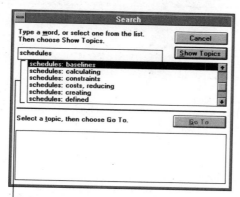

Related terms

In the middle box, the term "schedules: baseline" is selected.

4   Select the term "schedules: creating."

5   Click the Show Topics button to show a list of topics related to the term "schedules: creating."

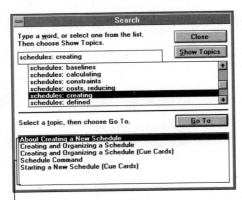

*Schedule-related
Help topics*

6   In the list of related topics, select "About Creating a New Schedule," and then click the Go To button.

Information appears about creating a schedule.

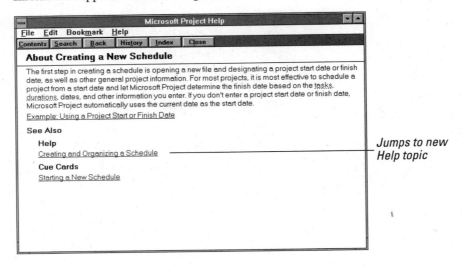

*Jumps to new
Help topic*

Online Help information appears in its own window. If you click in the application window, the Help window is covered by the Microsoft Project application window. To display the Help topic window again, hold down the ALT key, and then press and release the TAB key until you see the box for the Microsoft Project Help topic. When you see the Help topic box, release the ALT key to re-display the Help topic window.

Tip   To display the Help topic window on top of the application window, even as you work in the project, you can choose Always On Top from the Help menu in the Help window. The Help topic window will stay on top until you choose this command again or you close the Help window. Because you can size and move windows, you can display step-by-step instructions as you work in a project or a dialog box.

Display a definition

To get a definition of a word or term, you can click any text that is marked with a dotted underline. For example, you can get a definition of the words "tasks" and "durations" in this Help window.

1   Click the word "tasks" that is underlined with a dotted line.

When you point to an underlined word, the pointer changes to a hand with the index finger extended. A pop-up window displays a brief definition of this word.

2   After you finish reading the definition, click the pop-up window to close it.

Read an example

For more information about a topic, you can display an example or view Help information for a related topic by clicking any underlined term or phrase. For example, from this Help window you can read an example about using start and finish dates, or you can display the topic window for creating a schedule.

▶   Click the underlined phrase "Example: Using a Project Start or Finish Date."

An example appears. Take a moment to scan the topic, reading any definitions.

Return to the previous topic

You can easily backtrack through the Help topics you've displayed if you want to recall previous topics.

1   Click the Back button at the top of the Help window.

The previous topic appears.

2   Double-click the Control-menu box to close the Help topic window.

The Help topic window closes and you return to the application window.

Get Help about dialog box options

F1 is the Help key.

When you are working in a dialog box, you can read about the options by pressing the F1 key or by clicking the Help button. Start this step by first opening the Font dialog box.

1   From the Format menu, choose Font.

The Font dialog box appears.

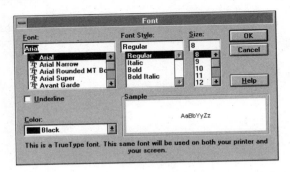

2 With the Font dialog box open, press the F1 key.

A Help window appears that describes the font command and the dialog box options.

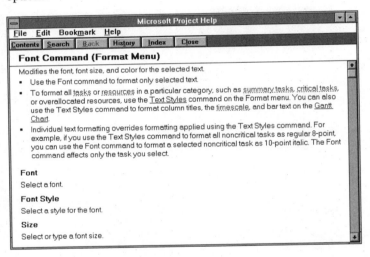

3 Double-click the Control-menu box to close the Help topic window.

The Help topic window closes and you return to the Font dialog box.

4 Click Cancel to close the dialog box.

Get information about a command

The Microsoft Project online Help contains a description of every command. If you are unsure of how to use a specific command, you can read about a command before you actually use it. Use the following procedure to learn about the Zoom command.

1 On the Standard toolbar, click the Help button.

Help

The Help button adds a question mark to the mouse pointer, indicating that you will choose a command for information only.

Tip   You can also press SHIFT+F1 to display the Help pointer.

2   From the View menu, choose Zoom.

A Help window appears that describes the Zoom command and shortcuts or options related to that command.

3   Click the down scroll arrow in the Help window to read more about the Zoom command.

4   When you finish reading about the command, double-click the Control-menu box.

If you accidentally choose the OK button in the dialog box, you can reverse the action by clicking the Undo button on the Standard toolbar.

Undo

Using Cue Cards

Another way you can get assistance as you learn to use Microsoft Project is by using Cue Cards. Like online Help topics, Cue Cards provide instructions for learning a new technique or completing a procedure. However, when you are unsure of which topics to look up or where to start, Cue Cards offer a more structured way to learn each step in a process.

Cue Cards typically give you the option to display step-by-step instructions, an illustration that provides an overview of the topic, or a useful tip. Choose the method that best suits the way you like to learn. Cue Cards also remain on top of the project window automatically, so that you can work in your project at the same time you follow the instructions.

Many Help topics provide the ability to jump directly to a specific Cue Card.

Cue Cards

Display Cue Cards for scheduling a project

You can display a menu of Cue Card topics by clicking the Cue Cards button on the Standard toolbar or by choosing the Cue Cards command from the Help menu.

1   On the Standard toolbar, click the Cue Cards button.

The Cue Cards window displays a menu of procedures related to the project planning process. By scanning this menu, you can quickly locate the part of the planning process for which you need information.

2   Click the button labeled "Create and organize a schedule."

Next you see a list of procedures related to creating and organizing a schedule.

3   Click the button labeled "Start a new schedule."

A Cue Card containing step-by-step instructions for starting a new project appears. Below the steps are buttons for getting background information and a tip related to starting a project.

4   Click the button labeled "Learn about setting the project start date."

You see a large Cue Card that illustrates the first step in starting a project.

5 Click the Next button in the lower-right corner.

Next, the Cue Card illustrates the concept of task durations, a critical part of planning a project. You will learn more about task durations in the next lesson.

6 Click the Next button.

Next, the Cue Card illustrates the concept of task relationships, another important element in scheduling a project.

7 Click the Next button.

You return to the Cue Card for starting a new schedule.

8 Click the button labeled "I've finished entering a project start or finish date."

You might need to scroll to see the last button on the Cue Card. By clicking the last button in each list of topics, you can return to the previous menu. Because you have finished using the Cue Cards for now, you can close the Cue Card window without returning to each list.

9 Double-click the Control-menu box on the Cue Cards window to close it.

Quitting Microsoft Project and Windows

After you have finished working in a project file, you close the file by double-clicking the Control-menu box for the project window. It is located next to the File menu in the menu bar. You can open another file if you wish or you can leave the Microsoft Project application. If you would like to quit Microsoft Project, follow these steps to close the file and exit the application at the same time.

Quit Microsoft Project

1 Hold down the ALT key and press F4.

2 If you see a message box asking whether you want to save changes, choose the No button.

If you have just quit Microsoft Project and would like to quit Windows, here is a simple way to exit from Windows.

Quit Microsoft Windows

1 Hold down the ALT key and press F4.

2 When you see a message box, "This will end your Windows session," press ENTER.

New Features in Project 4

If you are familiar with the previous version of Microsoft Project, you will notice some significant changes in how you use version 4. Although many features are the same, the enhancements in the new version are the result of a lot of research and testing. These enhancements are designed to make Microsoft Project easier to learn and use, even if you are new to project management.

The following table identifies the new features related to each topic in this book. Even if you are already familiar with Microsoft Project, focusing on these topics will help get you up to speed quickly.

To learn how to	See
Use Cue Cards and view helpful tips with the Tip Of The Day feature.	Getting Ready
Display context-sensitive menus with the right mouse button.	Getting Ready
Link tasks in a project by drawing a line connecting tasks in the default Gantt Chart view.	Lesson 4
Create recurring tasks that are placed at regular intervals in a schedule.	Lesson 5
Use the Resource Assignment dialog box that stays open on top of your project, so you can drag and drop a resource to its assigned task.	Lesson 6
Use the Change Working Time command to modify base and resource calendars for individual projects.	Lesson 7
Use the Resource Management toolbar for easy access to resource-related commands.	Lesson 9
Use new filtering options and apply filters with a button.	Lesson 10
Use new sorting options, and sort your project with a sort by date button.	Lesson 10
Use the GanttChartWizard to focus on specific information by customizing the formatting of your Gantt Chart view.	Lesson 12
Display project information in the new Calendar view.	Lesson 12

To learn how to	See
Use the Report Gallery to select from many different reports provided with Microsoft Project.	Lesson 12
Use the Tracking toolbar to get quick access to the commands you need when updating the project schedule.	Lesson 15
Work with the critical path and identify critical tasks.	Lesson 16
Customize tables, views, and reports in specific project files.	Lesson 17
Use the Organizer to copy customized features (filters, calendars, tables, views, reports, and macros) from one project file to another.	Lesson 17
Create your own toolbars to add to the GLOBAL.MPT file.	Lesson 18
Create a template that contains only the features you want in a project file.	Lesson 18
Use the sample templates provided with Project 4.	Appendix C

Understanding Project Management Basics

After you formulate your project goals, you need to determine what steps are required to meet your goals, and who will carry them out, taking into account personal schedules. And when they will start. And when they will finish. And how much it could cost. Of course, once the project is under way, you have to answer many questions about how the project is going. And adjust the schedule when the unexpected happens. And communicate with others so everyone works together. And...

As you can see, managing a project involves employing many different management and coordination activities. As you juggle all these tasks in a project, it can be a challenge to keep track of all aspects of the project and still keep everything moving forward.

The good news is that now you can take advantage of a lot of research and advances in the science of project management. Because Microsoft Project incorporates many proven project management techniques, you can benefit from these techniques without becoming a project management expert. With Microsoft Project as your project management resource, you can manage your projects with confidence and still have time to do your job.

You will learn how to:

- Use project management concepts and terms in Microsoft Project.
- Identify the phases of a project.
- Define project goals.

Estimated lesson time: 20 minutes

What is a Project?

A *project* is a well-defined sequence of events with a beginning and an end, directed toward achieving a clear goal, and conducted by people within such established parameters as time, cost, resources, and quality. A project is different from what you do every day, because a project goal is a specific, nonroutine event. Being nonroutine, a project requires some planning. How much planning you need depends on the complexity of the project. The more complex the project, the more you have to plan.

For example, if your job is to train employees on a regular basis to use a new spreadsheet application, for you the process requires little project management because the activities are familiar to you. On the other hand, it would be a significant project to develop a completely new course for a new financial reporting system. Similarly, if you spend your days developing financial reports, training even a few employees to use a new spreadsheet might require some project management on your part. Here are some other examples of projects for which using project management software can be a big help.

Category	Examples of projects
construction	building a house building a skyscraper developing a shopping mall
events planning	coordinating a retirement party moving to a new plant opening a new store putting on a marathon
product development	developing a new toy producing a software application creating a commercial frozen dinner entrée
publishing	producing a monthly newsletter writing a book creating an employee manual writing a software user guide publishing a magazine

As you can see, there are many different kinds of projects. These examples are only a few of the almost limitless endeavors that require planning.

Setting Project Goals

When you are about to begin a project, start your preparations by determining the goal of the project. Be as specific as you can. The following table provides some examples of how to make general goals more specific to facilitate better planning.

Too general	Better
Move company to new location	Move office and warehouse to new location by December 15.
Coordinate a retirement party for Julia Martinez	Host company-wide retirement party for company CEO to be held October 21.
Install new financial reporting system	Convert finance department and department heads to new financial reporting system by second quarter for pilot phase. Convert entire organization by year end.

Notice that the more specific goals clarify the scope or extent of the project, the people or groups affected, and the time frame.

Assess your project and define a goal

A little planning now (with old-fashioned pencil and paper) will help you when it comes time to use Microsoft Project for your own project. Complete the following steps for a project you are currently managing or preparing to manage. If you don't have a current project in mind, you could use "planning a vacation" as an example of a project.

1 Consider whether your project is complex and will require a great deal of planning. Does the project require many people, new procedures or technologies, tightly controlled costs, many variables, steps that depend on other steps, or several phases that need coordination?

Or will your project require less planning because it is relatively small? Does the project require only one or two people, familiar procedures, flexible budgets, or a simple sequence of events?

2 Write down the parameters or constraints within which you must work for your project to succeed.

Be sure to identify costs, deadlines, or other time constraints, and people whose approval is required.

3 Define a goal for your project.

Be sure that your goal includes the scope, who or how many are affected, and the time frame. Consider identifying criteria that will determine when the project is complete.

Developing the Parts of a Project

After defining your project goal, your next job is to develop the details of how and when you will get to your goal. A typical project is composed of these parts, or building blocks: tasks, milestones, and resources. Every sizable project can be broken down into a series of well-defined tasks. Each task takes a certain amount of time to complete. Some tasks can be done simultaneously, while other tasks must be carried out in sequence, one after the other. You might also want to define certain interim goals, or milestones, that can be used to mark the progress of your project before it is finished. Each task also requires the availability of appropriate resources—people, tools, or facilities.

Defining Project Tasks

The steps required to complete a project are called *tasks*. Tasks are performed in a sequence determined by the nature of the project. Some tasks occur sequentially, one after another, while other tasks can occur in parallel with one another. The following table identifies some typical tasks you might find in different kinds of projects.

Project category	Examples of tasks
construction	grade the site deliver roofing materials install security system pour asphalt for parking lot

Project category	Examples of tasks
events planning	hire caterers pack computers install shelving paint route markers
product development	test color fastness develop user specifications test market recipe
publishing	layout text and pictures write first draft review company policies define audience proofread articles

The simple list of tasks and the timetable for their completion is the project *schedule*. The schedule tells you when each task is scheduled to begin and end, and how long it will take. The amount of time it takes to complete a task is its *duration*. In Microsoft Project, a duration can be specified in weeks, days, hours, or minutes.

Identifying Project Milestones

A *milestone* represents an event or condition that marks the completion of a group of related tasks or the completion of a phase of the project. Milestones help you organize tasks into logical groups or sequences. They also help you note the progress of the project: As you complete a group of related tasks, you achieve a project milestone. When you achieve all the milestones in a project, the project is complete. The following table describes some sample milestones for different kinds of projects.

Project category	Examples of milestones
construction	site prepared roof complete security system enabled parking lot surfaced
events planning	contractors hired office equipment packed inventory stocked marathon route secured
product development	product testing complete specifications finalized recipe to manufacturing
publishing	camera-ready copy complete outline complete copy editing complete

In Microsoft Project, milestones, such as those listed above, usually have a duration of zero. This is because a milestone marks a specific point in the schedule that designates a phase of the project is complete.

Define project tasks and milestones in your own project

Identifying tasks in your own project is an important part of the planning process. Although Microsoft Project can be a big help in this part, it is a good idea to identify key tasks and milestones even before you begin entering information. To make it easier to rearrange tasks as the details of your project become clearer, consider writing each task on a separate sheet of paper, individual index cards, or on those popular, adhesive-backed sticky-notes.

1 List several important tasks for your project.

2 Determine which tasks (if any) depend on others. Can any tasks occur simultaneously? Do any tasks occur regularly throughout the project? Are there any constraints, such as specific dates when a task must begin or end?

3 Consider whether or not tasks are related in some way. Do they represent parts of the same process, or do they complete a phase in the project?

4 Identify points in the project that represent milestone tasks.

Assessing Project Resources

To accomplish a task you need *resources,* which can include people, equipment, and special facilities that are necessary to perform the task. The following table provides examples of different kinds of resources you might need to manage in the course of a project.

Resource type	Examples of resources
people	vice presidents
	carpenters
	caterers
	programmers
	writers
	names of specific individuals
equipment	computers
	printers
	copiers
	earth movers
	moving trucks
	fleet vehicles
facilities	conference rooms
	computer centers
	screening rooms
	warehouses

Because resources are seldom available 24 hours a day, seven days a week, you often need to consider resource availability. Be sure to take into account variables, such as vacation schedules, length of the work day, and access to buildings or equipment.

Identify resources in your own project

As you continue thinking about your own project, consider the resources you need to accomplish the tasks you've identified.

1 Identify the people or groups of people you need to perform specific tasks.

   To give you the most flexibility, use general titles (writer, analyst, carpenter, supervisor) rather than specific names (Mark, Maria, Smith).

2 Identify any equipment you need to accomplish tasks.

   Consider only equipment for which you must make special arrangements or which is in limited supply. For example, if everyone on your project team has a computer at their desk, you don't need to specify "computers" as an equipment resource. On the other hand, if your team must share computer equipment with others in your company, you should include "computers" in your project planning.

3 Identify any rooms or facilities that are required for your tasks.

   Be sure to consider space requirements for numbers of people or materials involved. Again, you only need to plan for facilities that are not continuously available or that require special arrangements.

Refining the Project Plan

Now that you have identified tasks, milestones, and resources, you need to refine your plan and fill in any missing information. Other information about project resources and tasks, such as the availability and cost of resources, scheduling constraints for tasks, or notes and background information, are also part of the *project plan*.

So far, you've answered the following questions about your project:

- What is the goal of your project?
- What steps are needed to accomplish your goal?
- Who or what is needed to perform each step?

Here are some additional questions to consider:

- How much will cost?
- What adjustments can be made to achieve the plan?
- How can project progress be presented to inform others?
- How will changes affect the plan?

Identify additional planning issues for your project

Now that you have gathered basic information about your project, think about other issues for which you are responsible in the project. Review the notes you made earlier on your initial project assessment while going through this exercise.

1 Does your project have a budget or other cost constraints that must be monitored?

For example, when producing a manual, are there specific costs (for freelance writers, for instance) that you cannot exceed?

2 Who needs to know about the status of your project? Would members of the project team benefit from to-do lists?

For instance, does a company vice-president need to know which tasks are on time and which are late for a software development project? Would the programmers on the development team better understand expectations if you provided them with a to-do list for programming tasks for the month?

3 How flexible are your deadlines? What are the consequences of missing a deadline?

For example, are your schedules allowed to slip without any negative consequences to the project, your company, or your career? Are there financial penalties for delays or rewards for being early?

How Microsoft Project Can Help

With Microsoft Project on your personal computer, it is easy to create and modify a set of tasks to meet your goals. Project management software is an invaluable tool for establishing an initial project plan. In addition, Microsoft Project quickly recalculates schedules and lets you see how changes in one part of the project can affect your overall plan. New tasks, obsolete tasks, interim dates that affect other tasks, or the irregular availability of a resource might otherwise slip by unnoticed; but with Microsoft Project you can keep it all under control.

In addition, keeping everyone informed by presenting only the information they need could be a lot of work without the aid of project management software like Microsoft Project. Some workers need to know what they are expected to do and when they are supposed to do it. Your management needs to be kept informed about the progress of the project. With Microsoft Project you can quickly get the reports and information you need.

Identifying Project Phases

The following illustration shows the different phases of a project and when they occur.

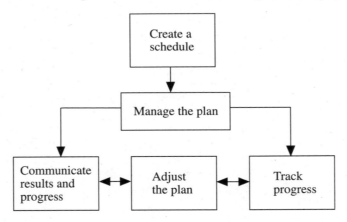

Microsoft Project can be used in each phase of a project. Use Microsoft Project to help you with the following tasks.

Create a realistic project schedule. When you first establish the tasks, schedules, and resources for a project, Microsoft Project helps by providing PlanningWizards, which keep track of the decisions and choices you make. Then, based on how you use Microsoft Project, the PlanningWizards offer suggestions and shortcuts to improve your effectiveness.

Microsoft Project also facilitates the "brainstorming" process that usually accompanies the creation of the project schedule. Features like drag and drop editing make it easy to move tasks around and enter new information quickly. For example, if after entering tasks you discover you need to add time for another site inspection, you can add the new task in the correct sequence in the project.

Manage the project and adjust to changes. Managing a project involves tracking the status of tasks and determining if tasks are proceeding as planned. If tasks fall behind schedule, you need to determine if you will still be able to meet your goals, and adjust the plan if necessary. In addition, you can always count on the unexpected in a project: A resource is suddenly unavailable; the budget is trimmed; new, faster equipment is available; another worker is hired. Because of the interdependent nature of a project, such changes usually affect not only a single task, but often the entire project.

Microsoft Project automatically adjusts the project schedule based on changes that you make. It even notifies you when resources are overcommitted or when a task cannot be completed in time for subsequent tasks to stay on schedule. In addition, with a variety of views and reports, you can quickly identify tasks that are late or over budget.

Communicate results and progress. By its very nature, a project typically involves more than one person. So everyone can work together effectively, it is important to communicate project schedules and expectations. By using a variety of reports (that you can customize), you can coordinate the project effectively. In addition, when your management requires information about the progress of the project, you want to be sure to present the project information concisely.

Use the reports available in Microsoft Project to present only the information you require. In addition, you can tailor each report to meet your communication needs or develop your own reports.

Using Project Management Tools

Two basic tools help you get the answers you need throughout the project. The Gantt Chart tells you when tasks are scheduled. The PERT Chart helps you understand the relationship between tasks and why they are scheduled the way they are. As your information requirements change in the course of a project, the tools you use will also change.

Using the Gantt Chart

One of the most familiar tools for visualizing progress in a project is the *Gantt Chart.* As the following illustration shows, the Gantt Chart uses horizontal bars, each representing a single task in the project.

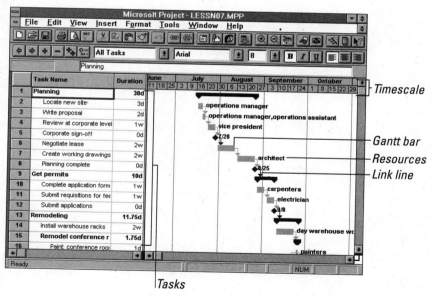

The bars are positioned across a period of time called a *timescale.* The relative length of an individual Gantt bar represents a task's duration, the length of time it takes to complete a task. A basic fixture in project management, the Gantt Chart is an excellent tool for quickly assessing the status of individual tasks over time in a project. Lines connecting individual bars in a Gantt Chart (a feature that is unique to Microsoft Project) reflect relationships between tasks—for example, if one task cannot start until another one is finished. The name of the resource assigned to a task also appears in the Gantt Chart.

Using the PERT Chart

When it is more important to focus on the relationships of the tasks in a project to one another (rather than on the schedule), the *PERT Chart* (also known as the network chart) can be more illustrative than the Gantt Chart. As shown in the following illustration, the PERT Chart displays the interdependencies among tasks.

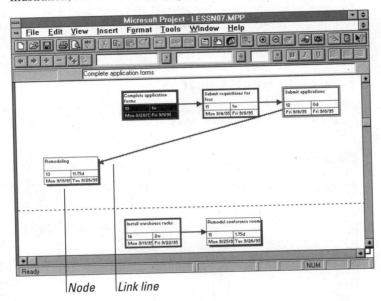

Each task is represented by a box, called a *node,* that contains basic information about the task. Tasks that depend on one another for completion or simply follow one another in a sequence of events are connected by lines. The PERT Chart gives you a graphical representation of how tasks are linked to each other in the project. In this book, detailed step-by-step exercises on using PERT Charts are in Appendix A.

Understanding Critical Tasks

A *critical task* is one that, if delayed, would also cause the completion of the project to be delayed. Critical tasks are said to be on the *critical path.* Changes to tasks not on the critical path will not have an effect on the completion date of the project. With Microsoft Project you can quickly identify the critical path, so you can focus on the tasks that require the closest management. Knowing which tasks are critical also helps you assess priorities, effectively assign resources, and determine the effect of changes on the project.

The *Critical Path Method* (CPM) is a standard project management technique for determining which tasks are critical. Based on a mathematical model that takes into account the relationships between tasks, their duration, and any constraints regarding the availability of resources, CPM is also used to schedule the start and finish dates for individual tasks. Historically, determining the critical path in a large or complicated project was a significant challenge for the project manager. Today, Microsoft Project brings the proven power of CPM to your project planning.

One Step Further

To review project management concepts and to begin getting acquainted with the capabilities of Microsoft Project, you can run the Microsoft Project Quick Preview. This animated overview shows you how Microsoft Project can be a valuable aid in project planning.

Microsoft Project

1   In Program Manager, double-click the Microsoft Project icon.

This starts the Microsoft Project program.

2   From the <u>H</u>elp menu, choose <u>Q</u>uick Preview.

3   Follow the instructions on the screen to view ways Microsoft Project 4 can help you plan each phase of a project.

As you read the information in the Quick Preview, think about which features can be helpful to you in your project.

When you have completed the lesson, you can go on to Lesson 2 in this book, "Learning Microsoft Project Basics."

If You Want to Quit Microsoft Project for Now

1   From the <u>F</u>ile menu, choose E<u>x</u>it.

2   Choose the No button if a message box asks whether you want to save your work.

Lesson Summary

To	Do this
Assess your project and set a project goal	Assess the complexity of your project and any constraints you must work within. Then formulate a goal that is specific: identify the project scope, who is affected, and the time frame.
Identify project tasks, milestones, and resources	List key tasks and durations. Note the relationship between tasks: which tasks depend on each other, which occur regularly, which are part of a larger category. Identify milestones and resources.

To	Do this
Refine the project plan	Review the requirements of the project: people needed; new procedures used. Identify project constraints: fixed deadlines and costs; anticipated changes. Who needs to know about the project and how is the information best presented?

For more information on	See in *Microsoft Project User's Guide*
Projects and project management	Chapter 2, "Managing Your Project with Microsoft Project"

Preview of the Next Lesson

In Lesson 2, you will learn about the Microsoft Project environment and the general steps for using the program to perform basic project management activities.

Learning Microsoft Project Basics

In this lesson, you'll get acquainted with the basics of using Microsoft Project by working in an existing project file. After you open and rename a practice project file, you'll see how Microsoft Project uses views to present the same project information in different ways. After moving around in the views and selecting project information, you'll learn how to supply general project information, such as when the project should start, so that Microsoft Project can schedule the project for you. In addition, you will edit task information in the schedule.

You will learn how to:

- Open and close a project file.
- Save a project file with a new name.
- Change the active view and move around within a view.
- Select information in the project.
- Use the Summary Information dialog box to schedule a project.
- Use the entry bar to edit task information.

Estimated lesson time: 35 minutes

Start Microsoft Project

If you see the Welcome dialog box, click the Close button to close it. If you see the Tip Of The Day dialog box, read the tip, and then click OK to close it.

If you quit Microsoft Project at the end of "Getting Ready," or if you are beginning with this lesson, start Microsoft Project now. For additional information about starting Microsoft Project, see "Starting Microsoft Project" in the "Getting Ready" section earlier in this book.

▶ Double-click the Microsoft Project icon.

The Gantt Chart view appears, ready for you to enter data. This view appears whenever you start a new project. You'll learn more about this and other views in this lesson.

Opening a Project File

A new, empty project window appears when you start Microsoft Project. If you already have a project file that you would like to work with, you can open that project file. To open an existing project file, you can choose the Open command from the File menu or you can click the Open button on the Standard toolbar.

Either technique displays the Open dialog box in which you specify the name of the file and where it's located. To help you explore Microsoft Project features, open a project file that already contains project information.

Open a project file

Open the project file called 02LESSN.MPP.

Open

If you do not see the PRACTICE directory, select a new drive (if necessary) and search first for the Project home directory, then search for the PRACTICE directory.

1   On the Standard toolbar, click the Open button.

Clicking the Open button is the same as choosing Open from the File menu.

2   In the Directories box, double-click the PRACTICE directory.

If the PRACTICE directory is on another drive, double-click the drive designation in the Drives box.

3   In the File Name box, select 02LESSN.MPP.

4   Choose the OK button.

5   After the project opens in the Gantt Chart, press ALT+HOME to move the timescale to the beginning of the project.

Saving a Project File

It's a good idea to save your work any time you have made important changes to the project. To store your work and changes in a project file, you have two options. You can use the Save command from the File menu, or you can click the Save button on the Standard toolbar.

You can use the Save As command (also on the File menu) to save a new version of the project file with a different name or to a different location. When you use the Save As command, Microsoft Project closes the original file, and the project file with the new name becomes the current file.

When you save a file, the PlanningWizard appears and asks if you want to save the project with a baseline. A *baseline* is a record or "snapshot" of the project at a specific point in the planning process or project. You will learn more about baselines later in this book, after you complete all your scheduling activities. For the lessons in Part 1 of this book, you will save your files without a baseline.

Save the file with a new name

The project practice file you opened contains some sample tasks that you might find in a project to move a company to a new location. Before you make any changes, save the project file with a new name so that you, or someone else, can reuse the original practice file.

1   From the File menu, choose Save As.

A PlanningWizard dialog box appears.

2   Click the second option button to save the project without a baseline.

3   Choose the OK button.

4   In the File Name box, type **lessn02.mpp**

The period and extension (.MPP) are optional; they are added automatically if you don't type them.

5   Choose the OK button.

Microsoft Project stores your project file on your hard disk with the filename LESSN02.MPP.

Displaying Project Information in Views

A *view* is one of several formats in which you can enter and display project information. The default view (the view you see when you first open Microsoft Project) is called the *Gantt Chart view*. This view includes the Gantt table on the left for quick entry of basic task information, and a bar chart—the Gantt chart—on the right.

The Gantt Chart view is just one of many ways in which you can examine project information. These views fall into three general categories: *sheet views, chart and graph views,* and *form views.* You can also display two views at one time, called a *combination view.* With Microsoft Project, you can even create your own custom views.

Throughout this book you'll have opportunities to work with a variety of views and learn about the important features of each. For now, here is a brief introduction of the different kinds of views you can use in Microsoft Project.

Sheet views display task or resource information in a rows-and-columns format, as in a spreadsheet. You can use sheet views to enter task or resource information. Use a sheet view when you want to see a lot of information at one time. The following illustration shows a Resource Sheet.

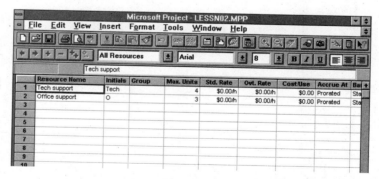

Chart and graph views provide graphical representations of project information. Use a chart or graph view when you need to present "the big picture" of the project plan to others. The following illustration shows a Resource Graph.

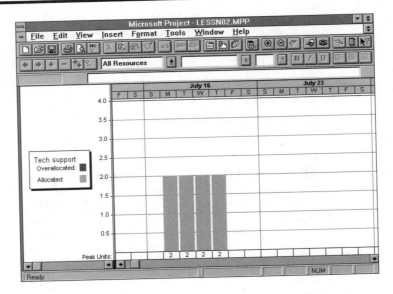

Form views display task or resource information in a format similar to that which you complete with pencil and paper. Forms contain the same information you see in the sheet view, but help you focus on information about a specific task or resource. Use a form view when you want to examine task or resource information in detail. The following illustration shows a Task Details Form.

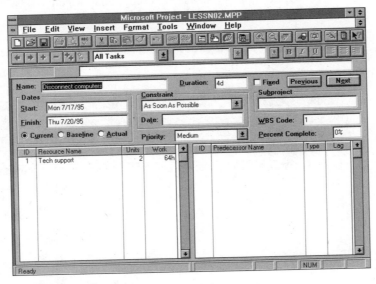

Moving Around in a View

A view often contains more information than what is currently displayed on the screen. For example, to see additional columns of task information in Gantt Chart view, you can scroll horizontally by using the horizontal scroll bar. You can scroll downward through the list of tasks to see additional tasks by using the vertical scroll bar.

To see more of the timescale, you can use the horizontal scroll bar on the Gantt Chart. There are also keyboard shortcuts that let you move quickly around the Gantt view. When you move around in the Gantt table (the left side of the view), the timescale on the Gantt Chart (right side of the view) does not move. Similarly, when you scroll through the timescale on the Gantt Chart, the Gantt table does not move. However, if you scroll vertically in the view, both the Gantt Chart and the Gantt table move simultaneously.

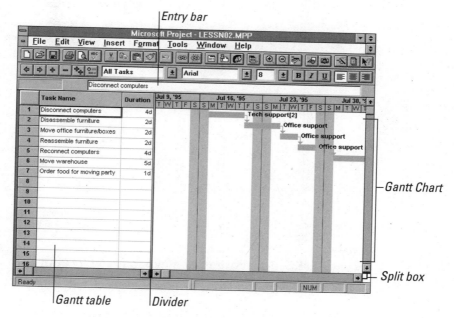

Moving in the Gantt Chart

In the Gantt Chart (on the right side of the view), Microsoft Project represents the current date (according to the Current Date in the Summary Info dialog box) with a dashed vertical line called the *date line*. The Gantt Chart displays the date line in the center of the Gantt Chart by default. Depending on the current date, the start of the project might not be visible in your project.

Scroll through the project

When you scroll horizontally through the Gantt Chart, you are moving through the timescale. Use the horizontal scroll bar to locate when the project is scheduled for completion.

1   Click the arrow at the right end of the horizontal scroll bar at the bottom of the Gantt Chart.

The timescale moves approximately one day further into the project.

Another way to display the Gantt bar for a specific task (without scrolling) is by selecting a task and clicking the Goto Selected Task button on the Standard toolbar.

2   Click in the area to the right of the scroll box in the horizontal scroll bar of the Gantt Chart.

The timescale moves further into the project, as shown in the following illustration.

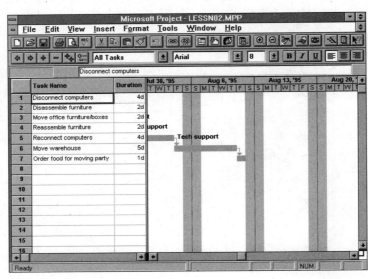

Use a keyboard shortcut to move to the start of the project

▶   Press ALT+HOME to move the timescale to the start of the project.

Moving in the Gantt Table

You enter specific project information in *fields* and *cells* in the Gantt table. In forms, the name of the field appears next to the box where you enter information. In tables, where information is aligned in rows and columns, field names appear at the top of the column. The intersection of a row and a column is a cell. This is where you enter your information.

Although you see only the first two columns of the Gantt table, there are actually additional columns that are hidden from view at the moment. For example, if you want to select the resource name for a task, you can scroll horizontally in the Gantt table to display additional fields.

Use the mouse to select cells

A cell is selected when it is surrounded by a bold, black border. You can use either the mouse or the keyboard to select cells in the Gantt table.

▶   Click the sixth cell of the Task Name column in the Gantt table. This cell contains the task name "Move warehouse."

The task name for task 6 is selected, as shown in the following illustration.

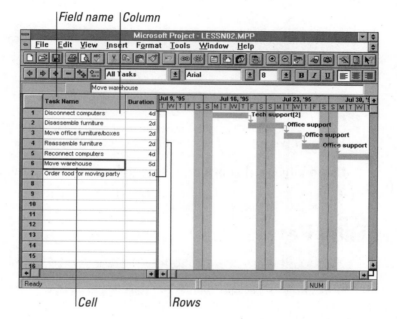

Use the keyboard to select fields

You can also use the keyboard to select the field where you want to work.

1   Press TAB to move to the Duration field.

2   Press TAB four more times to move to the Resource Names field.

The Resource Names field is the last field in the Gantt table. Notice that the first fields scroll off to the left of the screen as new fields you select scroll on to the screen from the right.

3   Press SHIFT+TAB to move to the previous field, Predecessors.

4   Press the DOWN ARROW twice to move down two rows.

Scroll in the Gantt table

If you have more tasks than will fit in the view, you need to use the vertical scroll bar to see the tasks and their corresponding Gantt bars. You can use the horizontal scroll bar in the Gantt table to see different parts of the table without selecting any field.

1   Click the left arrow of the horizontal scroll bar of the Gantt table.

The Gantt table and the Gantt Chart have their own horizontal scroll bars. Notice that the last field scrolls off the right edge of the table and a new field scrolls on from the left in small increments.

2   Click to the right of the scroll box in the horizontal scroll bar of the Gantt table.

Notice that more new fields scroll from the right as fields scroll off the left in larger increments.

3   Drag the scroll box all the way to the left edge of the horizontal scroll bar of the Gantt table.

The Task Name field appears as the first field in the table, but it is not selected. Moving around with the scroll bar does not change the selected cell.

Use a keyboard shortcut to select the first cell in the project

▶   Press CTRL+HOME to select the first cell in the first row.

Using the Entry Bar

You can use the *entry bar* to enter and edit text in specific fields. When you click in a field—either in a sheet view or in the table area of a chart view—the contents of the field appears in the entry bar. When you click in the entry area, the enter button (the check mark) and the cancel button (the "X") appear next to the entry area. Click the enter button when you complete an entry. Click the cancel button to retain the original entry. Making a selection from the entry bar is often faster than typing an entry in a field.

Enter button

Cancel button   *Entry area*

Select a cell

▶   Click the first cell of the Duration column.

The entry area contains the entry "4d."

Edit text in a cell

1 Click the last cell that contains text in the Task Name column.

The entry area contains the existing text.

2 Type **Moving day**

The entry area contains the text you type.

You can also press ENTER after typing text. The selection pointer moves to the next row in the Gantt table.

3 Choose the enter button on the entry bar to complete your entry in the Task Name column.

The enter button is the check mark next to the entry area. Your schedule looks like the following illustration.

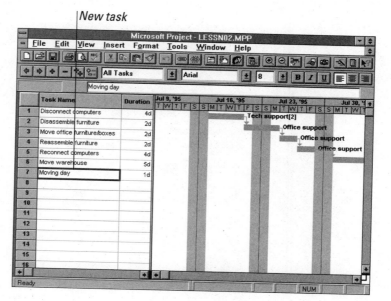

New task

Scheduling a Project

The Summary Info dialog box is where you enter the project start date or finish date to do basic project scheduling. If you do not enter a project start or finish date, Microsoft Project starts your project on the day to which your computer's system clock is set.

When you enter the project start date, Microsoft Project will compute a project finish date based on information entered in the project file. You also have the option to schedule a project based on a finish date you specify. In this case, Microsoft Project will determine a start date. The project file in this lesson was originally scheduled in this manner.

Tip For best results, schedule your projects from the start date. If you schedule from the finish date, you won't be able to level resources automatically or get a critical path. This topic will be covered in more detail later in this book.

Set a new start date

When your moving project was first planned, the kickoff date was July 17, 1995, based on a deadline of August 11, 1995. Because of other company priorities, the project will not be able to start until October 26, 1995. Enter the new start date and specify that you want Microsoft Project to schedule the project based on this new start date.

1 From the File menu, choose Summary Info.

The Summary Info dialog box appears, as shown in the following illustration. Click the Project tab if it is not already selected in the dialog box.

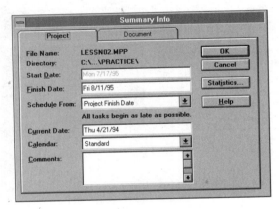

2 Click the down arrow in the Schedule From box, and select Project Start Date.

3 In the Start Date box, select the existing date and type **10/26/95**

Enter project information

In the following steps, you enter the project name, the company name, and your name as project manager. Although completing this dialog box is an optional step, you can choose to have this general project information appear when you print reports.

1 Click the Document tab.

2 In the Title box, type **Victory Sports Move** to name the project.

If you make a typing mistake, press BACKSPACE to remove the error.

3 In the Company box, select the existing name and type **Victory Sports, Inc.**

4   Complete the remaining fields, if you wish.

5   Choose the OK button.

You return to the Gantt Chart view and Microsoft Project recalculates the schedule based on the new start date.

Move to the end of the project

▶   Press ALT+END to move the timescale to the end of the project.

The new finish date is November 22, 1995.

Save your project

Save

1   On the Standard toolbar, click the Save button.

2   Click the second option button to save the project without a baseline.

3   Choose the OK button.

Your changes are saved in the project file.

One Step Further

Project notes are a great way to remind yourself to complete tasks or to leave information for others who might be working on the project. You can enter notes directly on the Gantt Chart so you (or others) are certain to get the message.

Drawing

1   On the Standard toolbar, click the Drawing button.

The Drawing toolbar appears. With the buttons on this toolbar you can draw objects and enter notes directly on the Gantt Chart.

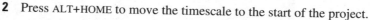

Tip If the toolbar appears to "float," double-click its title bar to "dock" it.

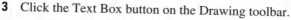

Text Box

2   Press ALT+HOME to move the timescale to the start of the project.

3   Click the Text Box button on the Drawing toolbar.

The pointer changes to a crosshair pointer.

4   Below the Gantt bar for the first task, drag a rectangle that is about one week long and about half as high as it is long.

You type text inside this area, but the exact size is not important.

5   Click in the text box you've drawn, and then type **Check vacation schedules**.

6   Click the right mouse button to the right of the Drawing toolbar to display the Toolbars shortcut menu.

7   From the Toolbars shortcut menu, choose Drawing.

The Drawing toolbar is no longer displayed.

Save

8   On the Standard toolbar, click the Save button.

9   Click the second option button to save the project without a baseline, and then choose the OK button.

Your changes are saved in the project file.

If You Want to Continue to the Next Lesson

1   From the File menu, choose Close to close your project file.

2   Choose the Yes button if you see the message box asking whether you want to save your work. Save the project without a baseline.

If You Want to Quit Microsoft Project for Now

1   From the File menu, choose Exit.

2   Choose the Yes button if you see the message box asking whether you want to save your work. Save the project without a baseline.

Lesson Summary

To	Do this	Button
Open a project file	On the Standard toolbar, click the Open button to display the Open dialog box. Double-click the name of the project to open. *or* From the File menu, choose Open. In the File Name box, double-click the name of the project to open.	
Save a project file	On the Standard toolbar, click the Save button to display the Save dialog box. *or* Choose the Save command from the File menu. If this is the first time you are saving this file, enter the name you want for the new file in the File Name box. Click OK.	

To	Do this
Save a file with a new name	From the File menu, choose the Save As command. Enter the name you want for the file in the File Name box.
Select a cell or field	Click in a cell or field. *or* Press TAB to select the next cell or field.
Enter text in a field	Select the field and begin typing.
Display columns currently hidden in a table	Click the right or left arrow on the horizontal scroll bar, or click to the right or the left of the scroll box.
Display the start of the project in the Gantt Chart	Press ALT+HOME.
Display the end of the project in the Gantt Chart	Press ALT+END.
Select the first cell in the first task	Press CTRL+HOME.
Close a project file	From the File menu, choose the Close command.
Schedule a project to finish as soon as possible	From the File menu, choose Summary Info. On the Project tab, click the Schedule From down arrow and select Project Start Date. In the Start Date box, enter the date you want the project to begin.
Schedule a project to finish on a specific date	From the File menu, choose Summary Info. On the Project tab, click the Schedule From down arrow, and select Project Finish Date. In the Finish Date box, enter the date you want the project to be complete.

For more information on	See in *Microsoft Project User's Guide*
Starting a project	Chapter 3, "Creating and Organizing a Schedule"
Displaying information in views	Chapter 9, "Working with Views"

For online information about	From the <u>H</u>elp menu, choose <u>S</u>earch and then type
Using the Gantt Chart	Gantt Chart
Starting a project	start date

For online information about	From the <u>H</u>elp menu, choose <u>S</u>earch and then type
Completing the Summary Info dialog box	Summary Info
Displaying information in views	Views

Preview of the Next Lesson

In the next lesson, you will learn to enter tasks in the task list and specify task durations. You'll also learn how to add, delete, move, and make changes to the task list.

Working with Project Tasks

As you saw in Lessons 1 and 2, project tasks are the basic building blocks of your project schedule. In this lesson, you will enter the tasks that constitute the framework of your project. After entering their duration, you will link the tasks to establish the relationship between them, creating a schedule of events. You will also insert, move, and delete tasks to adjust for changing conditions in the project.

You will learn how to:

- Enter tasks and durations.
- Enter milestones.
- Link and insert tasks.
- Move and delete tasks.

Estimated lesson time: 45 minutes

Start Microsoft Project

If you see the Welcome dialog box, click the Close button to close it. If you see the Tip Of The Day dialog box, read the tip, and then click OK to close it.

If you quit Microsoft Project in the last lesson, you need to restart the application before you can continue.

▶ Double-click the Microsoft Project icon.

If you need help starting Microsoft Project, see "Starting Microsoft Project" in the "Getting Ready" section earlier in this book.

Start the lesson

Open the project file called 03LESSN.MPP, and save it with the name LESSN03.MPP.

1 From the File menu, choose Open.

2 In the Directories box, double-click PRACTICE.

If necessary, scroll down the list to find it.

3 In the File Name box, double-click 03LESSN.MPP.

4 From the File menu, choose Save As.

If you don't see the PlanningWizard asking you to save the project without a baseline, continue with step 7.

5 Click the second option button to save the project without a baseline.

6 Choose the OK button.

7 In the File Name box, type **lessn03.mpp**

8   Choose the OK button.

Microsoft Project stores your project on the hard disk with the filename LESSN03.MPP. This file is a version of the project you opened in Lesson 2. However, its start date is July 17, 1995. There are no tasks in this project yet.

Specify the current date

Today's date (according to your computer's internal clock) is represented by a dotted line (called the *date line*) in the Gantt Chart. So that you get the same results as shown in the illustrations, you need to specify the same current date as in the exercises.

Note   When you are working on your own projects with your own schedule, you will not need to do this step.

---

1   From the File menu, choose Summary Info.

The Summary Info dialog box appears.

2   Click the Project tab (if it is not already selected in the dialog box).

3   In the Current Date box, select the entire existing date and then type **1/3/95**

The practice project files in this book work with a project that takes place in the summer of 1995; the project start date is already specified in this file. Assume you will begin planning the project early in the year.

4   Choose the OK button.

The dialog box closes and you return to the Gantt Chart. The date line has moved to the location of the current date you specified in the previous step and might not be visible in the project window.

Entering Tasks in the Gantt Chart

A task is an individual step that must be completed to complete the project. When you enter a task, you can be as detailed or as general as you wish, but you will want to enter those activities that need planning, require a measurable amount of time, or that you don't want to forget. When you enter a task, the task is assigned a task number. This number appears in the first column of the Gantt table.

After you enter a task, you enter a duration for the task in units of weeks, days, hours, or minutes. The following table lists abbreviations for entering durations.

Unit	Abbreviation
weeks	w
days	d (default)
hours	h
minutes	m

Enter a task and duration

For the Victory Sports move, you enter a list of the tasks that must occur after everything is packed. For example, before anything in the office can be moved, you need to disconnect the computers. You estimate this will take about two days to complete.

1   Click the first cell in the Task Name column to enter the first task in the project.

2   Type **Disconnect computers**

If you make a typing mistake, press BACKSPACE.

You can also press TAB to store a task name and move to the next column.

3   Click the Duration column for task 1.

By moving to another column, the data you typed in step 2 is automatically stored without your having to press ENTER. Notice that a duration of one day is already supplied for this task. The default duration for a task is 1d (one day).

Goto Selected Task

4   On the Standard toolbar, click the Goto Selected Task button.

Clicking the Goto Selected Task button is a fast way to see the Gantt bar for a selected task.

5   Type **2d** for a duration of two work days.

6   Click the enter button on the entry bar, or press ENTER.

Notice that a start date of 7/17/95 appears in the Start column for this task. Microsoft Project schedules each new task to begin on the first day of the project.

Note also that the bar on the Gantt Chart now indicates a two-day duration.

7   Click the Task Name cell for task 2.

Your project looks like the following illustration.

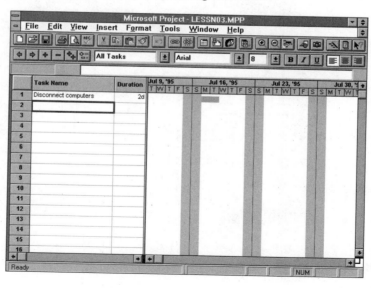

Save your project

It's a good idea to save your work any time you make important changes to the project.

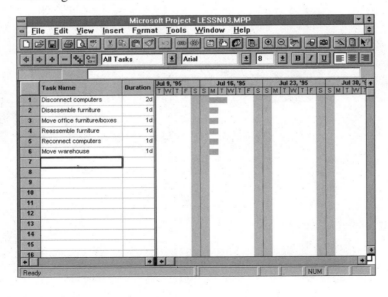

Save

▶ On the Standard toolbar, click the Save button and save without a baseline.

You can also choose the Save command from the File menu.

Adding Multiple Tasks

Although you can continue to enter each task and its duration individually, it is faster to enter several tasks and then go back and enter your estimates of the durations. First enter the following list of tasks, and then enter the durations.

Add several tasks

You can also click the mouse in a blank Task Name field to enter another task.

1   Type the following tasks, pressing the ENTER key after each task.

Disassemble furniture
Move office furniture/boxes
Reassemble furniture
Reconnect computers
Move warehouse

2   Proofread and correct tasks as necessary, so that the Gantt Chart looks like the following illustration.

You can also enter tasks by dragging in the Gantt Chart. Opposite a blank row, start dragging from the date in the Gantt Chart when you want the new task to start. The length of the rectangle you draw represents the task's duration.

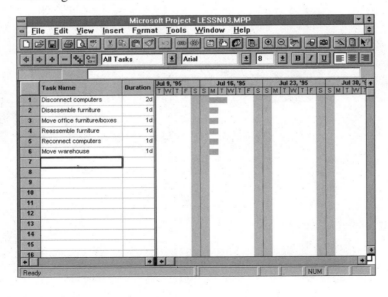

Add durations

When you enter a new task, Microsoft Project provides a default duration of 1d. Now that you have entered the tasks, you can go back and enter the actual duration you expect for each task.

1 Click the Duration column for task 2 to select it.

2 Type the following durations; after each one, press the ENTER key to enter the duration and move to the Duration field for the next task.

   1d (task 2)
   2d (task 3)
   1d (task 4)
   2d (task 5)
   5d (task 6)

Your Gantt Chart looks like the following illustration.

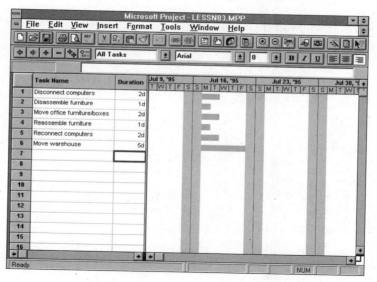

Enter a milestone

A *milestone* is an interim goal or checkpoint in your project. Entering a milestone is like entering a task, except that you type 0 (zero) for the duration. Follow the next steps to enter a milestone called "Move complete."

1 Click the Task Name cell for task 7 to select it.

2 Type **Move complete**

3   Click the Duration column for task 7.

4   Type **0**

5   Click the enter button on the entry bar.

Because the task has a duration of 0 (zero), the Gantt Chart shows the task as a diamond-shaped milestone, with the date next to it.

Save

Save your project

▶   On the Standard toolbar, click the Save button and save without a baseline.

Linking Tasks

A project is more than just a list of isolated tasks. Many tasks are related to each other. So far, although you've set up these tasks to follow one another in the task list, they all are scheduled to begin at the same time. Even though you've assigned durations to the tasks, you have not yet told Microsoft Project when each task is to begin in relation to the other tasks. The quickest way to relate tasks is to *link* them with the Link Tasks button on the Standard toolbar or the Link Tasks command on the Edit menu. You can also link two tasks by drawing a line connecting the two Gantt bars directly on the Gantt Chart.

Linking tasks sets up a *finish-to-start* relationship between selected tasks. When one task finishes, the next task starts. In addition, linking tasks allows Microsoft Project to automatically calculate a schedule for your project. When you link tasks, Microsoft Project determines the start and finish dates for each task in the project. By linking tasks, you relate them to one another with the click of a button.

Selecting Tasks

First you select the tasks you want to link. You can select all of your tasks or select only a few. To select a block of tasks, select the first task and drag until you've selected the last task you want.

You can also select a block of tasks by clicking the first task, then holding down SHIFT and clicking the last task in the group.

To select a set of individual tasks, click the first task you want to select, and then hold down CTRL and click each individual task you want to add to the selection.

Select and link all the tasks

First, select the tasks you want to link.

1   Select the task name for task 1 and drag the mouse through task 7 in the Gantt table.

Link Tasks

2   On the Standard toolbar, click the Link Tasks button.

You can also choose the Link Tasks command from the Edit menu. The Gantt Chart with linked tasks looks like the following illustration.

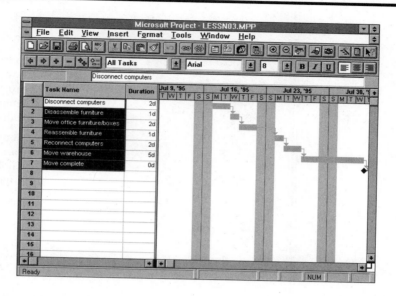

Microsoft Project links the tasks so that when one task finishes, the next task starts. A finish-to-start relationship is the most common type of relationship. In Lesson 4, you learn how to establish other kinds of relationships for tasks in a project.

Now that you've established task relationships, the bars on the Gantt Chart display the sequence of events. The Gantt bar for a subsequent task begins where the Gantt bar for the previous task ends.

Note You can *unlink* selected tasks by clicking the Unlink Tasks button on the Standard toolbar or by choosing Unlink Tasks from the Edit menu.

Save

Save your project

▶ On the Standard toolbar, click the Save button and save without a baseline.

Editing the Task List

Microsoft Project makes it easy to plan and schedule tasks in a project. In addition, you can quickly add, move, and delete tasks as the details of the project change or as the sequence of tasks becomes clearer to you. With the following Cut, Copy, and Paste commands on the Edit menu, you quickly modify the task list. Or, you can use the Cut, Copy, and Paste buttons on the Standard toolbar to perform the same actions.

Choose this command from the Edit menu	Or, click this button	To do this
Cut	✂	Remove the selected information from the project and store it in a temporary holding area called the Clipboard.
Copy	📋	Copy the selected information onto the Clipboard, leaving the original information intact.
Paste	📋	Insert the information currently on the Clipboard into the project. The Clipboard holds the most recently cut or copied information so you can paste it in as many places as you need.

Note   When you select a task name (or another field) for a task, only the selected cell is affected by the Cut and Copy commands or buttons. If you select an entire task (by clicking task number in the Gantt table), the Cut and Copy commands or buttons affect the entire task. Selecting the entire task is important when you want to copy and cut task information.

Undo

If you want to undo an editing change, select the Undo command on the Edit menu immediately after making the change. You can also click the Undo button on the Standard toolbar. The Undo feature reverses only the most recent change.

Inserting New Tasks

Before you can begin the packing activities in the project, you need to locate a new site and then write a proposal to get corporate approval for the new facilities. Then you'll need to get any necessary permits and remodel the new site as required. Before you can enter these tasks, you need to insert several blank rows at the beginning of the Gantt table using the Insert Task command from the Insert menu.

Insert new tasks

The Insert Task command inserts a blank row above the currently selected row. To insert several blank rows at once, select the tasks where you want the new tasks to appear. Insert blank rows so you can add the additional tasks to your project.

1 Select the first four task names in the Gantt table.

2 From the Insert menu, choose Insert Task.

Microsoft Project inserts four blank rows above the first task and all the remaining tasks move down to make room. Note that the task ID numbers are adjusted accordingly.

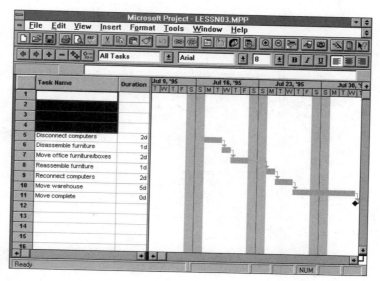

Enter new task information

In the new blank rows, enter the information for the additional tasks you've decided to add to the project.

▶ Type the following tasks and durations:

Locate a new site	**3d**
Write proposal	**2d**
Remodeling	**1d**
Get permits	**2w**

Moving a Task

When you move tasks from one location to the next, Microsoft Project automatically makes room at the new location; you don't need to insert blank rows first. One way to move a task to a new location is to first cut the selected task from its original place in the project, and then paste it in its new location. However, a faster way to move a task is to simply drag the task with the mouse to its new location.

Move a task

Move the "Remodeling" task from its current location to after the "Get permits" task.

1 Click task number 3 in the leftmost column of the Gantt table to select the entire row for the "Remodeling" task.

2 With the pointer still pointing to the task number, drag down slightly more than one row and release the mouse button.

A light gray bar appears below the current row as you drag, as shown in the following illustration.

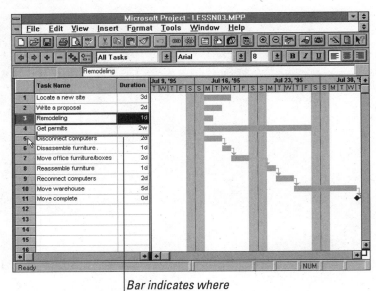

Bar indicates where
task will be moved.

The task numbers reflect the change.

Save your project

Save

▶ On the Standard toolbar, click the Save button and save without a baseline.

Delete a task

In your moving project, you realize that if you hire remodeling contractors, they can take care of the permits. You probably don't need to include the "Get permits" task in your project. Use the following steps to delete the task.

1 Select the "Get Permits" task.

You can also press the DELETE key on your keyboard to delete an entire task.

2   From the Edit menu, choose Delete Task.

Microsoft Project removes the task from the task list.

Undo the deletion

On the other hand, maybe "Get permits" should stay in the task list until you make sure the contractors can take care of it. Microsoft Project gives you the opportunity to undo most commands. The Undo command reverses only the most recent operation.

Undo

▶   On the Standard toolbar, click the Undo button.

If you change your mind about a command, the Undo command cancels your last editing command. "Get permits" is restored to the task list.

You can also choose Undo Delete from the Edit menu.

Link new tasks

The new tasks are all scheduled to start on the first day of the project. Because each of these tasks actually cannot start until the one before it is finished, you must link the new tasks to each other and to the "Disconnect computers" task.

1   Select task 1 and drag through task 5.

2   On the Standard toolbar, click the Link Tasks button.

Link Tasks

Microsoft Project reschedules the tasks so each task finishes before the next task begins in a finish-to-start relationship. In Lesson 4, you learn about other kinds of relationships you can specify for the tasks in your project.

Save your project

▶   On the Standard toolbar, click the Save button and save without a baseline.

One Step Further

Some tasks, such as status meetings, occur at regular intervals throughout a project. Instead of entering each of these tasks individually, you can add them all at once by using the Insert Recurring Task command from the Insert menu.

In the Victory Sports move project, you realize that you meet every week with your project team to get the status on individual tasks. Immediately after that meeting, you must report this status to senior management. Combined, these two meetings require about four hours. Add these meetings to your schedule as a recurring task to take place once a week.

1   Press CTRL+HOME to move to the first task in the Gantt table.

2   From the Insert menu, choose the Insert Recurring Task.

The Recurring Task Information dialog box appears. It looks like the following illustration.

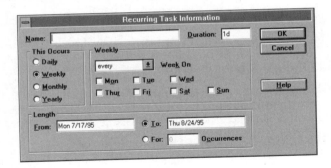

3   In the Name box, type **Project status meetings**

4   In the Duration box, type **4h**

5   In the Weekly area, click the Friday check box.

These meetings are scheduled every Friday. By default, recurring tasks start from the first day of the project until the project is complete.

6   Choose the OK button.

When you return to the Gantt Chart, you see Gantt bars representing each of the meetings. Also notice that the tasks have been renumbered to indicate additional tasks in the project—these new tasks are the recurring tasks.

7   Double-click the recurring task in the Gantt table.

Each of the recurring tasks appears below the "Project status meetings" task when you double-click the recurring task.

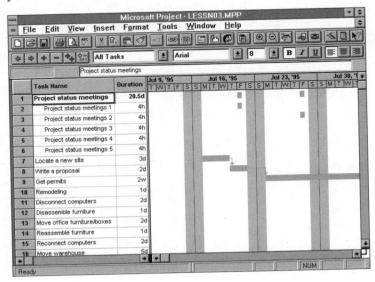

You can double-click the main recurring task again to hide the individual recurring tasks.

If You Want to Continue to the Next Lesson

1   From the File menu, choose Close to close your project.

2   Choose the Yes button if you see the message box asking whether you want to save your work. Save the project without a baseline.

If You Want to Quit Microsoft Project for Now

1   From the File menu, choose Exit.

2   Choose the Yes button if you see the message box asking whether you want to save your work. Save the project without a baseline.

Lesson Summary

To	Do this	Button
Enter a task	Click in a Task Name column and type the description of the task, and then click the enter button on the entry bar or press ENTER.	
Enter a duration	Click in the Duration column and type the duration of the task, and then click the enter button on the entry bar or press ENTER.	
Enter a milestone	Click in the Duration column and type 0 (zero) for the duration of the task; then click the enter button on the entry bar or press ENTER.	
Link tasks	Select the tasks and click the Link Tasks button on the Standard toolbar.	
Insert a task	Select the row where you want a task inserted, then, from the Insert menu, choose Insert Task to insert a blank row. Enter task information in the new row.	
Move a task	Select a task and drag the task to a new location. *or* Cut the selected task with the Cut button. Select a row in the new location; then click the Paste button to place your selection.	

To	Do this	Button
Delete a task	From the Edit menu, choose the Delete Task command to delete a selected task.	
Undo a command	From the Edit menu, choose the Undo command to reverse an action. *or* On the Standard toolbar, click the Undo button.	

For more information on	See in *Microsoft Project User's Guide*
Copying information	Chapter 14, "Copying and Moving Information"
Deleting information	Chapter 3, "Creating and Organizing a Schedule"
Durations	Chapter 3, "Creating and Organizing a Schedule"
Entering tasks	Chapter 3, "Creating and Organizing a Schedule"
Linking tasks	Chapter 4, "Scheduling Tasks"
Moving information	Chapter 14, "Copying and Moving Information"
Undoing a command	Chapter 3, "Creating and Organizing a Schedule"

For online information about	From the <u>H</u>elp menu, choose <u>S</u>earch and then type
Entering tasks	entering tasks tasks: entering
Copying tasks	copying tasks tasks: copying
Deleting tasks	deleting tasks
Inserting tasks	inserting tasks
Linking tasks	linking tasks
Moving tasks	moving tasks tasks: moving

Preview of the Next Lesson

In the next lesson, you'll learn how to schedule the sequence of tasks more precisely. You can use Microsoft Project to set up different task relationships, so that you can make the start or finish of one task depend on the start or finish of another task. You'll also learn how to schedule tasks so they occur simultaneously and how to schedule a delay between tasks.

Establishing Task Relationships

So far in this book, you have learned how to link tasks so that the next task begins when the previous task ends. In this lesson, you'll learn how to specify other types of relationships between the start and completion of tasks. You'll also specify lead and lag times to control the amount of overlap or time gaps between tasks. By specifying other kinds of task relationships you can gain greater control in the scheduling of tasks in your project.

You will learn how to:

- Specify finish-to-finish task relationships.
- Specify start-to-start task relationships.
- Specify lead and lag time task durations.

Estimated lesson time: 40 minutes

Start Microsoft Project

If you closed Microsoft Project in the last lesson, you need to restart the application before you can continue.

▶ Double-click the Microsoft Project icon.

If you need help starting Microsoft Project, see "Starting Microsoft Project" in the "Getting Ready" section earlier in this book.

Start the lesson

Open the project file called 04LESSN.MPP, and save it as LESSN04.MPP.

If you see the Welcome dialog box, click the Close button to close it. If you see the Tip Of The Day dialog box, read the tip, and then click OK to close it.

1   From the File menu, choose Open.

2   In the Directories box, double-click PRACTICE.

3   In the File Name box, double-click 04LESSN.MPP.

4   From the File menu, choose Save As.

If you don't see the PlanningWizard asking you to save the project without a baseline, continue with step 7.

5   Click the second option button to save the project without a baseline.

6   Choose the OK button.

7   In the File Name box, type **lessn04.mmp**

8   Choose the OK button.

Microsoft Project stores your project on your hard disk with the filename LESSN04.MPP. This file is a version of the project you opened in Lesson 3.

Understanding Relationships Between Tasks

You can use Microsoft Project to set up task relationships, also known as *dependencies* or *precedence* relationships, so that you can make the start or finish of one task depend on the start or finish of another task. A task that must start or finish before another task can begin is called a *predecessor* task. A task that depends on the start or completion of another task is called a *successor* task.

A *finish-to-start* relationship is the default relationship when you link tasks. Once the first task ends, the next task begins. Updating the mailing list before printing the labels is an example of a finish-to-start relationship.

A *finish-to-finish* relationship is one in which both tasks finish at the same time. For example, you want your new computer to be completely installed and operational at the same time you have finished backing up the information on your old computer.

In a *start-to-start* relationship, two tasks start at the same time. For example, when building a house, you might arrange to start laying tile on both the bathroom floors and the kitchen countertops at the same time. Such a relationship could save time and money if your resources charge you for each trip to the site.

The *start-to-finish* relationship is less common than the others. But it can occur when the completion of one task depends on the start of a later task. For example, if an information systems department is converting to a new financial reporting system, the task "Run reports on old system" would not stop until "Run reports on new system" has started.

Add a task

The moving project for Victory Sports is scheduled to complete on Thursday, August 24. But you realize you need to add a task to distribute boxes to office employees so they can pack their own offices. Because adding this task delays the completion of the project, you'll look for ways to tighten up the project schedule by modifying task relationships in the next exercise.

1 Select task 5, "Disconnect computers," and then from the Insert menu, choose Insert Task.

2 In the Task Name field, type **Distribute boxes**

3 Click the enter button on the entry bar.

4 On the Standard toolbar, click the Goto Selected Task button.

Goto Selected Task

Because you inserted the "Distribute boxes" task between two linked tasks, the new task is also linked to tasks 4 and 6.

5 In the Duration field, type **3h**

6 Click the enter button on the entry bar, or press ENTER.

7 Press ALT+END to see the end of the project in the Gantt Chart.

The project is now scheduled to be complete on August 25 as shown in the following illustration. You might need to scroll to the right to see the finish date.

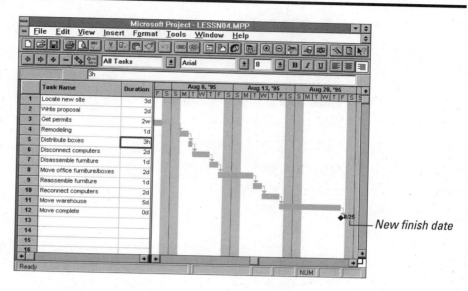

New finish date

Save the project

Save

▶ On the Standard toolbar, click the Save button, and save the project without a baseline.

All tasks are still scheduled in finish-to-start relationships. "Disconnect computers," task 6, is still a successor to task 3, "Get permits." In the next exercise, you specify different relationships to tighten up the schedule.

Specifying Task Relationships

You might need to define different types of relationships between tasks other than finish-to-start. For example, you might want the start of a task to be dependent on the start of another task—a start-to-start relationship—or want the finish date of a task to depend on the completion of another task—a finish-to-finish relationship. Establishing these relationships can often shorten the time it takes to complete the project and can make better use of your project's resources.

Entering Relationship Information

You can specify the task relationships in the Task Information dialog box or in the Gantt table. In this lesson, you practice using both methods, so you can determine what you prefer.

Tip   You can modify an existing task relationship by double-clicking a connecting line between two tasks in the Gantt Chart. This displays the Task Dependencies dialog box, in which you can specify the type of relationship and a lead or lag time.

On the Predecessors tab of the Task Information dialog box, you can include the task ID number of the predecessor, lead or lag time, and the abbreviation for type of relationship: finish-to-start (FS), start-to-start (SS), finish-to-finish (FF), or start-to-finish (SF).

Enter a new predecessor

So that the office workers can continue working for as long as possible before the move, the office manager has asked you not to finish moving the office furniture until the warehouse part of the move is completed. Use the Task Information dialog box to schedule a finish-to-finish relationship for these two tasks.

1 In the Gantt table, double-click task 11, "Move warehouse."

Double-clicking a task is a fast way to display the Task Information dialog box.

2 Click the Predecessors tab to make it active.

The current predecessor to the "Move warehouse" task is task 10, "Reconnect computers."

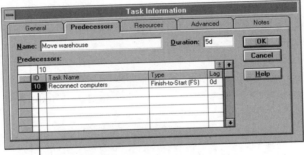

Current predecessor

3 On the Predecessors tab, click the ID number 10 in the ID column.

4 Press DELETE to remove this predecessor.

5 In the ID column, type **8**

This is the Task ID for the task "Move office furniture/boxes."

6 In the entry bar inside the dialog box, click the enter button, or press ENTER.

The task name and information appears.

Enter a finish-to-finish relationship

1 Click the Type cell for this task.

2 Click the down arrow at the right end of the entry bar to display a list of relationship types you can specify.

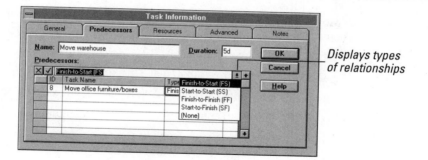

Displays types
of relationships

3   Select Finish-to-Finish (FF) from the list.

4   Choose the OK button.

5   Scroll to the left in the Gantt Chart (if necessary) to see the change in the project.

The Gantt bars for tasks 11 and 8 finish at the same time, displaying a finish-to-finish relationship, with both tasks finishing on August 15, as shown in the following illustration.

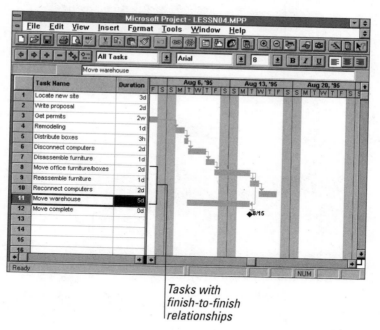

Tasks with
finish-to-finish
relationships

Add a predecessor to "Move complete"

With this finish-to-finish relationship, you scheduled to finish moving items from the office and the warehouse at the same time. Next you need to add a predecessor to the

"Move complete" milestone to indicate that the completion of the move project is dependent on the completion of the "Reconnect computers" task.

1   Double-click the milestone task 12, "Move complete."

2   Click the Predecessors tab to make it active.

3   In the Predecessors list, click the first blank field in the ID column.

4   Type **10**, the task ID number for "Reconnect computers."

5   In the entry bar inside the dialog box, click the enter button, or press ENTER.

6   Choose the OK button.

The "Move complete" milestone now occurs at the end of the "Reconnect computers" task, as shown in the following illustration.

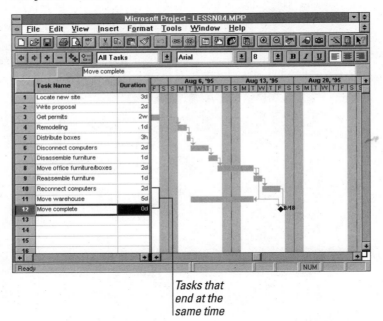

Tasks that
end at the
same time

Save the updated project

Save

▶   On the Standard toolbar, click the Save button, and save the project without a baseline.

Understanding Lag and Lead Time

With Microsoft Project you can include *lead* or *lag* (overlap or delay) time between tasks so you can accurately model real-world dependencies. An overlap between tasks is called lead time, where the start of the task precedes the finish of its predecessor.

For example, you might want to start painting conference room walls when half of the computer room walls have been completed.

The following illustration shows examples of lag and lead time in a project.

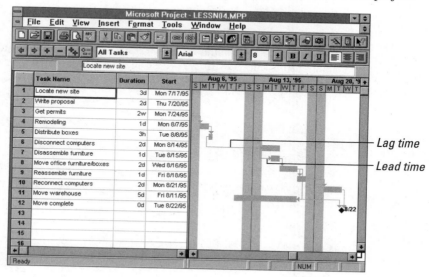

A gap or delay between two tasks is called lag time. For example, you might want to start laying carpet three days after painting is finished.

You can enter lead or lag time between tasks in minutes, hours, days, or weeks; elapsed minutes, hours, days, or weeks; or as a percentage of the duration of the predecessor task. For example, you can specify that a task start after half the duration of its predecessor.

Specifying Lag Time

To specify elapsed lag time as a percentage, you can enter the letter "e" before the percent (%) sign.

When you enter a lag time, you type a plus sign (+) in front of the duration. For example, to specify a lag time of four days, you would enter +4d.

Enter start-to-start and lag time relationships

In the Victory Sports move project, to allow sufficient time for everyone to pack their offices, you need to start distributing boxes four working days before the computers are disconnected. In the next exercise, you define a start-to-start relationship for the tasks "Distribute boxes" and "Disconnect computers." Then enter a lag time of four days for the task "Disconnect computers." This time, you use the Gantt table to specify a task relationship. You might find this technique faster than using the Task Information dialog box for specifying task relationships.

1   Drag the divider between the Gantt Chart and the Gantt table to the right until you see the Predecessors column in the Gantt table.

2 Select the Predecessors cell for task 6, "Disconnect computers."

3 Type **5ss+4d**

Task 6 "Disconnect computers" has a start-to-start relationship and a 4-day lag time with task 5, "Distribute boxes."

4 In the entry bar, click the enter button or press ENTER.

The Predecessors column for task 6 reads "5SS+4d." With a start-to-start task relationship with "Distribute boxes" and a 4-day lag time, "Disconnect computers" now begins on August 14.

After completing these steps, your project looks like the following illustration.

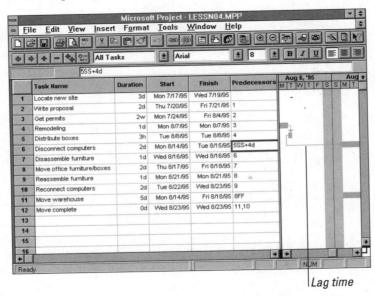

Lag time

Specifying Lead Time

Lead time is the amount of overlap between tasks. Currently all computers are scheduled to be disconnected before you start taking apart the furniture. You can save time by making these tasks overlap. In fact, you can start taking the furniture apart when 50 percent of the computers are disconnected. Since "Disconnect computers" is a two-day task, you can save a day by overlapping the tasks.

You can also enter multiple predecessor relationships in the Predecessors cell in the Gantt table by separating each with a comma.

If you want to enter a lead time in terms of days (rather than as a percentage of work complete), you need to include a minus sign (-) in front of the duration when you specify a lead time. For example, to enter a three-day lead time, you would type "-3d" in the Lag or Predecessors cell.

Enter percent lead time

Follow the next steps to schedule a start-to-start relationship with 50-percent lead time. By entering a percentage in the Lag cell in the Task Information dialog box, you actually create a lead-time relationship with the predecessor task.

1 Adjust the divider to the left so only the Task Name, Duration, and Start cells appear in the Gantt table.

2 Double-click task 7, "Disassemble furniture."

3 In the Task Information dialog box, click the Predecessors tab.

4 In the Predecessors list, click the Type cell and type **ss**

You can also enter lead time as a negative duration (such as -4d) in the Lag column.

5 Click the Lag cell and type **50%**

This indicates a start-to-start relationship with the second task starting after half of the first task is complete, creating a lead time of 50 percent.

6 In the entry bar inside the dialog box, click the enter button, or press ENTER.

7 Choose the OK button.

Now the tasks overlap, with "Disassemble furniture" starting one day after "Disconnect computers" begins. Your project looks like the following illustration.

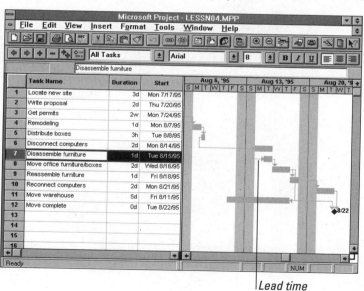

Lead time

Save the updated project

Save

▶ On the Standard toolbar, click the Save button, and save the project without a baseline.

One Step Further

You can also examine task relationships using the Task Form. The Task Form appears in the bottom half of the Gantt Chart view when you double-click the splitter located in the lower-right corner of the window. When you have two views open at one time, it is called a *combination* view. By working in one view while the other is displayed, you can instantly see the effects of each change. You can adjust the size of each half of the view by dragging the splitter to the size you want.

Display the Task Entry combination view.

1   When the cursor changes to a double-headed arrow, double-click the splitter located in the lower-right corner of the window.

 — Double-click here.

The Task Form appears in the bottom half of the Gantt Chart view as in the following illustration.

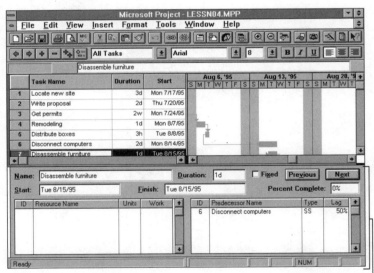

The Task Form displays information about the selected task.

2   Examine the task relationships for the previous three tasks by clicking the Previous button three times.

The task information about each task appears in the Task Form. The steps for entering relationships in this form are similar to specifying relationships in the Task Information dialog box.

3   Double-click the splitter to return to the full window view of the Gantt Chart.

If You Want to Continue to the Next Lesson

1   From the File menu, choose Close to close your project.

2   Choose the Yes button if you see the message box asking whether you want to save your work. Save the project without a baseline.

If You Want to Quit Microsoft Project for Now

1   From the File menu, choose Exit.

2   Choose the Yes button if you see the message box asking whether you want to save your work. Save the project without a baseline.

Lesson Summary

To	Do this
Specify a task relationship	In the Gantt table, double-click the task to display the Task Info dialog box. Click the Predecessors tab, and click in the Type column for the task. Enter the abbreviation for the relationship type, or click the down arrow in the entry bar and select a type. *or* In the Predecessors column in the Gantt table, type the relationship code.
Specify a lead or lag time task duration	In the Gantt table, double-click the task to display the Task Info dialog box. Click the Predecessors tab and, in the Lag column, enter the duration of the lead time preceded by a minus sign (–), or enter the duration of the lag time preceded by a plus sign (+). Lead time can also be specified as a percent completion of a predecessor task. *or* In the Predecessors column in the Gantt table, enter the duration of the lead time preceded by a minus sign (–), or enter the duration of the lag time preceded by a plus sign (+).

For more information on	See in *Microsoft Project User's Guide*
Lead and lag time	Chapter 4, "Scheduling Tasks"
Task relationships	Chapter 4, "Scheduling Tasks"

For online information about	From the <u>H</u>elp menu, choose <u>S</u>earch and then type
Assigning task relationships	task relationships
Overlapping tasks	lead time overlapping
Delaying tasks	lag time delaying tasks

Preview of the Next Lesson

Microsoft Project gives you control over the level of detail you see. In the next lesson, you'll learn how to outline a project to organize it into phases. With outlining, you hide detail tasks when you want to focus on the "big picture," or you can expand tasks to see just the detail you need.

Outlining Your Project

In this lesson, you'll learn how to outline your project tasks so you can see the structure of your project. You can arrange tasks in a hierarchical structure that helps you see how detail, or *subordinate*, tasks fit within broader categories, or *summary* tasks. With outlining, you also have the ability to collapse and expand the outline to present project information easily with just the right level of detail. To help you get the "big picture" when you need it, you'll learn how to adjust the timescale in the Gantt chart.

You will learn how to:

- Create a summary task.
- Demote tasks.
- Collapse and expand the outline.
- Adjust the timescale.
- Edit the outline and summary tasks.
- Collapse and expand summary tasks.

Estimated lesson time: 40 minutes

Start Microsoft Project

If you closed Microsoft Project in the last lesson, you need to restart the application before you can continue.

If you see the Welcome dialog box, click the Close button. If you see the Tip Of The Day dialog box, read the tip, and then click OK to close it.

▶ Double-click the Microsoft Project icon.

　　If you need help starting Microsoft Project, see "Starting Microsoft Project" in the "Getting Ready" section earlier in this book.

Start the lesson

Open the project file called 05LESSN.MPP, and save it as LESSN05.MPP.

1　From the File menu, choose Open.

2　In the Directories box, double-click PRACTICE.

3　In the File Name box, double-click 05LESSN.MPP.

4　From the File menu, choose Save As.

*If you see the
PlanningWizard
Click the second
option button and
click OK. Continue
with step 5.*

5 In the File Name box, type **lessn05.mpp**

6 Choose the OK button.

Microsoft Project stores your project on the hard disk with the filename
LESSN05.MPP.

Your project contains three new tasks: "Planning," "Moving," and "Move Office."
They have been entered near related tasks to illustrate how to use outlining in this
lesson.

Understanding Summary Tasks

Summary tasks are general headings with subordinate tasks (called *subtasks*) indented
below them. Summary tasks provide an outline structure that identifies the project's
major phases. As in any outline, each level of indentation represents an additional
level of detail for the task. You create a summary task when you indent (or *demote*)
the task below it. You remove the outline structure when you *promote* detail tasks
below a summary task.

A summary task is automatically scheduled to start on the earliest start date of its
earliest subtask; its finish date is the latest finish date of its last subtask. A summary
task's duration is the total working time between the earliest start and latest finish
dates of its subtasks; the duration for a summary task is not simply the sum of all the
durations of its subtasks.

Summary tasks also contain total work and cost information.

Creating an Outline

You can *collapse* the outline to show only the summary tasks and hide the more
detailed tasks. You can also *expand* summary tasks so that all the subtasks are revealed
in the plan. By collapsing and expanding specific summary tasks or all the summary
tasks in the project, you have the ability to view and print the amount of detail that you
need.

With the mouse, you can click an outline button to promote, demote, collapse, and
expand individual tasks, or expand all tasks. The following outline buttons are located
on the Formatting toolbar, near the left edge of the screen. You can also use the
Outlining commands on the Tools menu to promote and demote tasks, and to collapse
and expand the outline.

Use this outline button	To do this
	Demote a task to a lower level
	Promote a task to a higher level
	Expand a summary task to show its subtasks
	Collapse a summary task to hide its subtasks
	Expand all tasks to show all subtasks

Demoting tasks

Demoting tasks is how you establish an outline structure for your project. The task immediately above the first task you demote becomes a summary task.

Demote several tasks

Six of the tasks you entered earlier, from "Distribute boxes" through "Reconnect computers," are all part of moving the office. Demote these six tasks so they are indented under "Move office."

1 Select tasks 9 through 14.

Indent

2 On the Formatting toolbar, click the Indent button.

Goto Selected Task

3 With the tasks still selected, click the Goto Selected Task button on the Standard toolbar to view the new summary Gantt bar.

The selected tasks become subtasks. "Move office" is now a summary task because it has subtasks—tasks demoted under it. The duration of "Move office" changes to include the total duration of the six subtasks. Because the earliest task starts on 8/10/95, and the latest task finishes on 8/25/95, the duration is 12d.

Your Gantt Chart looks like the following illustration.

Outline buttons

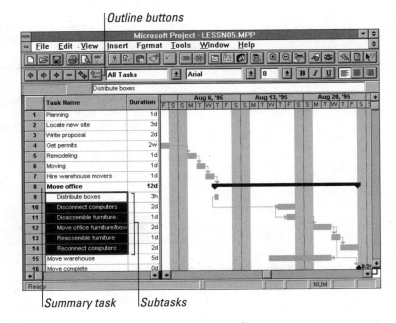

Summary task   *Subtasks*

4   Select tasks 7 through 16.

5   On the Formatting toolbar, click the Indent button.

Indent

The "Hire warehouse movers," "Move office," "Move warehouse," and "Move complete" tasks are demoted one level. The tasks you demoted earlier remain indented under the "Move office" task and their outline structure is maintained.

You've outlined the "Moving" phase of the project. It should look like the following illustration.

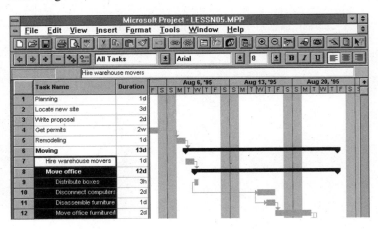

Save

Save your work

▶ On the Standard toolbar, click the Save button, and save without a baseline.

Collapsing and Expanding Tasks

Not everyone who is interested in your project requires the same level of detail as you do. For example, the regional manager of Victory Sports has requested an overview of the project. To help you focus on only the required information, you can collapse the "Move office" task. Collapsing a task means you can "hide" the subtasks. When you collapse the summary tasks, you can display the level of detail appropriate for the regional manager's request.

Collapse a summary task

Notice that "Moving" is a summary task. Collapsing it will hide all of its subtasks.

1 Select the summary task "Moving."

Hide Subtasks

2 On the Formatting toolbar, click the Hide Subtasks button.

All the tasks assigned to "Moving" are hidden.

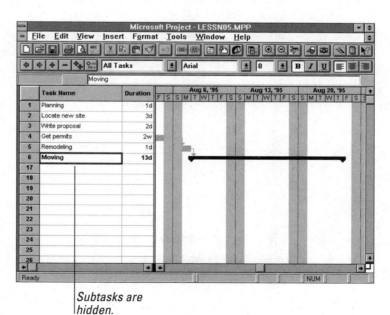

Subtasks are hidden.

Expand a summary task

The regional manager probably wants to see more details about the move than what is currently displayed in the Gantt Chart. By expanding the outline for the "Moving" summary task, you can increase the number of subtasks displayed by one outline level.

Show Subtasks

▶ With the "Moving" summary task still selected, click the Show Subtasks button on the Formatting toolbar.

The next level of subtasks appears in the Gantt Chart view. Notice that the subtasks under the "Move office" summary task are still hidden.

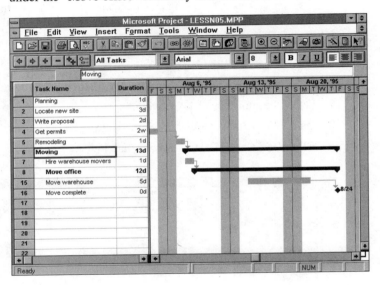

Adjusting the Timescale

Sometimes the results of displaying summary tasks can be clearer if you change the timescale range. The timescale, located across the top of your Gantt Chart, represents the period of time during which project tasks take place. The *major timescale* on top contains larger units (for example, weeks). It is paired with the *minor timescale* on the bottom that contains smaller units (for example, days).

With the Zoom In and Zoom Out buttons on the Standard toolbar, you can adjust the timescale units to give you more or less detail.

Each time you click the Zoom Out button, the size of the units increases to give you a "bigger picture" of the project. Each time you click the Zoom In button, the size of the units decreases to give you greater detail.

Change the units on the timescale

Your screen display currently shows weeks as the major timescale and days as the minor timescale. Change the units on the timescale to show a broader range of time—months and weeks—so all the summary task bars are visible on the Gantt Chart.

Zoom Out

▶ On the Standard toolbar, click the Zoom Out button twice to increase the units on the timescale.

Using Outline Symbols

As you demote tasks to form an outline, you can display outline symbols for the tasks. The outline symbols give you an additional visual indication of the outline's structure. By displaying outline symbols, you can easily see whether or not a task is a summary task, even if its subtasks are hidden.

Outline symbols appear in the Gantt table, but they do not print when you print your project file.

Outline symbol	Description
✛	Identifies a summary task
▬	Identifies tasks without subtasks

View the outline symbols

As you examine the tasks that are now summarized for the regional manager, display outline symbols so you can still identify the summary tasks in the project.

Outline Symbols

▶ On the Formatting toolbar, click the Outline Symbols button.

Outline symbols appear in front of each task name.

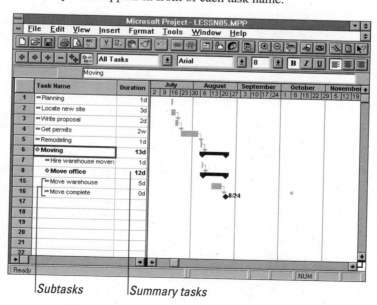

Subtasks   *Summary tasks*

Show all tasks by expanding them

After examining the project for the level required by the regional manager, you need to continue focusing on all of the subtasks of the project. To display all subtasks again, you can click the Show Subtasks button to expand a selected summary task one level at a time. On the other hand, if you want to quickly display all the subtasks for the entire project at once, click the Show All Tasks button.

Show All Tasks

▶ On the Formatting toolbar, click the Show All Tasks button.

All detail tasks appear as shown in the following illustration.

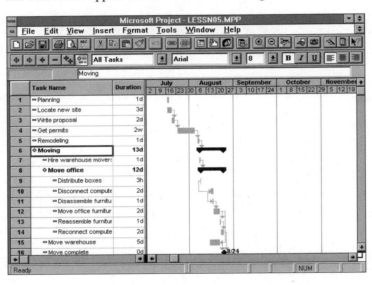

Save and close your project file

Now that you have learned the basics of project outlining, you will find out how outlining can save time when you want to move or delete tasks in a project. You'll close this project file and open another project that you will use in the remaining exercises in this lesson.

1   From the File menu, choose Close.

2   Choose the Yes button if you see the message box asking whether you want to save your work. Save the project without a baseline.

Editing Summary Tasks

In an earlier lesson, you learned how to edit the task list by moving, deleting, and copying tasks. Although the procedures for editing summary tasks are similar, there are a few important differences. Summary tasks actually represent a set of subtasks; therefore, when you edit a summary task, its subtasks are also affected.

For example, if you delete a summary task, the subtasks assigned to it are also deleted. Similarly, if you move a summary task, the subtasks are also moved. In this way, outlining your project makes it easy to rearrange and remove tasks.

Open a new project file

Do the following to open the project file called 05MOVE.MPP and save it as MOVE05.MPP.

1   From the File menu, choose Open.

2   In the Directories box, double-click PRACTICE.

3   In the File Name box, double-click 05MOVE.MPP.

4   From the File menu, choose Save As.

If you see the PlanningWizard, click the second option button and click OK. Continue with step 5.

5   In the File Name box, type **move05.mpp**

6   Choose the OK button.

Microsoft Project stores your project on the hard disk with the filename MOVE05.MPP.

The new project contains additional summary tasks and subtasks. This project is formatted with the default timescale.

Display first level subtasks

To make it easier to work with Remodeling tasks, hide all the subtasks, and then display only the next level of summary tasks.

1   Select summary task 10, "Remodeling," and then click the Hide Subtasks button on the Formatting toolbar.

All the subtasks under "Remodeling" are hidden.

Hide Subtasks

2   On the Formatting toolbar, click the Show Subtasks button.

Now only the next level of subtasks appears in the Gantt Chart view, as in the following illustration.

Show Subtasks

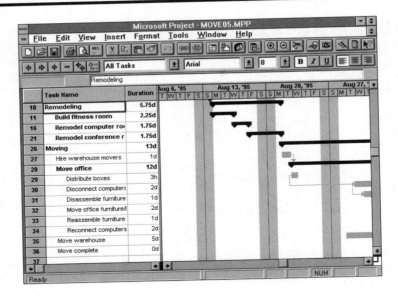

Delete a summary task

The plans to construct an employee fitness room as part of the Victory Sports move have been postponed by senior management. You need to remove all the tasks related to this activity in the project.

1   Select task 11, "Build fitness room," and then press DELETE.

A PlanningWizard informs you that the subtasks for this task will also be deleted.

2   Choose the OK button to continue.

3   In the next message box, choose the OK button to continue. To learn more about deleting the links, you can click the Help button.

The summary task, "Build fitness room," and all of its subtasks have been deleted from the project. Notice that the task IDs for the remaining tasks are renumbered to reflect the removal of the "Build fitness room" tasks.

Rearrange a summary task

To minimize interruptions to the computer support staff at Victory Sports, you decide to remodel the conference room before remodeling the computer room. You can quickly switch all the tasks related to these two activities by moving only the summary task for remodeling the conference room.

1   Select task 16, "Remodel conference room."

2   Drag the task up one row so it appears before task 11.

3   On the Formatting toolbar, click the Show All Tasks button to display all the subtasks.

Show All Tasks

Your Gantt Chart looks like the following illustration. Notice that the subtasks under each summary task moved along with their respective summary tasks. Also notice, however, that the original task relationships remain in effect. You need to establish new task relationships if you want the Gantt Chart to reflect a new sequence of tasks.

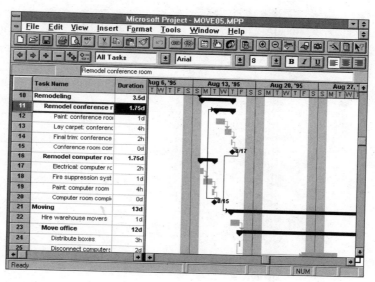

Establish new relationships between tasks

The milestone task for completing the computer room remodeling is still linked to the start of the conference room remodeling task. Before you can establish new task relationships, you must unlink task 20 and task 11.

Tip   If you have a clear idea of the structure of your project early in the planning process, you might prefer to outline the project before linking tasks and specifying task relationships. By outlining first, you will not need to establish new relationships later.

---

1   Select task 11, "Remodel conference room," and then press CTRL and select task 20, "Computer room complete."

Unlink Tasks

2   On the Standard toolbar, click the Unlink Tasks button.

Clicking this button unlinks the relationship between selected tasks.

3   Select tasks 15 and 16.

You want to create a finish-to-start relationship between the end of the conference room tasks and the start of the computer room tasks.

Link Tasks

4   On the Standard toolbar, click the Link Tasks button.

Your Gantt Chart looks like the following illustration. The completion of the remodeling conference room task is still linked to the start of the "Moving" summary task, and is actually still appropriate in this schedule.

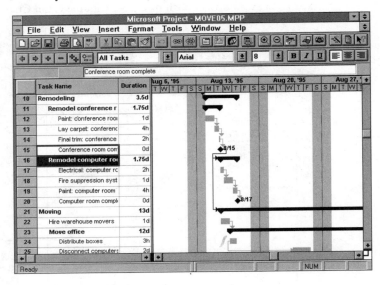

Save your work

Save

▶ On the Standard toolbar, click the Save button, and save your project without a baseline.

Print the current view

This is the information the plant supervisor wants to see. You can quickly print this information by clicking the Print button. But first, preview your project as it will look when you print. Even if your computer is not connected to a printer, you can see the view in Print Preview mode.

Print Preview

1   On the Standard toolbar, click the Print Preview button.

Microsoft Project prints only the active view of your project. A preview of your project looks like the following illustration.

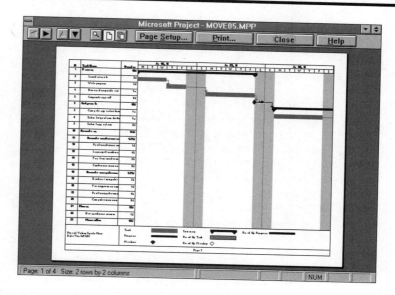

2 If your computer is connected to a printer, choose the Print button. If it is not connected to a printer, choose the Close button.

Microsoft Project prints the Gantt Chart you see on your screen. You'll learn more about printing in Lesson 12, "Printing Views and Reports."

One Step Further

Even though you don't see them, Microsoft Project assigns outline numbers to the tasks as you demote tasks to form an outline. The outline numbers indicate the levels of subtasks. Any changes you make to the outline of the task list are automatically reflected in the outline numbers. Using outline numbers is useful when you are organizing and viewing project tasks.

View the outline numbers

These numbers are useful for sorting your tasks into related groups. Display your project with outline numbers.

1 From the Tools menu, choose Options.

2 In the Options dialog box, click the View tab if it is not already activate.

3 Under View Options, click the Show Outline Number check box in the lower-right part of the dialog box.

Enabling this option displays outline numbers in your project. This option is enabled only in the currently open project.

4 Choose the OK button.

Your task list looks like the following illustration.

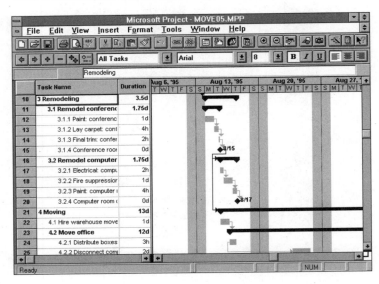

The outline numbers precede the task name to indicate the task's exact position in the outline. For example, the number 4.2 for "Move office" indicates that this is the second subtask for the fourth task in the project.

If You Want to Continue to the Next Lesson

1 From the File menu, choose Close to close your project.

2 Choose the Yes button if you see the message box asking whether you want to save your work. Save the project without a baseline.

If You Want to Quit Microsoft Project for Now

1 From the File menu, choose Exit.

2 Choose the Yes button if you see the message box asking whether you want to save your work. Save the project without a baseline.

Lesson Summary

To	Do this	Button
Create a summary task	Select the tasks below the one that is to be a summary task. On the Formatting toolbar, click the Indent button.	
Demote a task	Select the tasks to demote. On the Formatting toolbar, click the Indent button.	
Collapse a summary task	Select a summary task. On the Formatting toolbar, click the Hide Subtasks button.	
Expand a summary task one level at a time	Select a summary task. On the Formatting toolbar, click the Show Subtasks button.	
View outline symbols	On the Formatting toolbar, click the Outline Symbols button.	
Expand an outline	On the Formatting toolbar, click the Show All Tasks button.	
Adjust the timescale	Click the Zoom Out button to get a bigger picture, or click the Zoom In button to see more detail.	
View outline numbers	From the Tools menu, choose Options. On the View tab, click the Show Outline Number check box.	

For more information on	See in *Microsoft Project User's Guide*
Moving information	Chapter 14, "Copying and Moving Information"
Outlining	Chapter 3, "Creating and Organizing a Schedule"

For online information about	From the <u>H</u>elp menu, choose <u>S</u>earch, and then type
Outlining tasks	outlining
Outline numbering	outline numbers
Outline symbols	outline symbols

Preview of the Next Lessons

Throughout the lessons in Part 2, you will focus on assigning resources to each task, scheduling resources, and determining the cost of each task (and the project). In the next lesson, you'll begin to learn about working with the resources in your project.

Review & Practice

In the lessons in Part 1, "Learning the Basics," you learned skills to help you become familiar with planning a project and how to use Microsoft Project to start a project schedule and assign task relationships. If you want to practice these skills and test your knowledge before you proceed with the lessons in Part 2, you can work through the Review & Practice section following this lesson.

Part 1   Review & Practice

Before you begin planning a project of your own, practice the skills you learned in Part 1 by working through the project management activities in this Review & Practice section. In the following practice exercises, you open a practice project file and save it with a new name. Then you use the Summary Info dialog box to specify a new start date and enter general project information. After entering new tasks and milestones, you create a hierarchical structure to the project and assign task relationships.

Scenario

The Review & Practice sections of this book are based on a realistic scenario for which Microsoft Project can help you do your job more effectively. Imagine that you are the product manager in charge of new product development at Victory Sports, Inc. Your biggest responsibility this year is to lead the effort to design, market, manufacture, and distribute a new line of hiking boots, called Summit Boots. You will determine deadlines, assign resources to tasks, analyze costs, and communicate project progress. To help you in your role as project manager, you will enlist the aid of Microsoft Project to plan, schedule, coordinate, and report on the project.

You will review and practice how to:

- Develop an initial project schedule.
- Open a project file.
- Specify a start date for the project.
- Enter tasks and durations.
- Enter milestones.
- Link tasks and assign relationships.
- Save a project.

Estimated practice time: 20 minutes

Step 1: Before You Begin...Plan!

After thinking about the goal of the project and the major steps required to achieve the goal, your project plan might look like the following.

Project Name:
    Summit Boots Product Development

Project Goal:
    To produce and distribute a new line of hiking boots for a product roll-out at the spring Great Outdoors Expo '96.

Project Phases:
> Conduct a study of the marketplace
> Develop product design and cost specifications
> Produce prototype
> Test prototype
> Coordinate production with manufacturing team
> Design and produce packaging
> Coordinate advertising campaign for trade sell-in

Project Milestones:
> Market analysis complete
> Design and price approved
> Prototype completed for testing
> Prototype approved for production
> Product packaged and delivered to warehouse
> Product ready for roll-out

For more information on	See
Planning a project	Lesson 1

Step 2: Open and Save a Project File

1   Open the scenario project file called P1REVIEW.MPP. Before you make any changes in this project, save it with the new name **reviewp1.mpp**

2   This project file contains tasks and milestones that correspond to the Project Plan. Compare the task list in the project to the initial plan above.

For more information on	See
Opening a file	Lesson 2
Saving a file	Lesson 2

Step 3: Enter Project Information

This project was originally scheduled to start on March 14, 1996 and finish on May 29, 1996. Because you will be able to start the project one month earlier, your senior management wants to know how soon they can expect to see a new product. Change the scheduling method from Project Finish Date to Project Start Date to determine a new deadline based on the new start date and the addition of more tasks to the schedule.

▶   In the Summary Info dialog box, enter the following project information on the Project tab.

■   In the Schedule From box, select Project Start Date to schedule the project forward from start to finish.

■ Change the Start Date to 2/14/96.

Optionally, you can also enter general project information on the Document tab.

For more information on	See
Setting a start date	Lesson 2

Step 4: Enter Tasks and Durations

▶ Insert the following tasks and milestone with each duration so that they appear after task 9, "Prototype approved."

Task	Duration
Coordinate production	8w
Produce packaging	6w
Product ready to ship	0d

For more information on	See
Entering tasks and durations	Lesson 3

Step 5: Assign Task Relationships

Link tasks with finish-to-start and start-to-start relationships. Then schedule to begin producing packaging when production of the hiking boots is one-quarter complete.

1   Use the Link Tasks button to link tasks 9, 10, 11, and 12 with the default finish-to-start relationship.

2   Next, use the CTRL key to select tasks 5, 13, and 14, and then link them in a finish-to-start relationship.

3   Select task 11, "Produce packaging," and enter a start-to-start relationship with the predecessor task 10.

4   Enter a lead time of 25% for task 11.

For more information on	See
Linking and finish-to-start relationships	Lesson 3
Other task relationships	Lesson 4

Step 6: Outline the Project

1 Make task 10, "Coordinate production," a summary task for the subtasks 11 and 12.

2 Make task 4, "Develop design specs," a summary task for the subtasks 5, 6, and 7.

For more information on	See
Creating summary tasks	Lesson 5

Step 7: Determine the New Deadline

Based on the new start date and the addition of new tasks, Microsoft Project has scheduled a new finish date for your project. Use the Summary Info command to see the new finish date for the production of the new Summit Boots, and then save your project.

1 In the Summary Info dialog box, note the finish date on the Project tab. Close the dialog box when you are finished.

The project is now scheduled to be completed on May 8, 1996.

2 On the Standard toolbar, click the Save button, and save your project without a baseline.

For more information on	See
Saving a project	Lesson 2

If You Want to Continue to the Next Lesson

1 From the File menu, choose Close to close your project.

2 Choose the Yes button if you see the message box asking whether you want to save your work. Save the project without a baseline.

If You Want to Quit Microsoft Project for Now

1 From the File menu, choose Exit.

2 Choose the Yes button if you see the message box asking whether you want to save your work. Save the project without a baseline.

2 Working with Resources

Managing Project Resources

In this lesson, you will learn ways to manage *resources*: the people, equipment, facilities, and supplies required to accomplish project tasks. You will enter resources in your project and assign them to tasks. Then you will assign costs to resources and focus on viewing resource information.

You will learn how to:

- Enter and assign resources.
- Define a resource group name and code.
- Use a resource pool.
- Assign resource costs.
- Display resource information in a view.

Estimated lesson time: 30 minutes

Start Microsoft Project

If you closed Microsoft Project in the last lesson, you need to restart the application before you can continue.

If you see the Welcome dialog box, click the Close button. If you see the Tip Of The Day dialog box, read the tip, and then click OK.

▶ Double-click the Microsoft Project icon.

Start the lesson

Open the project file called 06LESSN.MPP, and save it as LESSN06.MPP.

1 From the File menu, choose Open.

2 In the Directories box, double-click PRACTICE.

3 In the File Name box, double-click 06LESSN.MPP.

4 From the File menu, choose Save As.

If you see the PlanningWizard, click the second option button, and then click OK. Continue with step 5.

5 In the File Name box, type **lessn06.mpp**

6 Choose the OK button.

Microsoft Project stores your project on your hard disk with the filename LESSN06.MPP. This file is similar to the project file you worked with in the last lesson; however, it contains several additional tasks.

Assigning Resources

The fastest way to assign resources is to select a task or group of tasks and then click the Resource Assignment button on the Standard toolbar. When you assign a new resource to a task, you can add optional details about the resource, such as salary information. There is also a Resource Management toolbar that contains the Resource Assignment button, as well as other buttons related to working with resources.

When you assign a new resource to a task, its resource name is added to the *resource pool*. Once a resource is defined in the resource pool, you can assign it to any task by typing its name, or by choosing it from the list of resource names in the pool.

Assign a resource

Begin by assigning yourself, as operations manager, the task of writing a proposal that describes the new office and warehouse site.

Resource Assignment

Drag the dialog box to one side if it obscures your view of the Gantt table.

1   On the Standard toolbar, click the Resource Assignment button.

The Resource Assignment dialog box appears. In this dialog box, you can enter new resource names and assign tasks to resources.

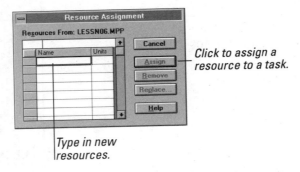

Click to assign a resource to a task.

Type in new resources.

2   Select task 3, "Write proposal."

The Resource Assignment dialog box stays on top of the project window, making it easy to assign a resource that is displayed in the dialog box.

3   Click in the Name cell, and then type **operations manager**

4   Click the enter button in the entry bar, or press ENTER.

After you enter a name, you can assign the resource to a specific task or several tasks. You can click the Assign button or you can drag with the Resource Assignment pointer to the appropriate task. In this lesson, you will have opportunities to try both methods.

5   In the Resource Assignment dialog box, click the Assign button.

The "operations manager" resource is assigned to task 3. Notice that a check mark appears in front of the resource name, indicating that it has been assigned to the selected task. Also notice that the Units cell contains a value of 1.00. By default, Microsoft Project assigns one *unit* of the resource to work full time on a task. A unit can be a person, a room, a computer, or whatever constitutes a single resource assigned to that task. By default, the resource name also appears next to the Gantt bar for the assigned task, as shown in the following illustration.

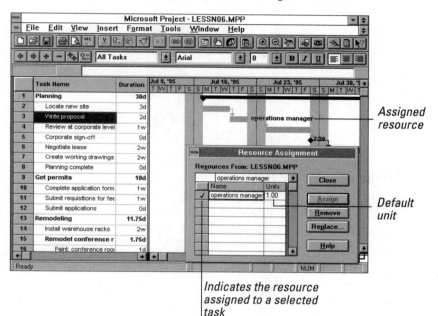

Assigned resource

Default unit

Indicates the resource assigned to a selected task

Adding Additional Resources

Entering resources into the resource pool as you assign them to tasks is fast and convenient for small projects, or when you are not sure of what resources the project requires. You can also enter resources directly into the resource pool before you assign them any tasks. Use this method if you are working on a large project for which you have a known set of resources, or anticipate using the same set of resources for future projects. This way, you can quickly assign existing resources to tasks. Remember, you only need to specify those resources that need managing, coordination, or planning.

Add resources to the resource pool

Although you haven't determined how to use them yet, you know of several more resources that will be involved in the project. You can enter these resource names now and assign them to tasks later.

1 In the next blank cell of the Name column, type **architect**

2 Click the enter button in the entry bar, or press ENTER.

3 Repeat steps 1 and 2 to enter the following additional resources to the project:
painters
carpenters
carpet layer

The Resource Assignment dialog box looks like the following illustration.

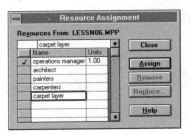

Providing Resource Details

You enter additional resource details in the Resource Information dialog box. You can provide additional information about a resource, such as initials, group names, or codes. You can also enter cost and calendar information. Completing this dialog box is optional, depending on your project. Nevertheless, providing these details about a resource allows you to take advantage of shortcuts, makes it easier to organize lists of resources, and facilitates better reporting. For example, if you enter cost information and group names for groups of resources, you can pull together reports on the costs or schedules for each group.

Display the Resource Information dialog box

You can quickly display the Resource Information dialog box by double-clicking a resource name in the Resource Assignment dialog box.

▶ In the Resource Assignment dialog box, double-click operations manager.

The Resource Information dialog box appears. In this dialog box, you can enter additional information about the currently selected resource.

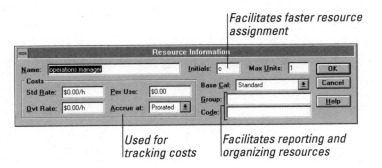

Facilitates faster resource assignment

Used for tracking costs

Facilitates reporting and organizing resources

Enter initials

Using a shorter name speeds up the job of making resource assignments. The next time you need to assign this resource to a task, you can type initials instead of the entire resource name.

▶ In the Initials box, type **opm**

Use these initials whenever you assign a task to yourself, the operations manager.

Enter a group name and code

The management at Victory Sports divides its resources into these groups: office staff, management, maintenance workers, warehouse staff, contractors, and equipment.

Assign yourself to the management group and enter an accounting code of 101-200.

1 In the Group box, type **management**

2 In the Code box, type **101-200**

3 Choose the OK button.

In your own projects for your own company, you will want to use whatever groups and codes are relevant for your reporting purposes.

Enter resource information for contractors

Earlier in this lesson, you added several resources to the resource pool. So that you can easily collect information about all the contractors later, complete the Resource Information dialog box for each of these resources as shown in the table.

▶ Double-click each of these resources, and enter the corresponding information for each one:

Resource	Group	Code
architect	contractor	501-100
painters	contractor	501-101
carpenters	contractor	501-102
carpet layer	contractor	501-103

Using the Resource Pool

Another way to assign a resource to a task is to select names from the resource pool. With the Resource Assignment dialog box open, you can select a task and then a resource and click the Assign button. If you select multiple tasks at one time, you can also assign the same resource to several tasks with the Assign button. If you prefer to use the mouse, you can drag a resource from the Resource Assignment dialog box to a task in the Gantt table.

Drag a resource to a task

Assign the architect to create the drawings.

1 In the Resource Assignment dialog box, select architect.

2 Position the pointer in the leftmost column until the pointer changes shape to resemble the Resource Assignment button.

3 Drag to task 7, "Create working drawings."

Notice that a check mark appears in front of the resource name, indicating this resource has been assigned to the selected task and that the Units cell contains a value of 1.00.

Goto Selected Task

4 On the Standard toolbar, click the Goto Selected Task button, and then scroll to view the resource assignment.

The Gantt bar for this task displays the name of the assigned resource.

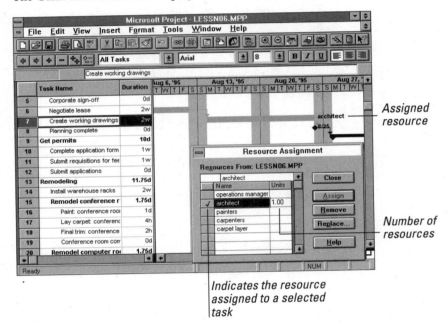

Assigned resource

Number of resources

Indicates the resource assigned to a selected task

Assign a resource to several tasks

There are several tasks in the moving project for which you are responsible. Assign yourself to these tasks by first selecting the tasks in the Gantt table, and then by using the Assign button in the Resource Assignment dialog box.

1 In the Resource Assignment dialog box, select operations manager.

2 In the Gantt table, select task 6, "Negotiate lease."

3   Scroll downward in the table (if necessary) to task 11, "Submit requisitions for fees," and press CTRL as you select this task.

By pressing CTRL as you click a task, you can select tasks that are not grouped together.

4   Scroll downward in the table (if necessary) to task 26, "Hire warehouse movers," and press CTRL as you select this task.

5   Hold down CTRL while selecting task 28, "Distribute boxes."

Tasks 6, 11, 26, and 28 are now selected.

6   In the Resource Assignment dialog box, click the Assign button.

You are now assigned to work full time on all the tasks you selected, and your resource name appears next to each Gantt bar.

Remove a resource

If you decide that a resource should not be assigned to a task, you can remove the resource from the task. In this exercise, you will not negotiate the lease for the new facility, so you need to remove yourself from this task.

1   In the Gantt table, select task 6, "Negotiate lease."

As the operations manager, you are currently assigned to this task.

2   In the Resource Assignment dialog box, click the Remove button.

You are no longer assigned to the task.

Add another resource to the resource pool

You plan to use 15 warehouse workers on the day shift for the task of moving the warehouse. You need to add these resources to the resource pool and then assign them to the task.

1   Select task 34, "Move warehouse."

2   In the next blank Name cell of the Resource Assignment dialog box, type **day warehouse workers**

3   Click the enter button on the entry bar, or press ENTER.

4   In the Units cell, type **15** and press ENTER.

Pressing ENTER enters the units and assigns all the workers to the task in one step. Notice that the status bar displays the message "Level: day warehouse workers." This means that the number of resources assigned to this task exceeds the maximum number of resources available. You need to specify that the maximum number of day warehouse workers is 15.

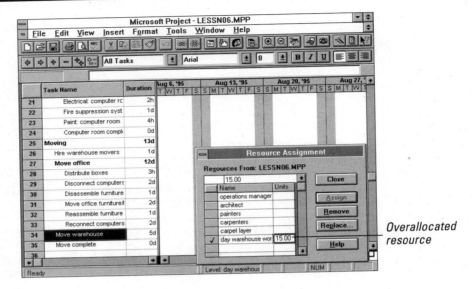

Overallocated resource

5   Double-click the Name cell for the day warehouse workers in the Resource Assignment dialog box.

6   In the Initials box, type **dww**

7   In the Max Units box, type **15**

Microsoft Project uses this limit for determining when the resources are overscheduled.

Keep the Resource Information dialog box open while you enter resource costs in the following exercises.

Working with Costs

Costs can be *fixed* or *variable*. Contractors, for example, often bid a fixed price for a job, meaning the cost remains the same even if the task takes more or less time than planned. Variable costs, on the other hand, typically include people and equipment that incur costs over time or per use. You can prorate costs for standard or overtime rates. You cannot prorate the cost per use.

Microsoft Project offers three cost accrual methods, which you can choose from the Accrue At list.

Start. Select as the accrual method if costs accrue as soon as a task using the resource begins.

End. Select as the accrual method if costs do not accrue until after the task finishes. Fixed costs for tasks are always accrued at the end of each task.

Prorated. Choose when costs accrue as the task using the resource progresses, based on the work done. Prorated is the default accrual method.

Enter an hourly rate

The warehouse workers normally earn $8 per hour. Their overtime rate is $12 per hour. Enter these standard and overtime rates. Use the default accrual rate for these resources.

1 In the Std Rate box, type **$8/h**

2 In the Ovt Rate box, type **$12/h**

3 In the Group box, type **warehouse**

4 In the Code box, type **301-110**

This code is the Victory Sports accounting code for the warehouse workers.

5 Choose the OK button.

Specify task details

After you assign the carpet contractor to task 17, "Lay carpet: conference room," specify that the cost will be incurred at the end of the project.

1 Select task 17, "Lay carpet: conference room."

2 In the Name cell of the Resource Assignment dialog box, select carpet layer.

3 Click the Assign button.

4 Double-click the Name cell for the carpet layer in the Resource Assignment dialog box to display the Resource Information dialog box.

5 In the Initials box, type **cl**

6 From the Accrue At list, select End.

7 Choose the OK button.

8 In the Resource Assignment dialog box, click the Close button.

Enter a fixed cost

The carpet contractor gives you a fixed price of $1,275 for carpeting the conference room. To enter fixed costs, you first need to apply the Cost table to the project. Use this table for entering and viewing cost information.

1 From the View menu, choose Table: Entry, and then choose Cost.

Choosing the Cost command replaces the Entry table with the Cost table in the left half of the Gantt Chart view. The Cost table looks like the following illustration.

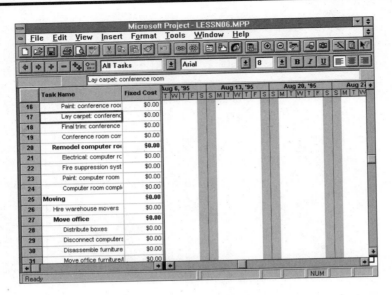

2 In the Fixed Cost column, click the cell for task 17 to select it, (if it is not already selected).

3 Type **1275**

Entering a dollar sign or a comma is not required.

4 Click the enter button on the entry bar, or press ENTER.

The fixed dollar amount for this resource appears in the Fixed Cost cell. You can scroll the Gantt table to verify that the Total Cost cell contains this value as well.

Viewing Resources

You can see all the people and equipment in the resource pool with the Resource Sheet. With its spreadsheet-like format, the Resource Sheet is a convenient way to review many resources at once. Change to the Resource Sheet view of the project and review the resources you have added.

View the resource pool

▶ From the View menu, choose Resource Sheet.

Your project in the Resource Sheet view looks like the following illustration.

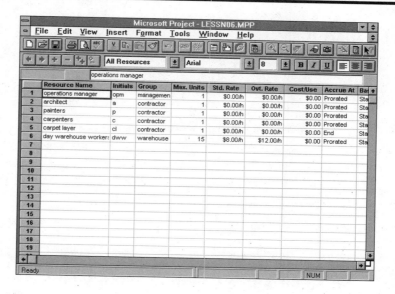

Edit several resources at once

Another benefit of this view is that it is easy to make the same change to several resources at one time. For example, the corporate office of Victory Sports has just decided that all contractors will have the same code. Rather than individually edit each code for each contractor, you change all the codes for all the contractors at one time.

1   Select all the contractor resources displayed in the Resource Sheet.

2   From the Insert menu, choose Resource Information.

    The Multiple Resource Information dialog box appears. This dialog box contains the same boxes as the Resource Information dialog box for an individual resource, but the information you enter in this dialog box will be entered for all the selected resources.

3   In the Code box, type **501-100**

4   Choose the OK button.

    In the Code column at the far right, verify that all the codes for the selected resources are updated with the new code.

Save your project

Save

▶   On the Standard toolbar, click the Save button, and save without a baseline.

One Step Further

To remind yourself of questions or issues related to a specific resource, you can enter a resource note. You can create and view a resource note when you are in the Resource Sheet view with the Resource Note command.

1   Select resource 2, "architect."

2   From the Insert menu, choose Resource Notes.

The Resource Notes dialog box for this resource appears. In this dialog box, you can enter important reminders about a resource.

3   Type **Find out about draftsman availability.**

4   Choose the OK button.

A note icon appears in the resource number column, indicating there is a note for this resource. To view a resource note, just select the resource that contains the note icon, and choose the Resource Notes command.

If You Want to Continue to the Next Lesson

1   From the File menu, choose Close to close your project file.

2   Choose the Yes button if you see the message box asking whether you want to save your work. Save the project without a baseline.

If You Want to Quit Microsoft Project for Now

1   From the File menu, choose Exit.

2   Choose the Yes button if you see the message box asking whether you want to save your work. Save the project without a baseline.

Lesson Summary

To	Do this	Button
Assign a resource to a task	Select a task in the Gantt table, and click the Resource Assignment button. In the dialog box, enter the resource name in the Name cell, and click Assign. *or* In the Resource Assignment dialog box, select an existing resource name. Drag to the task to which you want to assign the resource.	

To	Do this
Enter resource details	In the Resource Assignment dialog box, double-click the resource name to display the Resource Information dialog box.
Remove a resource from a task	In the Gantt table, select the task from which you want to delete the assigned resource. Click the Resource Assignment button. In the dialog box, click the Remove button.
Assign variable resource costs	In the Resource Information dialog box, enter variable costs in the Std Rate and Ovt Rate boxes. Select an accrual method from the Accrue At list.
Assign fixed resource costs	In the Resource Information dialog box, select End as the accrual method from the Accrue At list. From the View menu, choose Table, and then Cost. Enter the cost in the Fixed Cost column of the appropriate task. Click the enter button on the entry bar.
Edit several resources with the same information	From the View menu, choose Resource Sheet. Select the resources to be edited. From the Insert menu, choose Resource Information. In the Multiple Resource Information dialog box, enter the resource details you want applied to all selected resources.

For more information on	See in *Microsoft Project User's Guide*
Entering and assigning resources	Chapter 5, "Adding People and Equipment to Your Project"
Entering resource details and assigning resource costs	Chapter 5, "Adding People and Equipment to Your Project"

For online information about	From the Help menu, choose Search and then type
Adding resources	resources: adding
Assigning resources	resources: assigning
Assigning fixed costs	resources: fixed costs
Assigning a rate	resources: costs resources: rates

Preview of the Next Lesson

Coordinating the schedules of your resources can be a juggling act. Microsoft Project has a calendar system that does the trick by scheduling each task when the resources are available. In the next lesson, you'll learn several ways to enter exceptions to the standard Monday through Friday, 8:00 A.M. to 5:00 P.M. calendar.

Changing Working Time

When Microsoft Project calculates a schedule, it uses a standard 8-hour day and 40-hour week. Because not all resources in a project work according to this schedule all the time, you can use the calendar feature to adjust the working time for the entire project or for specific groups of resources. You can even adjust the working time for an individual resource. Using multiple calendars, Microsoft Project can schedule tasks to reflect the individual schedules of your resources. In this lesson, you will learn how to create calendars that are customized to the available hours of certain resources.

You will learn how to:

- Set holidays.
- Create new base calendars.
- Change the standard workdays.
- Change the standard work hours.
- Assign resources to a new base calendar.
- Edit resource calendars.

Estimated lesson time: 30 minutes

Start Microsoft Project

If you closed Microsoft Project in the last lesson, you need to restart the application before you can continue.

If you see the Welcome dialog box, click the Close button. If you see the Tip Of The Day dialog box, read the tip, and then click OK.

▶ Double-click the Microsoft Project icon.

Start the lesson

Open the project file called 07LESSN.MPP, and save it as LESSN07.MPP.

1 From the File menu, choose Open.

2 In the Directories box, double-click PRACTICE.

3 In the File Name box, double-click 07LESSN.MPP.

4 From the File menu, choose Save As.

5 In the File Name box, type **lessn07.mpp**

6 Choose the OK button.

If you see the PlanningWizard, click the second option button, and then click OK. Continue with step 5.

Microsoft Project stores your project on your hard disk with the filename LESSN07.MPP. This file is similar to the project file you worked with in the last lesson; however, it contains additional resources already assigned to tasks.

Changing Calendars

There are two types of calendars in Microsoft Project: *base* calendars and *resource* calendars. A base calendar defines the usual working and nonworking days and hours for the project or a group of resources. A resource calendar defines working and nonworking days for a specific resource whose availability does not conform to its base calendar.

The default base calendar (also known as the *project calendar*) is called Standard. It uses a Monday through Friday workweek, from 8:00 A.M. to 5:00 P.M., with an hour off at noon and no holidays. You must specify all nonworking days, even official, national holidays. You can create several base calendars and have them in effect for different groups of resources in the project.

A resource calendar contains exceptions to the base calendar for an individual resource. Adjust the resource calendar to schedule individual vacations, part-time hours, or regular overtime.

Using Base Calendars

Use base calendars for groups of resources. For example, if several resources work part time from 8:00 A.M. to 12:00 P.M., you can create a base calendar that shows these hours. You can give the new base calendar a name such as "Part-time" and use it with other projects as well. When you edit a base calendar, any changes you make are reflected in the resource calendars that depend on that base calendar. Changes you make to the Standard calendar affect only the current project, so each project can have its own set of calendars.

Set a holiday

The annual company meeting is on October 3. You need to make this a nonworking day in the Standard calendar.

1   From the Tools menu, choose Change Working Time.

   The Change Working Time dialog box looks like the following illustration.

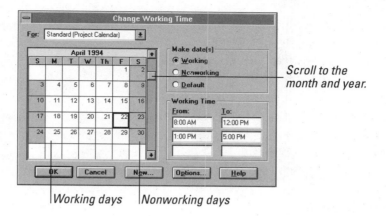

*Scroll to the
month and year.*

|Working days |Nonworking days

2   Scroll to October 1995, and then select October 3.

3   Under Make Date(s), select the Nonworking option button.

October 3 turns gray to indicate it is now a nonworking day. The working hours for this day disappear from the Working Time boxes.

4   Choose the OK button.

Your Standard calendar now includes the company meeting as a nonworking day.

Creating a New Base Calendar

You have three groups of resources that work at night: the night warehouse supervisor, the night warehouse workers, and the janitors. They work the same workweek and observe the same days off as the standard day workers, but their hours are different. You need to prepare a new base calendar to reflect their hours.

Copy a base calendar

So that the new calendar contains the same holidays as the current project calendar, you can copy the Standard calendar.

1 From the <u>T</u>ools menu, choose C<u>h</u>ange Working Time.

2 Click the New button.

The Create New Base Calendar dialog box appears. In this dialog box, you specify the name of the new base calendar you want to create. The Name box displays "Copy of Standard" by default. You can enter any name you wish.

If you have another calendar from which you want to create a new calendar, you can select that calendar from the list of calendars. You can also create a new calendar based on the settings in the default calendar.

Copies the current base calendar

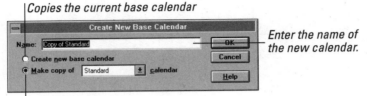

Enter the name of the new calendar.

Copies the dafault base calendar.

3 In the Name box, type **Night Shift**

This is the name of the calendar for the workers on the night shift.

4 Because you want to create a new calendar based on the current version of the Standard calendar (the default selection), choose the OK button.

A copy of the Standard calendar appears in the Change Working Time dialog box. The For box is updated to reflect the name of the new calendar you are creating. You can now edit this calendar to reflect the working hours for the night workers without affecting the Standard calendar.

Change the working hours

Do the following to set the hours for the night crews. Since the night shift spans more than one calendar day, enter the hours before midnight on one day and the hours after midnight on the next day.

1 Scroll in the calendar to display June 1995.

2 Select the Monday day title.

3 In the first set of Working Time boxes, type the following times to replace the existing values.

From   **To**
11:00 pm   **12:00 am**

Press TAB to move between boxes. If you make a mistake and need to move back to a previous box, press SHIFT + TAB.

4 In the second set of Working Time boxes, select the existing times and delete them.

5 Select the Tuesday through Friday day titles.

6 In the Working Time boxes, type the following times to replace the existing values.

From	To
12:00 am	3:00 am
3:30 am	7:00 am
11:00 pm	12:00 am

The night crew has a half-hour break from 3:00 A.M. to 3:30 A.M.

7 Select the Saturday day title.

Normally, Saturdays are nonworking days, but the night shift finishes their workweek on Saturday morning, so you need to change Saturday to a working day.

8 Select the Working option button.

Saturday is now a working day, so you can specify its working hours.

9 In the Working Time boxes, type the following times to replace the existing values.

From	To
12:00 am	3:00 am
3:30 am	7:00 am

Your calendar looks like the following illustration.

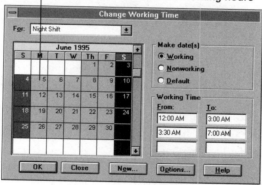

Shaded to indicate revised working hours

10 Choose the OK button to close the dialog box.

Save

Save your project

▶ On the Standard toolbar, click the Save button and save without a baseline.

Assigning Resources to a New Calendar

Microsoft Project assigns all the resources in this project to the Standard calendar. Use the Resource Information dialog box to assign resources to a new base calendar.

Specify a new calendar for a resource

You want the night crew to be scheduled according to the new base calendar, "Night Shift." Working in the Resource Sheet view, select the resources you want to reassign, then click the Information button on the Standard toolbar to display the Resource Information dialog box.

1 From the View menu, choose Resource Sheet.

2 Select janitors, and hold down CTRL as you select the "night supervisor" and "night warehouse workers."

Information

3 On the Standard toolbar, click the Information button.

The Multiple Resource Information dialog box appears.

4 In the Base Cal box, click the down arrow and select Night Shift from the list.

5 Choose the OK button.

These three resources are now scheduled according to the days and hours on the Night Shift base calendar. All other resources use the default base calendar called Standard.

Save your project

Save

▶ On the Standard toolbar, click the Save button, and save without a baseline.

Using Resource Calendars

Use a resource calendar for specifying working time for individual resources. Although resource calendars begin as exact copies of the Standard calendar, you can select a different base calendar and then easily customize each resource calendar to show the resource's personal vacation days, time away from the office, or individual work hours. In the case of equipment, a resource calendar can reflect scheduled maintenance, downtime, or any other exception to the normal schedule.

Edit a resource calendar

The night supervisor is scheduled to attend a safety seminar from 7:00 A.M. to 8:00 A.M., September 7. You will need to extend the supervisor's hours to 8:00 A.M.

for that day. To compensate the supervisor for the extra time, you can also specify that she doesn't need to arrive until the start of the next day. Enter these revised hours for this day in the supervisor's resource calendar.

1   In the Resource Sheet, select the night supervisor.

2   From the Tools menu, choose Change Working Time.

The resource calendar for the night supervisor appears in the dialog box. Right now, this calendar is the same as the Night Shift base calendar.

3   Scroll to September 7, 1995 and select this date in the calendar.

4   In the To box of the second set of hours, type **8** to replace the 7.

5   Select the times in the third set of hours and delete each time.

The supervisor is no longer scheduled from 11:00 P.M. to midnight.

6   Choose the OK button.

Microsoft Project reschedules the tasks around the resource's new hours.

7   From the View menu, choose Gantt Chart to return to the Gantt Chart view.

Save your project

▶   On the Standard toolbar, click the Save button, and save without a baseline.

One Step Further

The familiar monthly calendar is often an easy way to examine a project schedule instead of using the Gantt Chart. Add a new holiday to the base calendar for the move project and then view the project in the Calendar view.

1   From the Tools menu, choose Change Working Time.

The Change Working Time dialog box appears. Be sure Standard (Project Calendar) appears in the For box.

2   Scroll to September 4, 1995 and select this date in the calendar.

This is a nonworking day at Victory Sports.

3   Click the Nonworking option button.

4   Choose the OK button.

5   From the View menu, choose Calendar.

6   Click the down arrow button in the upper-right corner of the calendar window until September appears.

Notice the shaded box on the date September 4, indicating a nonworking day. Your project looks like the following illustration.

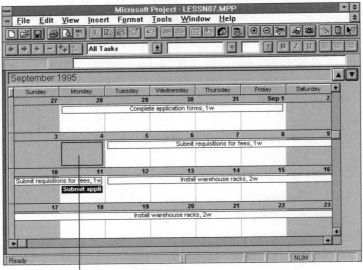

New nonworking day

No tasks are scheduled for this day.

If You Want to Continue to the Next Lesson

1   From the File menu, choose Close to save your project file.

2   Choose the Yes button if you see the message box asking whether you want to save your work. Save the project without a baseline.

If You Want to Quit Microsoft Project for Now

1   From the File menu, choose Exit.

2   Choose the Yes button if you see the message box asking whether you want to save your work. Save the project without a baseline.

Lesson Summary

To	Do this	Button
Create new base calendars	Choose Change Working Time from the Tools menu. Select the New button to display the Create New Base Calendar dialog box. Choose an option button to create a new calendar based on an existing one or to create a new calendar not based on an existing calendar.	
Change the standard workdays	Choose Change Working Time from the Tools menu. Select the base calendar you want to change. Select the day of the week you wish to change. Then select the Working or Nonworking option button.	
Change the standard work hours	Choose Change Working Time from the Tools menu to access the base calendars. Select the base calendar you want to change. Then select the days of the week you wish to change. Enter the working hours in the Working Time boxes.	
Assign a resource to a new base calendar	In Resource Sheet view, select the resource. On the Standard toolbar, click the Information button. In the Resource Information dialog box, select the appropriate base calendar from the Base Cal list. *or* Double-click a resource name in the Resource Sheet view.	
Edit resource calendar	In Resource Sheet view, select the resource. Choose Change Working Time from the Tools menu to display the resource calendar for the selected resource. Enter appropriate edits.	

For more information on	See in *Microsoft Project User's Guide*
Calendars	Chapter 5, "Adding People and Equipment to Your Project"

For online information about	From the **Help** menu, choose **Search** and then type
Creating calendars	Calendar command
Changing working time	calendars: timescale
Assigning resources to a calendar	calendars: assigning

Preview of the Next Lesson

In the next lesson, you will learn to specify both *resource-driven* scheduling, where availability of resources controls the schedule, and *fixed-duration* scheduling, where time controls the schedule regardless of the resources assigned.

Scheduling with Resources

Some tasks can be completed in less time if you assign them additional resources. Other tasks require the same amount of time no matter how many people are assigned. In this lesson, you will learn to specify whether the number of resources will affect how quickly a task can be completed. You will also change a schedule by varying the number of resources used.

You will learn how to:

- Use resource-driven scheduling.
- Use fixed-duration scheduling.

Estimated lesson time: 25 minutes

Start Microsoft Project

If you closed Microsoft Project in the last lesson, you need to restart the application before you can continue.

If you see the Welcome dialog box, click the Close button. If you see the Tip Of The Day dialog box, read the tip, and then click OK.

▶ Double-click the Microsoft Project icon.

Start the lesson

Open the project file called 08LESSN.MPP, and save it as LESSN08.MPP.

1 From the File menu, choose Open.

2 In the Directories box, double-click PRACTICE.

3 In the File Name box, double-click 08LESSN.MPP.

4 From the File menu, choose Save As.

If you see the PlanningWizard, click the second option button, and then click OK. Continue with step 5.

5 In the File Name box, type **lessn08.mpp**

6 Choose the OK button.

Microsoft Project stores your project on your hard disk with the filename LESSN08.MPP. This file is similar to the project file you worked with in the last lesson; however, it contains additional resources already assigned to tasks.

Establishing a Scheduling Method

Microsoft Project provides two scheduling methods: *resource-driven* and *fixed-duration*. By default, Microsoft Project schedules resource-driven tasks, whose duration depends on the available resources. There are times, however, when adding resources will not affect task duration. Such tasks are called fixed-duration tasks. The scheduling method you use depends on the nature of the task.

Resource-Driven Scheduling

If you want resource assignments to determine the duration and the start and finish dates of a task, use resource-driven scheduling. With resource-driven scheduling, the task duration is based on the amount of work and the number of resource units assigned to a task. Resource calendars determine the start and finish dates for the task.

For example, suppose the "Move warehouse" task has two movers assigned. With resource-driven scheduling, if you assign another mover, Microsoft Project shortens the task duration. The start and finish dates are determined by when the movers are available based on their resource calendars.

Resource-driven scheduling is helpful when you have limited resources to share among tasks. As you move resources from one task to another, or split resource time between tasks, Microsoft Project gives you instant updates on how long each task will take with the current number of resources.

In earlier lessons, you entered durations for your tasks based on your estimate of the total work for the amount of resources you planned to assign. For instance, if you estimated that a plumbing task takes three plumbers 10 hours to complete, you would enter a task duration of 10 hours. If you changed the number of resources, the duration for the task would also change.

Changing Resource Quantities

Resource-driven scheduling is Microsoft Project's default scheduling method, which means that each task you enter is initially set as resource-driven. You can change the scheduling method for a specific task on the Resource tab of the Task Information dialog box. For tasks that are resource-driven, you can change the task duration when you change the number of *units* (the number of individual instances of a resource) for the same resource assigned to a task. For example, by adding additional resources to a task, you can reduce the amount of time required to complete the task to meet a deadline.

Note You can change the default scheduling method for all *new* tasks on the Schedule tab of the Options dialog box. You can set the Default Duration Type option to Resource Driven or Fixed Duration. Changing the default scheduling method affects only new tasks—not tasks you've already entered.

Display the details of a resource-driven task

The day warehouse supervisor estimates it takes two weeks for eight warehouse workers to install inventory racks in the new warehouse. The supervisor needs to oversee the work as well.

1   Double-click task 14, "Install warehouse racks."

The Task Information dialog box appears.

2   Click the Resources tab.

Notice that the Duration Type is set as Resource Driven as shown in the following illustration.

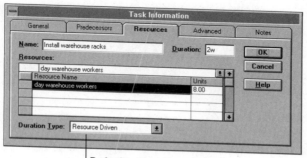

Default scheduling method

Change units of an assigned resource

Now that you know how much work the task requires, you can use resource-driven scheduling to quickly test some "what if" scenarios. You can use Microsoft Project to see how changing the resource assignments affects the duration of this task.

You need to shorten the task to a week so you can start the warehouse move earlier. Try doubling the number of day warehouse workers.

1   Select the Units cell for day warehouse workers.

2   Type **16**

3   Click the enter button in the entry bar, or press ENTER.

4   Choose the OK button.

The duration changes from two weeks (2w) to one week (1w) in the Gantt table.

Goto Selected Task

5   On the Standard toolbar, click the Goto Selected Task button.

The Gantt bar for this task reflects the new duration.

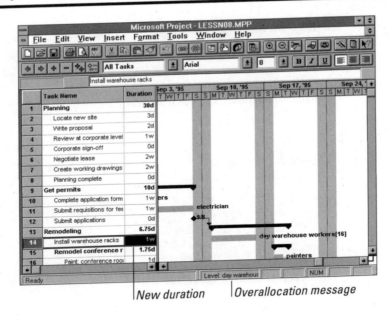

New duration | Overallocation message

Note The message "Level: day warehouse workers" appears at the bottom of your screen. This means that this resource is overallocated; you'll examine the workload for this resource in Lesson 9, "Resource Workloads."

Save

Save your project

▶ On the Standard toolbar, click the Save button, and save without a baseline.

Assigning Multiple Resources to One Task

If two different resources are assigned to the same task, Microsoft Project calculates the duration as the largest amount of work per unit done by any one resource. For example, if a piece of equipment must run for two hours while a laboratory researcher works three hours on the same task, the task duration is three hours. However, if you add a second researcher, thus reducing the hours per researcher to 1.5 hours, the task duration is now two hours because the equipment resource is now driving the task.

Add another resource to the task

Now that you've reduced the duration of the "Install warehouse racks" task, assign the day warehouse supervisor to the task while the day warehouse workers are at the warehouse.

1 Double-click task 14 again to display the Task Information dialog box.

2 Click the Resources tab.

3 Click in the first blank row of the Resource Name column.

4 Click the Resources arrow in the entry box to display a list of resources you can assign to tasks.

Earlier, you learned how to assign resources in the Resource Assignment dialog box. Selecting resources from the Resources tab in the Task Information dialog box is another way to assign resources.

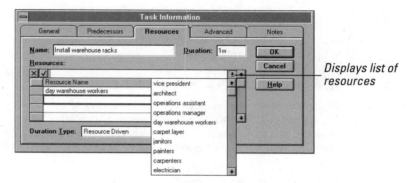

Displays list of resources

5 From the list of resources, select day warehouse supervisor.

6 Choose the OK button to return to the Gantt Chart.

Notice that the duration of the task does not change. Microsoft Project assumes that the additional resource works in parallel with the other resources assigned to the task. In other words, adding additional resources of the same type will change the duration of the task. Adding a different resource does not affect the task's duration.

Save your project

▶ On the Standard toolbar, click the Save button, and save without a baseline.

Using Fixed-Duration Tasks

You might prefer to use the fixed-duration scheduling method for certain tasks, especially when you expect a task to take a fixed amount of time to complete regardless of assigned resources.

Select fixed-duration scheduling when you want a duration to remain unchanged, or if you want to estimate the duration yourself. You can still assign resources to tasks, but Microsoft Project won't change the duration as you adjust resource assignments.

For example, you might know that it takes two hours to drive a truckload of office furniture 50 miles. No matter how many workers you assign to make the trip, the task duration remains two hours. In this case, using fixed-duration scheduling ensures that your task duration remains the same regardless of the resource assignments you make.

Designate a task as fixed-duration

You want to allow everyone one week for the "Review at corporate level" task, because each reviewer reads the project proposal independently. Designate this task as fixed-duration so you can add reviewers without changing the duration.

1   In the Gantt table, double-click task 4, "Review at corporate level."

2   Click the Resources tab.

3   Click the Duration Type arrow and select Fixed Duration.

Leave the dialog box open for now, so you can also change the number of vice presidents assigned to the task.

Add resources to a fixed-duration task

Originally, when the resource for this task was entered, there was only one vice president. However, Victory Sports has just completed reorganizing its rapidly growing groups, so there are now three vice presidents, all of whom want to review your proposal. Increase the number of reviewers for the "Review at corporate level" task.

1   In the Units column, type **3**

2   Click the enter button in the entry bar, or press ENTER.

3   Choose the OK button.

Note that the duration is still one week. No matter how many vice presidents review the project proposal, each needs one week to finish the job.

Goto Selected Task

4   On the Standard toolbar, click the Goto Selected Task button.

The Gantt bar reflects the number of resources assigned to the task.

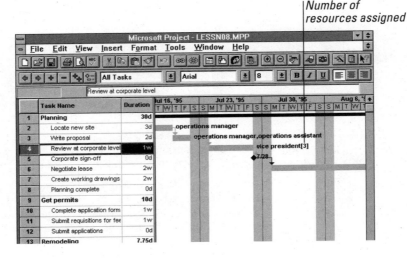

Save

Save your project

▶ On the Standard toolbar, click the Save button, and save without a baseline.

One Step Further

In addition to the duration, it is often useful to see the total hours of work scheduled for a task. Microsoft Project calculates work hours by multiplying the duration for the task by the hours specified in the work day of the base calendar for each different resource. To see the work hours for a task, display the project using the Work Table.

▶ From the View menu, choose Table: Entry, and then choose Work.

The Gantt table displays scheduled work hours for each task, as shown in the following illustration.

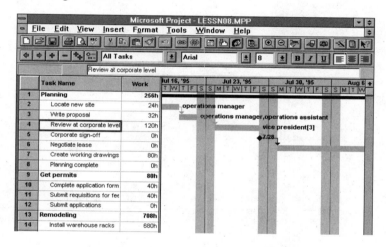

Notice that the total work hours for task 14, "Install warehouse racks," is 680 hours. This value is the total of 16 warehouse workers assigned to work one week on the task (16 workers at 40 hours each is 640 hours) plus the warehouse supervisor at 40 hours, for a total of 680 hours.

If You Want to Continue to the Next Lesson

1 From the File menu, choose Close to close your project file.

2 Choose the Yes button if you see the message box asking whether you want to save your work. Save the project without a baseline.

If You Want to Quit Microsoft Project for Now

1 From the File menu, choose Exit.

2 Choose the Yes button if you see the message box asking whether you want to save your work. Save the project without a baseline.

Lesson Summary

To	Do this
Use resource-driven scheduling	This is the default scheduling method. You do not need to make any special selections. As you add resources to a resource-driven task, its duration decreases.
Change the number of resource units for a selected task	Click the Resource Assignment button. In the Resource Assignment dialog box, click in the Units cell for the assigned resource and enter the number of units. Click the enter button.
Add a new resource to a selected task	Click the Resource Assignment button. In the Resource Assignment dialog box, click in the Units cell for the additional resource you want to assign. Click the Assign button.
Use fixed-duration scheduling for a selected task	Double-click the task to open the Task Information dialog box. On the Resources tab, change the Duration Type option to Fixed Duration.

For more information on	See in *Microsoft Project User's Guide*
Scheduling methods	Chapter 5, "Adding People and Equipment to Your Project"

For online information about	From the <u>H</u>elp menu, choose <u>S</u>earch and then type
Adjusting schedules	scheduling

Preview of the Next Lesson

In the next lesson, you'll learn how to use different views to examine and identify resource allocations. You will learn a variety of ways to resolve resource conflicts. In addition, you'll set a baseline for the project, so that in later lessons you can compare your current schedule with original plan information.

Managing Resource Workloads

In this lesson, you'll learn about ways you can manage overallocated resources to resolve resource conflicts. You'll adjust resource workloads and learn to identify and resolve delays caused when you assign a resource too many tasks scheduled at the same time.

You will learn how to:

- View resource workloads.
- Identify overallocated resources.
- Resolve resource conflicts.
- Set a baseline for the project.

Estimated lesson time: 30 minutes

Start Microsoft Project

If you closed Microsoft Project in the last lesson, you need to restart the application before you can continue.

▶ Double-click the Microsoft Project icon.

Start the lesson

Open the project file called 09LESSN.MPP, and save it as LESSN09.MPP.

If you see the Welcome dialog box, click Close. If you see the Tip Of The Day dialog box, read the tip, and then click OK.

1 From the File menu, choose Open.

2 In the Directories box, double-click PRACTICE.

3 In the File Name box, double-click 09LESSN.MPP.

4 From the File menu, choose Save As.

If you see the PlanningWizard, click the second option button and click OK. Continue with step 5.

5 In the File Name box, type **lessn09.mpp**

6 Choose the OK button.

Microsoft Project stores your project on your hard disk with the filename LESSN09.MPP. This file is similar to the project file you worked with in the last lesson; however, it contains additional resources already assigned to tasks.

Resolving Resource Conflicts

Resource conflicts occur when the amount of a particular resource required at a given time exceeds the specified maximum units for that resource. For example, in the previous lesson, you decreased the duration for the task to install warehouse racks by increasing the number of resources assigned to it from 8 to 16. This immediately resulted in a resource overallocation. Because the maximum number of resources is 15, and the task requires 16, you have overallocated the day warehouse workers resources.

Resource conflicts don't always occur in the same task. It is common to assign the same resource to more than one task. If the tasks overlap, the resource could be overallocated. For example, you might have two painters assigned to paint the conference room at the same time three painters are scheduled to paint the executive offices. Even though you might have a maximum of four painters on your team, you need *five* painters to complete both tasks on time. You have a resource allocation conflict because the number of painters you need at a given time exceeds the maximum number of painters available for the project.

Microsoft Project displays a message in the status bar when it finds a resource conflict. Although you can continue to work on your plan, you need to *level* the resources so that your plan accurately reflects the resources required to complete all the tasks. Leveling resources means ensuring that peak usage of a particular resource never exceeds the maximum number of available units for that resource.

For example, in the case of the overallocated painters, you need to make adjustments to the plan so that you never need more than four painters at one time, or else you would need to increase the number of painters on the project team. Microsoft Project offers several ways to resolve a resource conflict.

- You can choose to level resources manually if your project requires using several strategies to level resources. Leveling resources yourself allows you to try a variety of other adjustments to resource assignments or to task schedules according to the specific needs in your project.

- You can use resource leveling commands to have Microsoft Project resolve resource conflicts for you. These commands resolve the conflict by delaying overlapping tasks that caused the conflict. If you use the commands, Microsoft Project resolves the resource conflict with the painters, mentioned above, by rescheduling the start of painting the executive offices after painting the conference room has been completed.

- You can also enlist the aid of *Cue Cards*, which are built-in "coaches" that guide you step-by-step in using Microsoft Project features, including the process of leveling resources. At the end of this lesson, the "One Step Further" section guides you in using a Cue Card to level resources.

Resolving Resource Conflicts Yourself

When you need to resolve the conflict yourself, you can use any one or a combination of the following strategies. The steps in this lesson help you discover the different alternatives you might try in your own projects.

Increase the maximum units of a resource available. If you really have additional resources available, enter a larger number of maximum units in the Resource Information dialog box or on the Resource Sheet.

Assign a different resource to the overallocated task.   Determine whether you have another comparable resource available that could do the work. For example, assigning the operations assistant to a task might free the operations manager for another task. You can do this in any view in which you can assign resources to tasks.

Adjust task relationships or constraints.   When two overlapping tasks cause an allocation conflict, you might be able to reschedule a task so that one task starts later.

Allow overtime.   You can enter overtime work for the resource in the Ovt Work field in the Task Form or in the Resource Form. Overtime work is paid at the overtime rate.

Extend working days and hours on the resource calendar.   Use this method (instead of entering overtime work) if you don't want the additional work to be incurred at the overtime rate, and if you want the additional work to be included in the task schedule.

Using Resource Management Tools

The status bar displays a message when the first resource in the project is overallocated. To see whether there are other overallocated resources, you display the project in the Resource Sheet view. In this view, the overallocated resources are displayed in red if you are using a color monitor. If you are using a monochrome monitor, overallocated resources appear in bold. Begin resolving resource conflicts by displaying the Resource Sheet view.

Display the Resource Sheet view

▶ From the View menu, choose Resource Sheet.

The Resource Sheet looks like the following illustration.

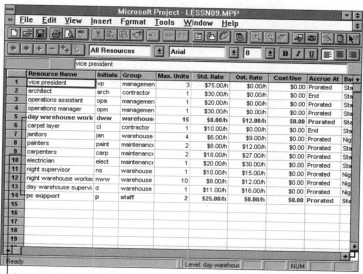

Overallocated resources

Two resources, "day warehouse workers" and "pc support," are overallocated in the project. First you will resolve the day warehouse workers overallocation; then you will level the pc support resource.

Change the number of maximum units

After explaining the benefits of adding an additional worker to the day warehouse crew, you have received approval to hire an additional day warehouse worker. With the Resource Sheet open, change the maximum number of units to 16.

1   Select the Max. Units cell for the day warehouse workers, and then type **16**

2   Click the enter button in the entry bar, or press ENTER.

Notice that even after increasing the maximum number of units for this resource, the resource is still overallocated. You will need to explore other strategies to level the workload for the day warehouse workers.

Using the Resource Usage View

The Resource Usage view displays resource usage over time in a table format. Use this view to determine to what extent a resource is overused or underused. By locating underallocated resources you can identify resources that can assist or replace overallocated resources.

Display the Resource Usage view

1   From the View menu, choose Resource Usage.

The Resource Usage view appears, displaying a list of resources and a timescale that shows allocations.

2   Press ALT+HOME to move quickly to the beginning of the project, if it is not already there.

Your Resource Usage view looks like the following illustration.

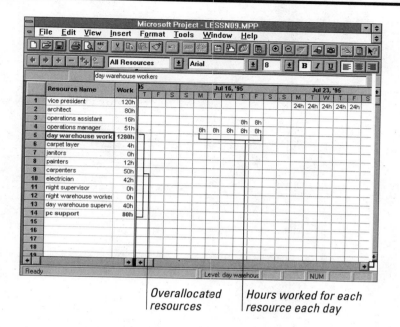

Overallocated resources

Hours worked for each resource each day

3 In the calendar side of the view, scroll through the dates horizontally until you see the week of September 10, 1995.

The #'s mean that the number in the cell is too wide to fit in the column. You need to adjust the width of the columns.

4 Double-click in the timescale area at the top of the date columns.

The Timescale dialog box appears.

5 In the Enlarge box, select the existing value, and then type **120**

This number increases the column width by 20 percent.

6 Choose the OK button.

The columns are now wide enough to display all the information.

7 Continue scrolling until you see the week of October 1, 1995.

Notice that several of the tasks scheduled during this week are highlighted in red (or bold). The tasks during this period are causing the resource overallocation of the day warehouse workers.

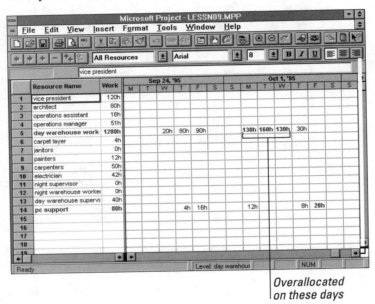

Overallocated
on these days

Display the Resource Graph

The *Resource Graph* provides a graphical representation of resource usage over time. Use the Resource Graph to see a profile of a resource's allocation and determine by how many hours a resource is overallocated.

In the following steps, you first select the overallocated day warehouse workers. Then you display the Resource Graph to see the peak units for this resource.

1 Select the day warehouse workers resource.

2 From the View menu, choose Resource Graph.

3 Scroll to the week of October 1, 1995.

The resource graph for the day warehouse worker looks like the following illustration.

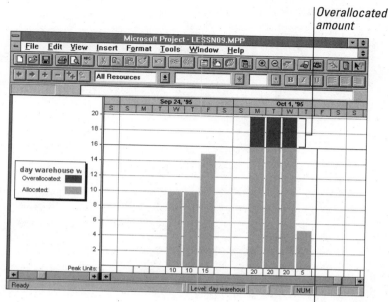

The Resource Graph shows that during the week of October 1, the peak usage for day warehouse workers is 20 but the maximum number of workers available is 16. (The maximum number of workers is specified in the Maximum Units field in the Resource Information dialog box and indicated on the Resource Graph as a bold line.) The day warehouse workers resource is overallocated by 4 units. Because you are unable to convince management to hire additional workers (thus increasing the maximum units) to address the overallocation, you need to explore other alternatives for leveling this resource.

View Task Assignments

To find out which tasks the overallocated day warehouse workers are assigned to, use the Resource Allocation view. This is a combination view that consists of the Resource Usage view over the Delay Gantt view. It does not appear on the View menu, but you can display it using the More Views command. You can also display the Resource Management toolbar and display the Resource Allocation view. Because using this toolbar is faster than making menu selections and using dialog boxes, display the Resource Management toolbar.

Display the Resource Management Toolbar and Resource Allocation view

1   Click a toolbar with the right mouse button, and from the shortcut menu, choose Resource Management.

The Resource Management toolbar appears. This toolbar contains the buttons for commands you use when working with resources.

Displays Resource Allocation view

   Displays Resource Graph

      Displays tasks assigned to a specific resource

Displays Cue Cards for resource leveling

Displays Resource Assignment dialog box

Displays Task Entry view

Resource Allocation View

2   On the Resource Management toolbar, click the Resource Allocation View button. The Resource Allocation view appears. It looks like the following illustration.

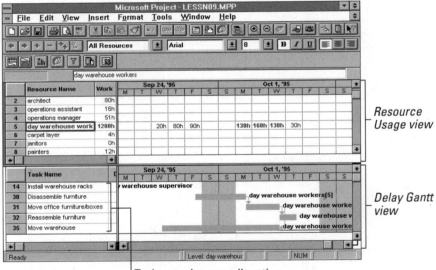

Resource Usage view

Delay Gantt view

Tasks causing overallocation

The Delay Gantt view shows all the tasks to which the day warehouse workers are assigned. Note that the "Move office furniture/boxes" and "Move warehouse" tasks overlap, which is when the peak usage occurs.

Review resource workload

▶ In the Resource Usage area (in the top half of the view), scroll downward (if necessary) until you see the night warehouse workers resource. Be sure the day warehouse workers resource name is still selected.

You can see in the Resource Usage view that the night warehouse workers are not assigned to any moving tasks during the period when the day warehouse workers are overallocated.

Substitute a resource

One way to level resources is to assign a different resource to the task. Because the night warehouse workers appear to be available, replace the day warehouse workers with the night warehouse workers for one of these moving tasks.

1   In the Delay Gantt view (in the bottom half of the view), select task 31, "Move office furniture/boxes."

Resource
Assignment

2   On the Resource Management toolbar, click the Resource Assignment button.

The Resource Assignment dialog box appears. Drag the dialog box near the top of the window to get a clear view of the Gantt bars.

3   In the Name column of this dialog box, select day warehouse workers from the list.

4   Click the Replace button.

The Replace Resource dialog box appears.

5   In the Units column for night warehouse workers, type **10**

You need to assign 10 night warehouse workers.

6   Click the enter button in the entry bar, or press ENTER.

7   Choose the OK button and then click the Close button.

The Resource Assignment dialog box closes. The message "Level: pc support" replaces the previous overallocation message in the status bar. The Delay Gantt view displays the tasks now assigned to the day warehouse workers; task 31 has been removed from the list.

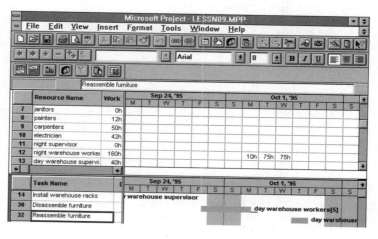

By assigning a different, equally capable resource to move the furniture and boxes, you have solved the overallocation problems for the day warehouse workers. Later in this lesson, you will level the pc support resource using a different resource leveling technique.

8   Click a toolbar with the right mouse button, and from the shortcut menu, choose Resource Management to hide the Resource Management toolbar.

9   In the top part of the view, select resource 12, "night warehouse workers."

Task 31 is now assigned to the night warehouse workers.

Returning to the Gantt Chart View

When you have a combination view open (such as the Resource Allocation view), choosing a view from the View menu displays the new view only in the currently active part of the window. The currently active part of the window is the one you clicked in last. The dark bar at the left indicates the active view. The following illustration indicates that the currently active view is the Resource Usage view in the top half of the window.

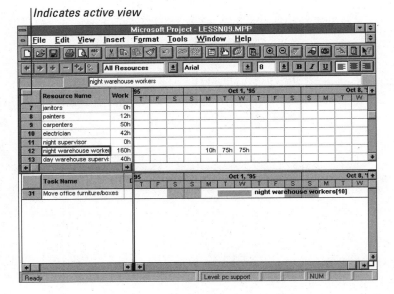

To display a full screen view when you have a combination view, you must first press SHIFT as you select the new view from the View menu.

Return to the Gantt Chart view

Display a full screen view of the Gantt Chart view.

▶   Hold down SHIFT and from the View menu, choose Gantt Chart.

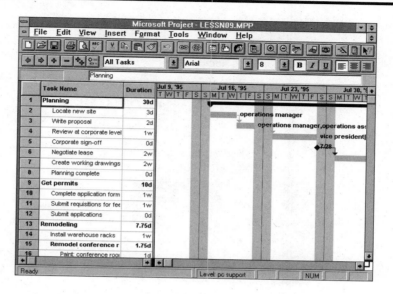

Leveling Resources Automatically

If the best solution for leveling resources is to delay overlapping tasks (tasks that occur at the same time), you can have Microsoft Project resolve resource conflicts for you by using the Resource Leveling command on the Tools menu. In the Resource Leveling dialog box, you can specify manual or automatic leveling.

With manual leveling (the default option), you must resolve resource conflicts yourself, as you did in this lesson, or you can click the Level Now button to have Microsoft Project level the resource. When you enable automatic leveling with the Automatic option button, Microsoft Project levels the overallocated resource as soon as it becomes overallocated.

When Microsoft Project levels a resource, it adds a delay in the Delay field in the Delay Gantt view for the task (except for tasks already in progress). You can choose Undo Level from the Edit menu immediately after leveling to remove all changes, or you can click the Remove Leveling button in the Resource Leveling dialog box.

Note If you have scheduled your project from Finish to Start (in the Summary Info dialog box), you will not be able to take advantage of the automatic leveling feature. Other factors preventing automatic leveling include specifying conflicting task constraints and conflicting predecessor relationships. You might need to remove constraints or links to allow automatic leveling.

Level another resource by delaying a task

The pc support resource is still overallocated. Because you cannot substitute or hire additional pc support resources, you need to level the pc support workload by delaying the overlapping tasks 33 and 34. You can have Microsoft Project delay and reschedule the tasks for you by using the Level Now button.

1 Click in the Task Name cell for task 33.

2 On the Standard toolbar, click the Goto Selected Task button.

3 From the Tools menu, choose Resource Leveling.

The Resource Leveling dialog box appears.

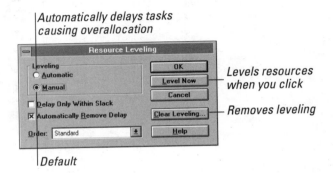

Automatically delays tasks causing overallocation

Levels resources when you click

Removes leveling

Default

4 Click the Level Now button.

The dialog box closes and you return to the Gantt Chart. Notice that task 34, "Install network software," is scheduled to start after the previous task ends.

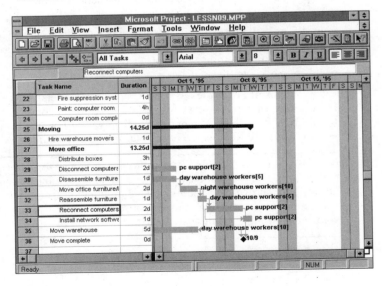

Goto Selected Task

Tip   To see how Microsoft Project delayed each overallocated task, you can use the Delay Gantt view to display Gantt bars that show delay and *slack* (the amount of time between the end of one task and the start of its successor).

Creating a Baseline

Now that you have resolved the resource conflict in the schedule, the current plan represents your best estimate of how the project should proceed and what resources it will take to accomplish the move. You can now save your project information as a *baseline* for future comparisons to actual progress. The Save Baseline command on the Tracking menu (from the Tools menu) stores a copy of task and resource information. The information is "frozen" and is used for reference purposes only.

Note   If you have enabled the option to have the PlanningWizard prompt you to save a baseline whenever you save the project, you see a PlanningWizard message giving you a choice to save the project with or without a baseline. With this PlanningWizard option enabled, click the Save button on the Standard toolbar. Then you can choose the option button to save the baseline.

Microsoft Project uses the baseline data to calculate and display *variance*—the difference between what was originally planned and what is currently scheduled after you make changes.

Create a baseline for future comparisons

Save the plan for the project as your baseline. In later lessons, you'll compare this data to updated project information.

1   From the Tools menu, choose Tracking, then choose Save Baseline.

The Save Baseline dialog box appears. In this dialog box, you can specify different baseline saving options.

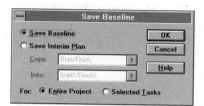

The options selected in the dialog box are all correct for setting the plan, so you don't need to change them. In Lesson 14, "Tracking Project Progress," you learn more about the different options available when setting the plan.

2   Choose the OK button.

3   From the File menu, choose Save.

One Step Further

Microsoft Project provides many tools and techniques for resolving resource conflicts. To help understand the tools you have available, you can use Cue Cards, which display valuable illustrations and provide useful tips for leveling resources.

1   Click a toolbar with the right mouse button and, from the shortcut menu, choose Resource Management.

The Resource Management toolbar appears.

Leveling CueCards

2   On the Resource Management toolbar, click the Leveling CueCards button.

The Cue Cards window displays the steps for resolving resource conflicts yourself (as you did in this lesson).

3   In the Cue Cards window, click the Back button to see the previous Cue Card that lists other Cue Card topics related to resolving resource conflicts.

The Cue Cards window displays a list of strategies for resolving resource conflicts.

4   Click the button labeled "Learn about strategies for resolving resource overallocations."

A Cue Card appears that explains how resource overallocations occur and how to resolve them. Read this Cue Card before you continue.

5   Click the Next button.

You return to the Cue Card menu.

6   Double-click the Control-menu box in the Cue Cards window to close it.

7   Click a toolbar with the right mouse button, and then choose Resource Management to hide the Resource Management toolbar.

If You Want to Continue to the Next Lesson

1   From the File menu, choose Close to close your project file.

2   Choose the Yes button if you see the message box asking whether you want to save your work.

If You Want to Quit Microsoft Project for Now

1   From the File menu, choose Exit.

2   Choose the Yes button if you see the message box asking whether you want to save your work.

Lesson Summary

To	Do this	Button
View resource workloads	Click the Resource Sheet, Resource Graph or Resource Usage views on the View menu. On the Resource Management toolbar, click the Resource Allocation View button.	
Resolve resource conflicts	Resolve the conflicts yourself by adjusting individual resource assignments and task schedules. *or* Choose the Resource Leveling command on the Tools menu. Specify manual or automatic leveling in the Resource Leveling dialog box. *or* Click the Leveling CueCards button on the Resource Management toolbar to guide you through the process.	
Set a baseline for the project	Choose the Save Baseline command on the Tracking submenu of the Tools menu. Specify saving options in the Save Baseline dialog box.	

For more information on	See in *Microsoft Project User's Guide*
Leveling resources	Chapter 7, "Evaluating and Adjusting Your Schedule"
Resource Graph	Chapter 7, "Evaluating and Adjusting Your Schedule"
Resource Usage View	Chapter 7, "Evaluating and Adjusting Your Schedule"

For online information about	From the <u>H</u>elp menu, choose <u>S</u>earch and then type
Managing resources	resources: overallocated Resource Allocation Resource Usage view resolving overallocated resources

Preview of the Next Lessons

In the next part of the book, you will learn about viewing and organizing your project in different ways. In the next lesson, you will learn how to display only the information you need at a specific time or to answer a specifc question about the project.

Review & Practice

In the lessons in Part 2 "Working with Resources," you learned skills to help you enter and schedule resource information in a project. If you want to practice these skills and test your knowledge before you proceed with the lessons in Part 3, you can work through the Review & Practice section following this lesson.

Part 2   Review & Practice

Before you begin planning a project of your own, practice the skills you learned in Part 2 by working through the resource management activities in this Review & Practice section. You'll define the people, equipment, and materials needed to introduce a new line of hiking boots, called Summit Boots. You will assign resources to the tasks you entered in the project from the Part 1 Review & Practice. You'll also set up a resource calendar to define a resource's availability, check resource usage, resolve overallocations, and obtain cost estimates to complete specific tasks.

Scenario

As product manager for the Summit Boots product launch, you have enlisted resources from your department as well as other resources inside Victory Sports. You will also have outside resources to complete specialized tasks. In your role as product manager, you need to coordinate who will do each task, when they will do it, and when they are available.

You will review and practice how to:

- Enter resources.

- Enter cost information.

- Change calendars.

- Resolve resource overallocations.

- Save the project with a baseline.

Estimated practice time: 30 minutes

Before You Begin

1 Open the scenario project file called P2REVIEW.MPP. Before you make any changes in this project, save it with the new name REVIEWP2.MPP. Be sure to save the project without a baseline.

   This project file should look similar to the file you saved after completing the steps in the Part 1 Review & Practice. However, notice that your assistant has already entered some resources in the resource pool and has assigned specific resources to several tasks. Because some resources are overallocated, you need to resolve the resource conflict.

2 Display the Resource Management toolbar for easy access to useful resource-related features.

Step 1: **Enter New Resources**

To help develop the new hiking boots, Victory Sports has hired a boot designer and a marketing analyst. Add these two resources to the resource pool.

1   Use the Resource Assignment dialog box to add the following resources:

designer
analyst

2   Double-click each resource name and enter the following resource details:

Resource	Group	Code
designer	**Staff**	**100**
analyst	**Marketing**	**300**

After closing the Resource Information dialog box for the last resource, you can keep the Resource Assignment dialog box open for the next step.

For more information on	See
Entering resources	Lesson 6

Step 2: **Assign Resources to Tasks**

After entering new resources to the resource pool, you can assign the resources to tasks. You will also assign yourself (as the product manager) and a marketing analyst to several tasks. These resources are already in the resource pool.

▶   Assign the following resources to the following tasks:

Resource	Task ID
product manager	2, 3, 5, 15
designer	10, 12
analyst	7, 21

For more information on	See
Assigning resources to tasks	Lesson 6

Step 3: **Change the Calendar**

Now that you have assigned resources to tasks, you are ready to adjust the working times for different resources in the project.

Specify a holiday

April 19, 1996 is Spring Fever day and a company holiday. Change this day to a nonworking day in the base calendar.

▶ In the Base calendar for the project, scroll to April 1996, and change the day from working to nonworking.

Create a new base calendar

To alleviate traffic congestion, Victory Sports has decided to stagger work hours for some employees. Create a copy of the Standard base calendar, and call it Line Workers. Then adjust the working hours for the line workers.

1 Copy the base calendar and name it Line Workers.

2 Select all working day headings (Monday through Friday), and change the working hours to be from 7:00 A.M. to 11:00 A.M. and from 12:00 P.M. to 4:00 P.M.

3 Assign the Line Workers calendar to the line workers resource. (Hint: Double-click the resource name in the Resource Assignment dialog box to display the Resource Information dialog box.)

Modify a Resource Calendar

▶ Change the resource calendar for the product manager to reflect the fact that you will be taking a vacation day on March 14, 1996.

For more information on	See
Changing the Standard calendar	Lesson 7
Editing a resource calendar	Lesson 7

Step 4: Schedule Resources

Specify that the duration for task 4 is not affected by the number of senior managers assigned to the task, and then assign all three senior managers to the task of reviewing your plan.

1 Change the duration for task 4 to Fixed Duration. (Hint: Double-click the task to display the Task Information dialog box.)

2 Assign three senior managers to task 4.

Be sure to assign the resources to the task by pressing ENTER.

For more information on	See
Scheduling with resources	Lesson 8

Step 5: Review and Level Resource Workloads

Review your resource workloads to determine any overallocations, and then resolve any resource conflicts.

Review Resource Workloads

▶ Use the Resource Graph and Resource Usage views to display resource workloads over time. Look for overallocated resources. Then use the Resource Allocation view to locate tasks causing overallocation.

Level Overallocated Resources

Resolve overallocated resource conflicts for the line workers by replacing them with another resource for task 19, "Produce packaging." The resources from Morton Marketing will take over this task.

1 For task 19, use the Resource Assignment dialog box to replace the line workers with 4 units of the Morton Marketing resource.

2 Close the Resource Assignment dialog box.

For more information on	See
Examining workloads	Lesson 9
Resolving resource conflicts	Lesson 9

Step 6: Save a Baseline

After making resource assignments and leveling the workload, you and your project team are ready to commit to the current finish date (May 16, 1996) as a deadline. To establish a baseline against which you can compare and track project progress and results, save the project with a baseline.

1 Display a full screen Gantt Chart view.

2 Hide the Resource Management toolbar.

3 Save the baseline and save the project file.

For more information on	See
Saving a baseline	Lesson 9

If You Want to Continue to the Next Lesson

▶ From the File menu, choose Close to close your project file.

If You Want to Quit Microsoft Project for Now

▶ From the File menu, choose Exit.

3 Viewing the Plan

Applying Project Filters and Sorting

As you saw in Lesson 5, outlining allows you to view different levels of detail in your project. In this lesson, you'll learn a way to view only the tasks you want by applying *filters*. You'll use filters provided in Microsoft Project, and you'll create custom filters to display information that is unique to your project. In addition, you'll learn to use sorting as a quick and easy way to rearrange a project's tasks and resources.

You will learn how to:

- Apply a filter to display information.
- Apply a filter to highlight information.
- Create a custom filter.
- Sort tasks using one field.
- Sort tasks using multiple fields.

Estimated lesson time: 45 minutes

Start Microsoft Project

If you closed Microsoft Project in the last lesson, you need to restart the application before you can continue.

If you see the Welcome dialog box, click the Close button. If you see the Tip Of The Day dialog box, read the tip, and then click OK.

▶ Double-click the Microsoft Project icon.

Start the lesson

Open the project file called 10LESSN.MPP, and save it as LESSN10.MPP.

1 From the File menu, choose Open.

2 In the Directories box, double-click PRACTICE.

3 In the File Name box, double-click 10LESSN.MPP.

4 From the File menu, choose Save As.

5 In the File Name box, type **lessn10.mpp**

6 Choose the OK button.

Microsoft Project stores your project on the hard disk with the filename LESSN10.MPP. This project file is similar to the one used in the previous lesson. The timescale in this project has been adjusted so that you can better observe the results of the exercises in this lesson.

Filtering Your Project Tasks

As the number of tasks in your project increases, you might find it useful to display only certain tasks in which you are interested at the moment. Filters make it easier to manage large projects by displaying or highlighting only the information you currently need. For example, Microsoft Project supplies a Milestones filter that displays or highlights only milestone tasks, along with the associated summary tasks. All other tasks are temporarily hidden or, with the highlight option, not highlighted. Interactive filters allow you to enter criteria you specify (such as a date) or display data within a range of values.

In this lesson, you will use *task filters* to focus on task-related information and *resource filters* to focus on resource-related information.

Note   Remember that filters affect the screen display, but not the tasks in the project itself.

Filtering Project Information

There are two ways to display the information presented by a filter. By default, the filter displays only the information that matches the criteria; it hides the information that does not match. You also have the option to have the filter highlight (display in another color or in bold) the data that matches the criteria. You are still able to see the tasks that do not match.

Display the milestones

The plant supervisor would like to see a list of the milestones in this project. Milestones are scattered throughout the project, but Microsoft Project provides a filter that displays only the milestones and their associated summary tasks.

▶ On the Formatting toolbar, click the down arrow next to the Filter list box, and then select Milestones.

In the Gantt table, only the names of the milestone tasks and their corresponding summary tasks appear. In the Gantt Chart, only the Gantt bars for the milestone and summary tasks appear. The Gantt bars for all the other tasks are hidden.

Your view looks similar to the following illustration.

Milestone filter selected

[Microsoft Project screenshot - LESSN10.MPP]

	Task Name	Duration
1	Planning	30d
5	Corporate sign-off	0d
8	Planning complete	0d
9	Get permits	10d
12	Submit applications	0d
13	Remodeling	7.75d
15	Remodel conference r	1.75d
19	Conference room com	0d
20	Remodel computer ro	1.75d
24	Computer room comp	0d
25	Moving	13.25d
35	Move complete	0d
36		
37		
38		
39		

Milestones

Print the active view

This is the information the plant supervisor wants to see. You can quickly print this information by clicking the Print button. But first, preview your project as it will look when you print it. Even if your computer is not connected to a printer, you can see the view in Print Preview mode.

Print Preview

1 On the Standard toolbar, click the Print Preview button.

Microsoft Project prints only the active view of your project. A preview of your project looks like the following illustration.

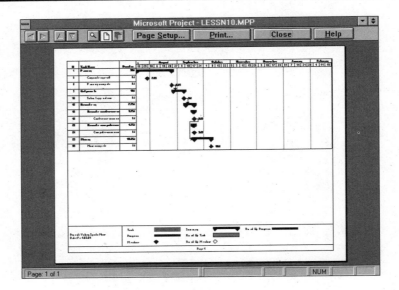

2 If your computer is connected to a printer, choose the Print button and then choose the OK button. If it is not connected to a printer, choose the Close button.

Microsoft Project prints the Gantt Chart you see on your screen. You'll learn more about printing in Lesson 12, "Printing Views and Reports."

Highlight the milestones

So that you can see the other tasks, but still focus on milestones, use the highlighting option (by holding down SHIFT) when using the Milestones filter.

▶ Hold down SHIFT and then, from the Tools menu, choose Filtered For: Milestones, and then choose Milestones.

All the tasks are displayed again, but the milestones are now highlighted in the table either in blue or in bold. The highlighting you see depends on the kind of monitor you are using. Your project looks like the following illustration.

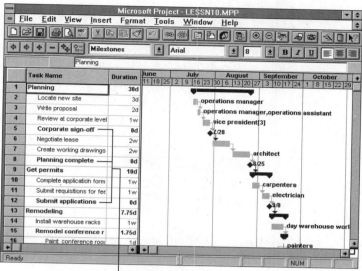

Highlighted tasks

Remove the filter and display all tasks

After you have reviewed the milestones with the plant supervisor, you can remove the highlighting filter.

▶ From the Filter list box on the Formatting toolbar, select All Tasks.

Specifying Filter Criteria

If you want to specify different criteria each time you use a filter (such as a date or range of task IDs), you can use an interactive filter. When you choose an interactive filter, you can specify a value or range of values to be applied in the filter. Filters displayed with an ellipsis (...) in the Filtered For submenu and in the Filters box on the Formatting toolbar are interactive filters.

Display tasks for a specific period in the project

On August 16 and 17, all the office employees at Victory Sports are required to attend a presentation about the company retirement program. In planning the move, you want to focus on the tasks in the schedule that could be affected during this time. Using the Date Range interactive filter, you can display tasks that take place on these two days.

1   From the Filter list box on the Formatting toolbar, select Date Range.

The Date Range dialog box appears. In this dialog box, you enter the start of the date range.

2   In the box, type **8/16/95** and then choose the OK button.

The next dialog box appears. In this dialog box, you enter the last date in the range.

3   In the box, type **8/17/95** and then choose the OK button.

Only the tasks that occur between 8/16/95 and 8/17/95 appear. The only task in this period is task 7, "Create working drawings." Because the architect is a contractor and will not attend the meeting, the employee meetings will not have a significant effect on this task.

Tip   To see the start and finish dates in the Gantt table, you can drag the divider that separates the Gantt table from the Gantt Chart to the right until you see the Start and Finish columns.

Remove the filter and display all tasks

After you have reviewed the filtered tasks, you can display all the tasks in the project by removing the filter.

▶   From the Filter list box on the Formatting toolbar, select All Tasks.

Displaying Tasks for a Specific Resource

When working with resources, you can display the Resource Management toolbar for easy access to resource-related commands.

When you want to see only those tasks assigned to specific resources, you can use the Using Resource and Resource Group filters. With the Using Resource filter, you can specify the name of a specific resource. Similarly, you can use the Resource Group filter to display tasks for a specific group of resources. For example, to prepare for a meeting in which senior management wants to know about the role of contractors in the project, you can use the Resource Group filter to display those tasks assigned to contractors (such as architects, carpenters, carpet layers, electricians, and painters).

Display tasks assigned to contractors

When contractor resources were entered into the resource pool for the project, "contractor" was entered in the Group box of the Resource Information dialog box. Use the Resource Group filter to display tasks assigned to contractor resources.

1   From the Filter list box on the Formatting toolbar, select Resource Group.

The Resource Group dialog box appears, where you can specify the group you want to filter.

2   In the Group Name box, type **contractor**

3   Choose the OK button.

The tasks assigned to the contractor resources appear in the Gantt Chart view.

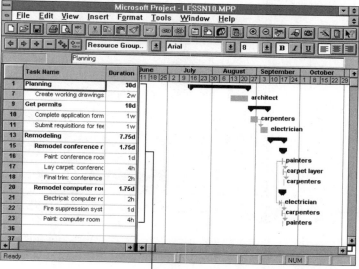

| Tasks assigned to contractor resources

Creating a Custom Filter

Even though Microsoft Project supplies several filters, it is easy for you to create your own. For example, if you frequently want to focus on tasks that start after a particular date, you can create a filter so that you don't have to enter the date each time.

To define your own filter, you name the new filter and enter filter criteria in a dialog box. For quick access, you can add any filter you create to the Filtered For submenu.

Name a custom filter

To assist you in the Victory Sports move project, you are looking for short tasks that could be assigned to temporary resources. To help you identify short tasks requiring one day or less, create a custom filter.

1 From the Tools menu, choose Filtered For: Resource Group, and then choose More Filters.

The More Filters dialog box appears. It contains additional Task and Resource filters you can apply. You can also choose to create a new filter in this dialog box.

If you are in a Task view, the More Filters dialog box displays task-related filters. If you are in a Resource view, the dialog box displays resource-related filters.

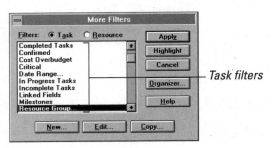

— *Task filters*

2 Click the New button.

The Filter Definition dialog box appears. You enter filter criteria in this dialog box.

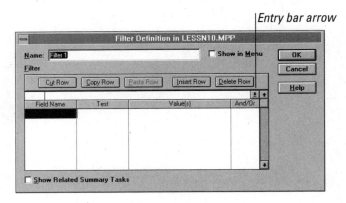

|*Entry bar arrow*

3 In the Name box, type **ShortTasks**

Enter the filter criteria

1   Click the Field Name column.

In this part of the dialog box, you enter each of the filter criteria in its own row. Later you will learn to combine filter criteria by entering multiple filters in separate rows.

2   Click the entry bar down arrow (at the right end of the dialog box) to display the list of fields.

You can filter tasks by any of these fields.

3   Select Duration from the list.

You might need to scroll downward to locate the field.

4   Move to the Test column.

In this column, you select how you want each task duration compared to the search criteria.

5   Click the entry bar arrow to display the list of tests, and then select Less Or Equal from the list.

6   Move to the Value(s) column and type **1d**

7   Click the enter button on the entry bar, or press ENTER.

Adds filter to Filtered For submenu

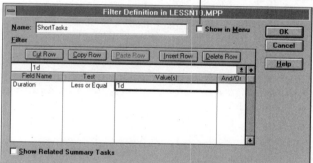

8   Choose the OK button to return to the More Filters dialog box.

Notice that the "ShortTasks" filter is selected in the list of filters.

9   Click the Apply button to apply the filter.

Only the tasks with a duration of one day or less appear in the Gantt table and Gantt Chart. Because milestones have a duration of 0d (that is, less than 1), the milestone tasks also appear.

Remove the filter and display all tasks

After you have reviewed the tasks displayed by the custom filter, you can display all the tasks in the project by removing the filter.

▶ From the Filter list box on the Formatting toolbar, select All Tasks.

Save your project

▶ On the Standard toolbar, click the Save button.

Customized filters are saved in the project file.

Save

With the Organizer available in the More Filters dialog box, you can copy filters and other features to other project files. See the One Step Further activity in Lesson 17 to learn about the Organizer.

Combining Filter Criteria

You might want to display tasks with a range of values or with specific values in two or more fields. You can create filters that display exactly what you want by using the And or Or operators. *Operators* allow you to combine filter criteria that are specified in multiple rows of the Filter Definition dialog box.

For example, to help focus on October's activities for a specific resource, you might wish to display only those tasks that begin *and* end in October, and that are performed by a resource you specify. To create such a filter, you need to define and combine three filters in the Filter box. The first filter looks for tasks with a Scheduled Start date greater than or equal to 10/1/95; the second filter looks for tasks with a Scheduled Finish date less than or equal to 10/31/95. From this list of tasks, the third filter looks for tasks assigned to the resource you specify. Using the And filter operator means that all three filters are in effect at the same time, so that a task must meet the criteria specified in all filters to be displayed.

Name another custom filter

The warehouse supervisor has asked to see a list of tasks to which all the warehouse workers are assigned in October. To prepare this information for the supervisor, create a filter that displays these tasks.

1   From the Tools menu, choose Filtered For: All Tasks, and then choose More Filters.

The More Filters dialog box appears.

2   Click the New button.

The Filter Definition dialog box appears.

3   In the Name box, type **October Warehouse**

Enter the first filter criterion

1   In the Field Name column, click the entry bar arrow to display the list of fields.

2   Select Start from the list.

You might need to scroll downward to locate the field.

3   In the Test column, click the entry bar arrow to display the list of tests.

4   Select Gtr Or Equal from the list.

5   In the Value(s) column, type **10/1/95**

6   Click the enter button on the entry bar, or press ENTER.

Combine filter criteria

1   In the And/Or column, click the entry bar arrow to display the two operators you can use, and then select And from the list.

2   Click in the Field Name column below Start, click the entry bar arrow to display the list of fields, and then select Finish from the list.

3   Move to the Test column, click the entry bar arrow to display the list of tests, and then select Less Or Equal from the list.

4   In the Value(s) column, type **10/31/95**

5   Click the enter button on the entry bar, or press ENTER.

Add a third criterion to combine

1   In the And/Or column, click the entry bar arrow to display the two operators you can use, and then select And from the list.

2   Click in the Field Name column below Finish, click the entry bar arrow to display the list of fields, and then select Resource Group from the list.

3   In the Test column, click the entry bar arrow to display the list of tests, and then select Equals from the list.

4   In the Value(s) column, type **warehouse**

5   Click the enter button in the entry bar, or press ENTER.

The completed dialog box looks like the following illustration.

First criterion

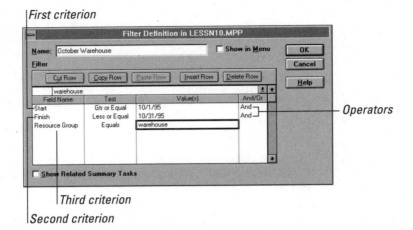

Operators

Third criterion

Second criterion

6   Choose the OK button.

7   In the More Filters dialog box, click the Apply button.

Only those tasks appear that begin and end in October and are performed by warehouse workers.

8   Select the first task in the Gantt table, and then click the Goto Selected Task button on the Standard toolbar.

Your project looks like the following illustration.

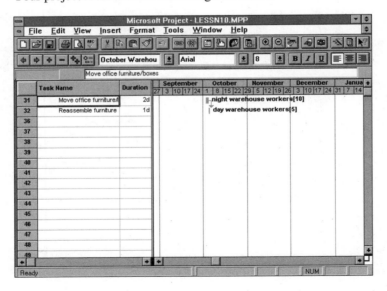

Change the timescale

To see the timescale in more detail, change the units on the timescale back to weeks over days.

Zoom In

1 On the Standard toolbar, click the Zoom In button twice to decrease the size of the units on the timescale.

The Gantt bars appear for warehouse worker tasks beginning on or after October 1, and ending on or before October 31.

2 In the Filters list box on the Formatting toolbar, select All Tasks.

Save your project

Save

▶ On the Standard toolbar, click the Save button.

Sorting Tasks

Sorting tasks and resources is another way you can organize project information. As you enter a task or resource, Microsoft Project assigns an ID number to it. By default, tasks and resources are listed in ascending (smallest to largest) order by ID number. When you sort a project, you rearrange the tasks or resources by specifying the fields that should control the order of the tasks. The Sort command on the Tools menu displays a submenu of fields by which you might wish to sort most often. With the Sort By command on the Sort submenu, you can specify up to three fields or *keys* at one time.

When you sort tasks or resources, the ID numbers of tasks or resources reflect the new sort order by default. By clearing the Permanently Renumber Tasks (or Resources) check box in the Sort By dialog box, you can rearrange tasks (and resources) without affecting the ID numbers. This option is in effect every time you sort in Microsoft Project.

Ascending and Descending Sort Orders

Microsoft Project can sort tasks in ascending or descending order. When a field contains text, it is sorted in ascending order from A through Z. When sorting date fields, Microsoft Project arranges their corresponding tasks in ascending order from the earliest date to the latest date. When sorting numeric fields, Microsoft Project arranges their corresponding tasks in ascending order from the lowest number to the highest number.

You select the Descending option button in the Sort dialog box to sort from Z through A or from the highest number to the lowest number. Microsoft Project ignores case when sorting text; uppercase and lowercase letters are sorted together.

Display the Task Sheet view

Use the Task Sheet view when you want to see task information in a spreadsheet-style format. Without the Gantt bars, this view helps you focus on task start and finish dates as well as resources. In some ways, you can use this view as a "to do" list for the project.

1 From the View menu, choose More Views.

2 In the More Views dialog box, scroll to Task Sheet and select it.

3 Click the Apply button.

Your project looks like the following illustration.

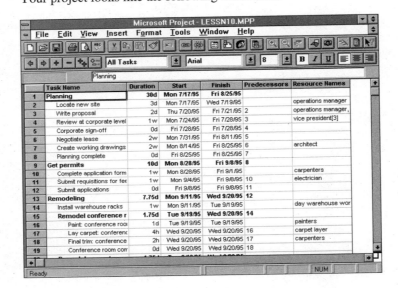

Sort the task list by duration

The tasks are currently listed in ascending order by ID number—the order in which you entered them. Because you now want to focus on those tasks that require the most time, follow these steps to sort tasks by the Duration field. Use descending order to ensure that the tasks requiring the most time appear first in the view.

1 From the Tools menu, choose Sort, and then choose Sort By.

The Sort dialog box appears. In this dialog box, you specify the fields by which you want to sort. You can also indicate ascending or descending order for each field.

2 Clear the Permanently Renumber Tasks check box, located near the bottom of the dialog box.

3 Click the Sort By down arrow to display the list of task field names.

The list of task field names appears.

Default sort order

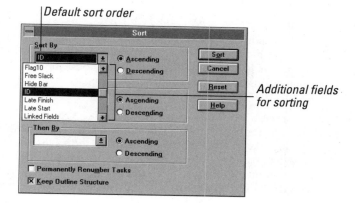

Additional fields for sorting

4   Scroll to and select Duration.

Duration appears in the Sort By box.

5   Click the Descending option button to sort the tasks from longest duration to shortest.

6   Click the Sort button.

The tasks under each summary task are sorted in descending order according to the contents of the Duration field. The original task ID numbers are retained. Your project in the Task Sheet view looks like the following illustration.

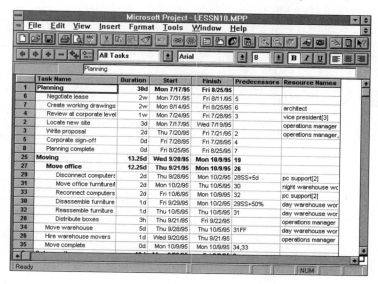

Sorting an Outlined Project

As you have learned, when you apply a filter or collapse part of an outlined project, some tasks are hidden from view. When you sort a filtered or collapsed task list, the outline structure is retained if the Keep Outline Structure check box is selected. This means that the tasks are sorted under each summary task. This option is the default setting.

If you clear the Keep Outline Structure check box, your task list is sorted without regard to outline structure. Once the outline no longer has its original structure, you cannot change the structure of the outline. This means that the outline buttons on the Formatting toolbar are disabled, and you cannot promote, demote, collapse, or expand tasks. If you want to use the outline buttons, you first need to return the task list to its original order by clicking the Reset button in the Sort dialog box.

Reset the task list to ID number order

Your new sort order replaces the previous one. You cannot use the Undo command to reverse the Sort command. To return your task list to ascending order by ID number, use the Reset button in the Sort dialog box. The Reset button also returns the Permanently Renumber Tasks check box to the default.

1   From the Tools menu, choose Sort, and then choose Sort By.

2   Click the Reset button to return the task list to ID number order.

3   Click the Sort button.

Now the Task Sheet displays tasks in the order in which you entered them.

Save

Save your project

▶   On the Standard toolbar, click the Save button.

Sorting by Multiple Fields

Another way to tap the power of sorting is to sort by two or more fields. When you specify two fields by which you want to sort, Microsoft Project sorts by the first field, and then sorts the tasks again within each grouping by the second field. For example, if you are working in the Resource Sheet view, it makes sense to first sort the resources by group and then by the hourly rate within each group of resources.

Display the Resource Sheet view

Use the Resource Sheet view to see resource information in a spreadsheet-style format.

▶ From the View menu, choose Resource Sheet.

Your project looks like the following illustration.

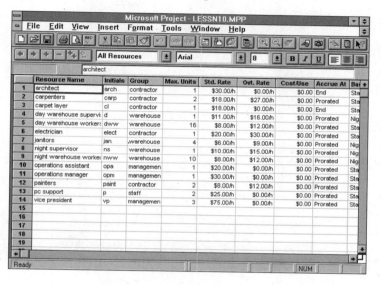

	Resource Name	Initials	Group	Max. Units	Std. Rate	Ovt. Rate	Cost/Use	Accrue At	Ba
1	architect	arch	contractor	1	$30.00/h	$0.00/h	$0.00	End	Sta
2	carpenters	carp	contractor	2	$18.00/h	$27.00/h	$0.00	Prorated	Sta
3	carpet layer	cl	contractor	1	$18.00/h	$0.00/h	$0.00	End	Sta
4	day warehouse supervi	d	warehouse	1	$11.00/h	$16.00/h	$0.00	Prorated	Nig
5	day warehouse worker	dww	warehouse	16	$8.00/h	$12.00/h	$0.00	Prorated	Sta
6	electrician	elect	contractor	1	$20.00/h	$30.00/h	$0.00	Prorated	Sta
7	janitors	jan	warehouse	4	$6.00/h	$9.00/h	$0.00	Prorated	Nig
8	night supervisor	ns	warehouse	1	$10.00/h	$15.00/h	$0.00	Prorated	Nig
9	night warehouse worke	nww	warehouse	10	$8.00/h	$12.00/h	$0.00	Prorated	Nig
10	operations assistant	opa	managemen	1	$20.00/h	$0.00/h	$0.00	Prorated	Sta
11	operations manager	opm	managemen	1	$30.00/h	$0.00/h	$0.00	Prorated	Sta
12	painters	paint	contractor	2	$8.00/h	$12.00/h	$0.00	Prorated	Sta
13	pc support	p	staff	2	$25.00/h	$0.00/h	$0.00	Prorated	Sta
14	vice president	vp	managemen	3	$75.00/h	$0.00/h	$0.00	Prorated	Sta

Sort resources by group and rate

To display the resources by group and then by rate, follow these steps.

1 From the Tools menu, choose Sort, and then choose Sort By.

2 Click the down arrow next to the Sort By box to display the list of fields by which you can sort.

3 Select Group and, under Sort By, be sure the Ascending option button is selected.

4 Click the down arrow next to the Then By box, and then scroll to and select Standard Rate.

The Standard Rate field is the hourly rate for a resource.

5 Under Then By, click the Descending option button.

The completed Sort dialog box looks like the following illustration.

Sort first by Group...

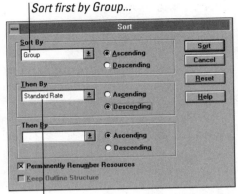

...and then, within each group, by Standard Rate.

6 Click the Sort button.

Microsoft Project sorts the resource names according to their group. Within each group, the resources are sorted by highest rate to lowest.

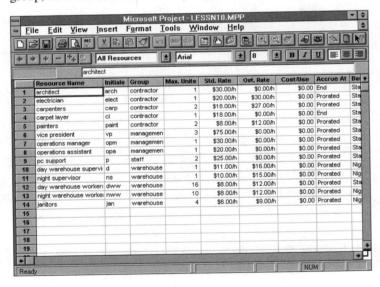

Save

Save your project

▶ On the Standard toolbar, click the Save button.

One Step Further

As you have already learned, clicking the Zoom In button expands the timescale to allow you a closer look at the Gantt bars. Similarly, clicking the Zoom Out button decreases the timescale, giving the "big picture" of the project by allowing you to see more Gantt bars at one time. To give you even greater control over the detail you see in the Gantt Chart, you can customize the increments displayed in either the major or minor timescale. You can also change the appearance of the headings in either timescale.

Change the major timescale increments

By changing the increments in the major timescale from one week to two, you are able to see more tasks in the Gantt Chart at one time.

1   From the <u>V</u>iew menu, choose <u>G</u>antt Chart.

2   On the Standard toolbar, click the Zoom Out button three times.

Zoom Out

The timescale now displays quarters over months, allowing you to see more of your project at once.

You can also choose the Timescale command on the Format menu, but double-clicking is a faster way to display this dialog box.

3   Double-click anywhere in the timescale heading to display the Timescale dialog box.

|Major timescale

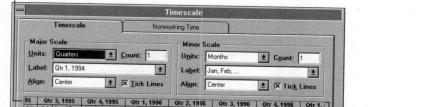

— Preview area

|Minor timescale

4   Click the Timescale tab if it is not already active.

5   In the Major Scale area, change the Units to Weeks.

6   In the Count box, type **2** to replace the previous value.

The Count box indicates the increments for the units of the major timescale. In this case, the major timescale displays headings of every two weeks, rather than every week.

7   From the Label box, select Jan 31, Feb 7.

By reducing the amount of text in the label, you can display even more of the project.

Change the minor timescale units

By changing the increments in the minor timescale from days to weeks, you are able to see more tasks in the Gantt Chart at one time.

▶   In the Minor Scale area, change the Units to Weeks.

The preview area of the dialog box displays headings for every two weeks in one-week increments.

Reduce the column width of the Gantt Chart

1   Select the value in the Enlarge box in the lower-left corner of the dialog box, and then type **90**

The size of the column width in the Gantt Chart is reduced to 90%.

2   Choose the OK button.

You might need to scroll to the left so your Gantt Chart looks like the following illustration.

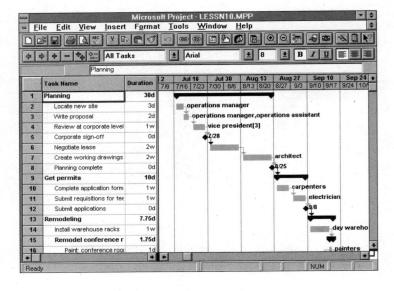

If You Want to Continue to the Next Lesson

1   From the File menu, choose Close to save your project file.

2   Choose the Yes button if you see the message box asking whether you want to save your work. Leave the baseline unchanged for now.

If You Want to Quit Microsoft Project for Now

1   From the File menu, choose Exit.

2   Choose the Yes button if you see the message box asking whether you want to save your work. Leave the baseline unchanged for now.

Lesson Summary

To	Do this
Apply a display filter	On the Formatting toolbar, choose the filter you want from the Filter list box. *or* From the Tools menu, choose the filter you want from the Filtered For submenu.
Apply a highlighting filter	On the Tools menu, hold down SHIFT and choose the filter you want from the Filtered For submenu.
Remove a filter and display all tasks	On the Formatting toolbar, choose the All Tasks filter from the Filter box.
Apply an interactive filter	Choose a filter with an ellipsis in the Filter box on the Formating toolbar or on the Filtered For submenu. In the next dialog box, specify the criteria you want the filter to match.
Create a custom filter	From the Tools menu, choose the Filtered For command, and then choose More Filters. Click the New button, then enter the filter criteria.
Change the timescale of the Gantt Chart	Click the Zoom In and Zoom Out buttons on the Standard toolbar. *or* Double-click the timescale heading to customize the settings in the Timescale dialog box.

To	Do this
Sort by a single field	From the Tools menu, choose the Sort command, and then choose Sort By. Select the name of the field by which you want to sort and the sort method. Then click Sort.
Sort by multiple fields	From the Tools menu, choose the Sort command, and then choose Sort By. Select the name of the first field by which you want to sort. Then in the Then By areas, select additional fields by which you want to sort. Then click Sort.
Retain the original task ID numbers during a sort	From the Tools menu, choose the Sort command, and then choose Sort By. In the Sort By dialog box, clear the Permanently Renumber Tasks check box, and then click Sort.
Reset the task list to its original ID number order	From the Tools menu, choose the Sort command, and then choose Sort By. In the Sort By dialog box, click the Reset button, and then click Sort.

For more information on	See in *Microsoft Project User's Guide*
Filters	Chapter 9, "Working with Views"
Sorting information	Chapter 3, "Creating and Organizing a Schedule"

For online information about	From the <u>H</u>elp menu, choose <u>S</u>earch and then type
Filters	Filters Tab filters: customizing
Changing the timescale	timescale: changing
Sorting	Sort Command sorting by

Preview of the Next Lesson

Another way to manage the amount of project information you see is to work with multiple project files. In the next lesson, you will learn how to combine project information from other project files by using the Consolidate Project and master project features.

Working with Multiple Projects

When you are managing more than one project, it is often useful to see project information for all the projects at one time. In this lesson, you will learn to open several projects at once and to use the Consolidate feature to review workloads and schedules for all projects in progress.

With a very large project, it can be awkward to scroll through many tasks or resources, or to focus on the information you need. In many cases, it is easier to work with separate subprojects that are related together through a master project. In this lesson, you will also learn to assign a subproject to a master project.

You will learn how to:

- Create a project workspace.
- Consolidate information from independent projects.
- Combine subproject information into a master project.

Estimated lesson time: 35 minutes

Start Microsoft Project

If you closed Microsoft Project in the last lesson, you need to restart the application before you can continue.

▶ Double-click the Microsoft Project icon.

Start the lesson

If you see the Welcome dialog box, click the Close button. If you see the Tip Of The Day dialog box, read the tip, and then click OK.

Open the project file called 11LESSN.MPP, and save it as LESSN11.MPP.

1 From the File menu, choose Open.
2 In the Directories box, double-click PRACTICE.
3 In the File Name box, double-click 11LESSN.MPP.
4 From the File menu, choose Save As.
5 In the File Name box, type **lessn11.mpp**
6 Choose the OK button.

Microsoft Project stores your project on your hard disk with the filename LESSN11.MPP. This file is similar to the project file you worked with in the previous lesson; however, the timescale has been adjusted to the default setting of weeks over days.

Working with Multiple Open Projects

Like many project managers, you might be responsible for several projects that take place at the same time. With Microsoft Project, you can have multiple project files open at one time, so that you can review all the projects. If you open the same group of project files frequently, you can open all the project files at one time by creating a *workspace*. When you create a workspace, you identify the project files you wish to have open. Then, when you open the workspace, all the files you need to review are opened automatically.

Open other project files

As operations manager at Victory Sports, you are also responsible for managing the computer-related operations at the company. Although the data processing manager is directly responsible for computer-related projects, you must review these projects and report results to your management. Because you regularly review the same project files, you plan to create a workspace for these projects. Begin by opening the other project files.

Open

1   On the Standard toolbar, click the Open button.

The Open dialog box appears.

2   In the File Name box, double-click 11MOVSUB.MPP.

The project file opens.

3   Repeat steps 1 and 2 to open the following files:

11RLLOUT.MPP
11SFTDEV.MPP

You now have four project files open.

Switch to another project

With the commands on the Window menu, you can work efficiently with multiple files by quickly displaying the files you want. The Window menu also contains a list of open files that you can display individually by selecting the filename.

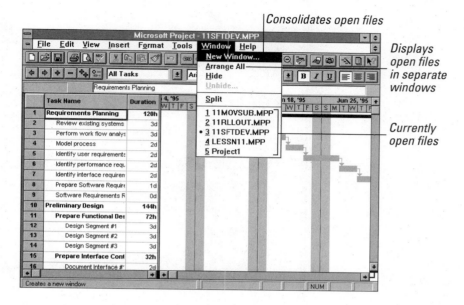

1 From the Window menu, choose PROJECT1.

   The empty project file PROJECT1 appears in the Gantt Chart.

2 From the File menu, choose Close.

3 Choose the No button if you see the message box asking whether you want to save your work.

4 From the Window menu, choose Arrange All.

   This command displays all the open projects in their own separate windows, as shown in the following illustration.

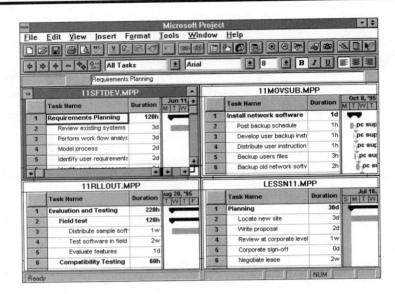

You can scroll and work in each window independently.

5   Click the project window for LESSN11.MPP to make it the active window, and then click the Maximize button.

Although the other projects are still open, project LESSN11.MPP appears maximized in the project window.

Create a workspace

Because you plan to use this set of files often, create a workspace that contains all four files. By creating a workspace, you are able to open all the files at once.

1   From the File menu, choose Save Workspace.

The Save Workspace dialog box appears. In this dialog box, you enter a name for your workspace.

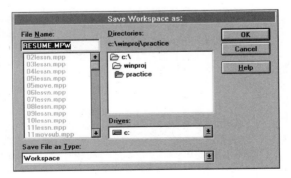

2   In the File Name box, type **operpr11**

Microsoft Project provides the extension "MPW" when you create a workspace.

3   Choose the OK button.

Your workspace is saved.

If you see the
PlanningWizard,
click the third option
button to leave the
baseline unchanged
for now and click OK.

4   From the File menu, choose Close.

5   Choose the No button if you see the message box asking whether you want to save your work.

6   Repeat steps 4 and 5 to close each of the project files you have open.

No projects are open right now.

Consolidating Projects

Although you can easily work with multiple projects in open but separate project windows, it is often easier to display all the projects in a single window. For example, to provide complete information about all of the operations projects for which you are responsible at Victory Sports, you don't need to switch between each project window. Instead, you can use the Consolidate feature to combine all the projects into one window. With all the project information displayed as a single project, you can view and even print the consolidated project as if it were one large project.

There are two ways to consolidate projects. If the projects you want to consolidate are already open, you can combine them quickly with the New Window command on the Window menu. You can also use the Consolidate Project command on the Multiple Projects submenu (from the Tools menu) to consolidate selected project files without opening them first. With this command, you also have the option to specify the order in which the files will appear in the project window. You can also specify that you want to combine the resource pools, attach the projects to the source project, work with copies of the project files, or hide subtasks.

Using the Consolidate Command

To make it even easier to review all the projects for your department, consolidate all the projects into a single Gantt Chart. The resulting combined project file is the *consolidated project,* and the individual project files are the *source files.*

Consolidate the projects

1   From the Tools menu, choose Multiple Projects, and then choose Consolidate Projects.

The Consolidate Projects dialog box appears. In this dialog box, you can specify the options you want to use when you consolidate projects.

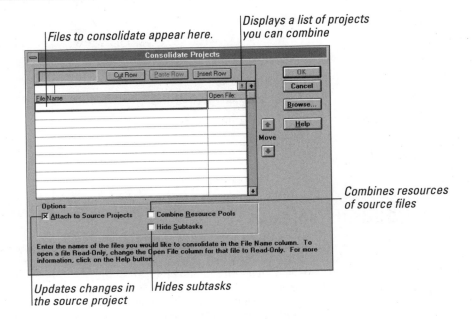

Files to consolidate appear here.

Displays a list of projects you can combine

Combines resources of source files

Updates changes in the source project

Hides subtasks

2   Click the Browse button.

The Browse dialog box appears. In this dialog box, you can select the files you want to consolidate.

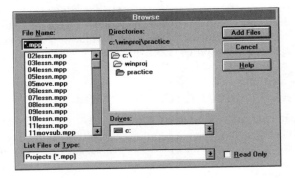

3   In the File Name list box, select 11MOVSUB.MPP, and then hold down SHIFT and click 11SFTDEV.MPP.

All the files between the first one you clicked and the last one are selected.

4   Hold down CTRL, scroll downward to LESSN11.MPP, and then click this file to
select it.

You want to consolidate these four project files.

5   Click the Add Files button.

The Browse dialog box closes and the file names appear in the Consolidate
Projects dialog box, as shown in the following illustration.

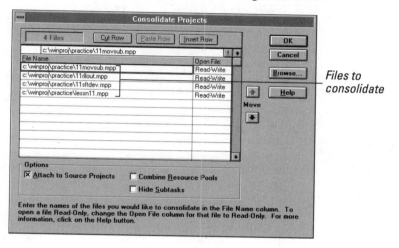

*Files to
consolidate*

*By clearing this
check box, the
changes to the
consolidated project
are not reflected in
the source files. The
tasks will be
renumbered.*

6   Clear the Attach To Source Projects check box.

The default setting attaches the consolidated project to the source projects (the
tasks retain their original task ID numbers).

7   Click the last project in the list, and then click the Move up arrow.

The last project appears as the third project in the list. This project will appear third
in the consolidated file.

8   Choose the OK button.

The dialog box closes and Microsoft Project consolidates all the selected projects.

Goto Selected Task

9   When the consolidation is complete, click the Goto Selected Task button on the
Standard toolbar to display the Gantt bars for the first project.

Your project window looks like the following illustration.

Consolidated file

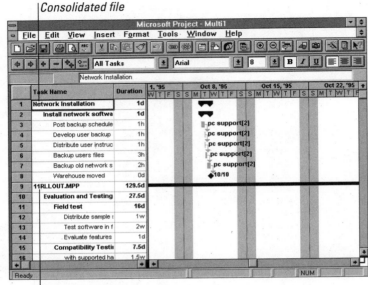

Consolidated file

Notice that each project in the Gantt table is separated with the title of the project as specified in the Summary Info dialog box. If no title is specified, the project filename appears in the Gantt table.

Viewing the Consolidated Project

Now that all the projects are in a single project window, you can get the big picture for all the projects. To view how the projects are organized, you adjust the timescale and then scroll through the list of tasks.

Adjust the timescale

Zoom Out

▶ On the Standard toolbar, click the Zoom Out button two times until you see months over weeks on the timescale.

View specific tasks

With all the tasks for all the projects displayed, you can use filters to focus on specific tasks. See which tasks the pc support resources are assigned.

1 From the Filter box on the Formatting toolbar, select Using Resource.

The Using Resource dialog box appears.

2 In the Resource box, type **pc support**

3 Choose the OK button.

4   All the tasks assigned to this resource appear.

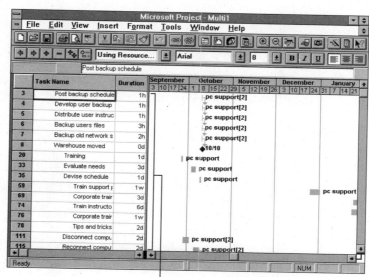

Tasks assigned to PC support resource

Save and close your project file

1   From the File menu, choose Close.

2   Choose the Yes button if you see the message box asking whether you want to save your work. Leave the baseline unchanged for now.

3   In the File Name box, type **consl11**

The consolidated project is saved with the name CONSL11.MPP.

Using Master Projects and Subprojects

When you are working with a very large project, the file can become so large that it is cumbersome to use, requiring you to scroll frequently, change the timescale, or wait for the screen to re-display. This is because very large files also use large amounts of computer memory, causing Microsoft Project to run slower. As the size of the project file increases, it will take more time to move around and perform operations. By creating a master project with related subprojects, you can focus on only those parts of the project you need at the moment.

Assigning a Subproject to a Master Project

One of the tasks in the move project is "Install network software." This task is actually a small project you have delegated to the data processing manager. To help keep track of the process, the data processing manager created a project plan for this task in

Microsoft Project. To incorporate this information into your move project, begin by opening the main project file (LESSN11.MPP).

Open a master project

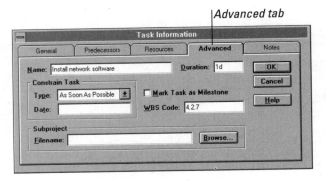
Open

1   On the Standard toolbar, click the Open button.

The Open dialog box appears.

2   In the File Name box, double-click LESSN11.MPP.

The project file opens.

Specify a subproject

With the master project open, you select the task into which the subproject information will go. This task cannot have a finish-to-finish or start-to-start relationship specified. Then you use the Advanced tab in the Task Information dialog box to specify the subproject. For example, the subproject contains a more detailed list of tasks for the "Install network software" task.

1   Scroll to task 34, "Install network software."

You can also click the Information button on the Standard toolbar.

2   Double-click this task to display the Task Information dialog box.

3   Click the Advanced tab to make it active, as shown in the following illustration.

Advanced tab

On the Advanced tab, you can specify additional options and details about the selected task, including the subproject.

4   In the Subproject area, click the Browse button.

The Subproject dialog box appears. In this dialog box, you can select the file you want to include as the subproject.

5   In the File Name list box, double-click 11MOVSUB.MPP.

You return to the Advanced tab. The name of the subproject file appears in the Filename text box.

6   Choose the OK button.

Examine subproject information

You won't notice any significant change in the master project file but, by double-clicking the "Install network software" task, you can examine tasks subordinate to it.

▶ Double-click task 34, "Install network software."

The subproject file, 11MOVSUB.MPP, appears in the project window. This project contains detail information about the task to install the network software.

Close the subproject and master project

1   From the File menu, choose Close to close the subproject.

You return to the master project.

2   From the File menu, choose Close to close the master project.

3   Choose the Yes button if you see the message box asking whether you want to save your work. Leave the baseline unchanged for now.

One Step Further

With the New Window command on the Window menu, you can quickly combine open files using default settings. (Changes that you make in the consolidated file are reflected in the source files, and each of the tasks in a project retain their original task IDs.) You also have the option to select the view in which the project will appear. Explore the New Window feature, but first open the project files you need by opening the workspace you created earlier in this lesson.

Open a workspace

1   On the Standard toolbar, click the Open button.

The Open dialog box appears.

2   In the File Name box, double-click OPERPR11.MPW.

All the project files open.

3   If you see the message asking whether you want to update links to the other files, click the Yes button.

Display files in Resource Sheet view

1   From the Window menu, choose New Window.

The New Window dialog box appears. In this dialog box, you can select the open documents you want to combine.

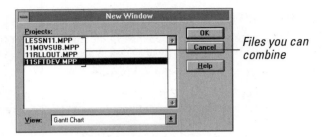

Files you can combine

2   Select the first file in the list and hold down SHIFT while you click the last file in the list, to select all four files.

3   From the View box, select Resource Sheet.

With this view you can see information about all the resources from all the projects in a spreadsheet-style view.

4   Choose the OK button.

All the files are displayed in a single Resource Sheet view. The resource names for each project are grouped together. Projects are listed in the same order as they appear in the Gantt Chart view.

Change a source file

1   In the first occurrence of the electricians resource, change the maximum number to 2.

This changes the number of electricians in the LESSN11.MPP file.

2   From the File menu, choose Close.

3   When you see the message box asking you to save changes, click the Yes button.

4   When you see the message box asking you to save changes to LESSN11.MPP, click the Yes button.

5   When you see the message box asking you to save changes to 11MOVSUB.MPP, click the Yes button.

6   In the File Name box, type **consl11a**

7   Choose the OK button.

With project files saved in a workspace, you can open multiple projects quickly; and with the New Window command, you can specify the view in which you want all the projects to appear, making it easy to work in all the files at once. Combined, these two features help you work efficiently when you must manage several projects at the same time.

If You Want to Continue to the Next Lesson

1   From the File menu, choose Close to close your project file.

2   Choose the Yes button if you see the message box asking whether you want to save your work. Leave the baseline unchanged for now.

3   Repeat steps 1 and 2 for all of the remaining open files.

If You Want to Quit Microsoft Project for Now

1   From the File menu, choose Exit.

2   Choose the Yes button if you see the message box asking whether you want to save your work. Leave the baseline unchanged for now.

Lesson Summary

To	Do this
Create a project workspace	With all the project files open, choose Save Workspace from the File menu.
Consolidate project files	From the Tools menu, choose Multiple Projects, then choose Consolidate Projects. Click the Browse button, and then select the files you want to consolidate. Change any default settings you do not want to include. *or* With all the project files open, choose New Window from the Window menu. Select the files you want to consolidate (the default settings will be in effect).
Assign a subproject to a master project	Open the master project file. Double-click the task to which you want to add the subproject information (or click the Information button on the Standard toolbar). In the Task Information dialog box, click the Advanced tab. Click the Browse button and select the subproject file. Double-click the task in the master file to view the subproject information.

For more information on	See in *Microsoft Project User's Guide*
Creating a workspace	Chapter 11, "Working with Multiple Projects"
Consolidating projects	Chapter 11, "Working with Multiple Projects"
Working with subprojects and master projects	Chapter 11, "Working with Multiple Projects"

For online information about	From the <u>H</u>elp menu, choose <u>S</u>earch and then type
Creating workspaces	workspaces
Consolidating projects	consolidating projects consolidating resources
Subprojects	subprojects: creating subprojects: working with

Preview of the Next Lesson

In the next lesson, you'll learn more ways to view information in your project. You will also learn how to use and customize reports provided with Microsoft Project. With a printed hard copy of your project, you can communicate project expectations and results to others.

Printing Views and Reports

In this lesson, you'll learn several ways to print project information. After you learn how to select the printer on which to print, you will use the Page Setup command to specify header and footer information, as well as other adjustments to the appearance of the printed page. You will also learn how to preview and print a view and a report.

You will learn how to:

- Format with the GanttChartWizard.
- Select your printer.
- Change the page setup, including headers and footers.
- Preview and print a view.
- Preview and print a report.

Estimated lesson time: 40 minutes

Start Microsoft Project

If you closed Microsoft Project in the last lesson, you need to restart the application before you can continue.

▶ Double-click the Microsoft Project icon.

Start the lesson

If you see the Welcome dialog box, click the Close button. If you see the Tip Of The Day dialog box, read the tip, and then click OK.

Open the project file called 12LESSN.MPP, and save it as LESSN12.MPP.

1 From the File menu, choose Open.

2 In the Directories box, double-click PRACTICE.

3 In the File Name box, double-click 12LESSN.MPP.

4 From the File menu, choose Save As.

5 In the File Name box, type **lessn12.mpp**

6 Choose the OK button.

Microsoft Project stores your project on your hard disk with the filename LESSN12.MPP. This file is similar to the project file you worked with in the previous lesson; however, the timescale has been adjusted to the default setting of weeks over days.

Communicating Project Information

Communicating project plans and progress with your project team and management is critical to executing a successful project plan. Microsoft Project provides many alternatives for conveying project information to those who need to know about your project. Printing views is a fast way to get a hard copy of what you see in the active view on your screen. You can also choose from many reports provided with Microsoft Project. In addition, you can customize views and reports to get the information you need in the format you want.

Using the GanttChartWizard

The GanttChartWizard provides an easy way to enhance the appearance of your project. When you use this wizard, you are asked a number of questions about the information you want to emphasize and how you want the project to look. The wizard displays sample formats to choose from, and you can also select custom formatting to customize the project's appearance in specific ways. After you answer all the questions, Microsoft Project formats the project according to your responses.

Enhance the appearance of the project

Use the GanttChartWizard to format the project so that you can easily see the status of tasks in progress.

GanttChartWizard

1 On the Standard toolbar, click the GanttChartWizard button.

The GanttChartWizard starts.

2 Click the Next button.

The second wizard window looks like the following illustration.

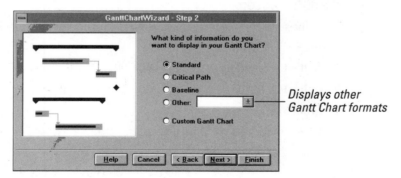

Displays other Gantt Chart formats

3 Click the Other option button, and then click the down arrow to display the list of Gantt Chart formats.

4 Select Standard 2 from the list, and then click the Next button.

The next wizard window displays options for the information you want to appear near the Gantt bars.

5 Click the Next button to accept the default setting (Resources and Dates).

The next wizard window appears. In this window you can choose whether the linking lines between tasks should appear in the Gantt Chart.

6 Click the Next button to accept the default setting (Yes) to show links between dependent tasks.

The next wizard window informs you that you are done using the GanttChartWizard.

7 Click the Format It button.

After formatting your Gantt Chart, you see the last wizard window.

8 Click the Exit Wizard button.

After you return to the Gantt Chart, you see that it is formatted the way you specified.

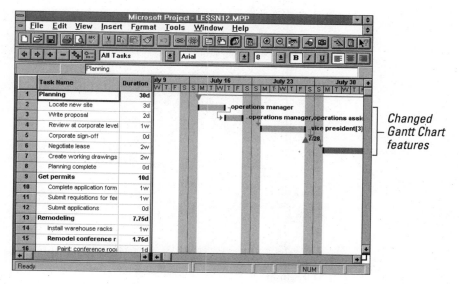

Changed Gantt Chart features

Using Page Setup

A vice president has requested a report on the current status of the move. You want to show graphically what has been planned for the project, so you need to print a Gantt Chart view of the project. You also want to provide the vice president with a summary of the project that can be taken in at a glance. The project summary report provides a one-page summary of the entire project.

Before you print this information, you need to specify the printer you want to use. You also want to specify header, footer, and legend text that will appear on every page.

Setting Up Your Printer

You must install (or attach) a printer before you can select it in Microsoft Project.
From Windows Control Panel, you specify which printers are attached to your
computer. Then, using the Page Setup command in Microsoft Project, you select the
printer or plotter you want to use from the list of attached printers or plotters. You can
also select the page orientation, scaling, margins, header, footer, legend, and view
when you print. See your *Microsoft Windows User's Guide* if you need more
information about installing printers.

Select a printer

First, be sure the printer or plotter connected to your computer is selected.

1   From the File menu, choose Page Setup.

The Page Setup dialog box appears.

2   Click the Printer button.

The Print Setup dialog box appears. In this dialog box, you see a list of printers
installed on your computer.

Note   The printers you see on your computer might be different than those shown in
the illustration.

3   Select the printer you want to use.

4   Choose the OK button.

You return to the Page Setup dialog box.

Specifying Page Orientation

The *page orientation* setting determines whether your report prints with the page taller
than it is wide (called *portrait*) or wider than it is tall (called *landscape*). If your
project has many short tasks, you might prefer using the portrait setting. Use landscape
when you have fewer tasks, but with longer durations. You select page orientation in
the Page Setup dialog box. Landscape is the default setting when printing views.

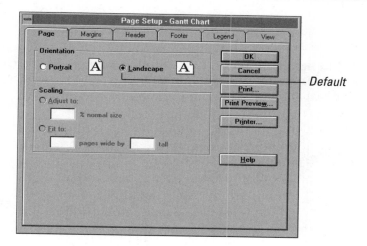

Note Some of the printing and page features you can use depend on the kind of printer you have selected in the Printer Setup dialog box. For example, some printers cannot print in the landscape orientation. With other printers, you can use the Scaling features to adjust the size of the project to the number of pages on which you want to print.

Specifying Headers, Footers, and Legends

A *header* is text that appears at the top of every page; a *footer* is text that appears at the bottom of every page. In both the header and footer, you can specify the kind of information that should appear on each page. You can also specify the alignment of the header and footer information. In addition to text you enter, you can also include the following information in the header or footer.

- company name
- project current date
- current system date*
- project file name*
- current system time
- project start date
- filter name

- project title
- last saved date
- report name
- manager name
- total pages*
- page number*
- view name

* Indicates that you can use a button to insert this information.

On the bottom of every page, you also have the option to print a legend. The legend is a graphical key to the symbols and shading in the Gantt bars.

Change the Gantt Chart header

1   Click the Header tab, if it is not already active.

The Header tab appears in the dialog box, where you can specify the information you want to appear at the top of every page. You can also specify how you want the information aligned.

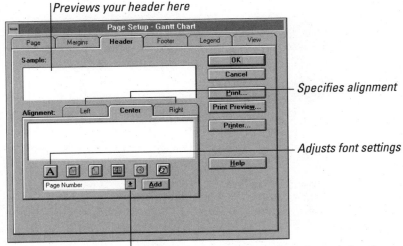

Previews your header here

Specifies alignment

Adjusts font settings

Displays additional information to insert in header

2   In the Alignment area, click the Left tab.

The information you enter in the text box on this tab will appear at the left edge of the project when you print it.

Date

3   Click the Date button.

The date appears as a code in the Alignment text box. The actual date, as it will appear when you print, appears in the Sample text box. This is the date that your computer is currently programmed to display.

4   Press HOME to move the insertion point to the beginning of the line, and then type **Project Status as of:**

Be sure you type two spaces after the colon (:). This text will appear before the date in the header.

5   Press END to move the insertion point to the end of the line, and then press SHIFT+ENTER.

When you press SHIFT+ENTER, the insertion point moves to the next line.

Note   If you press ENTER in this dialog box, it is the same as choosing the OK button. Press ENTER only when you have completed using this dialog box and you want to close it.

6   Type **Project Start Date:**

Be sure you type two spaces after the colon (:).

7   Click the down arrow below the buttons to display a complete list of information you can include in the header. Scroll downward in the list and select Project Start Date.

8   Click the Add button.

The date appears as a code in the Left Alignment text box. The actual date, as it will appear when you print, appears in the Sample text box. This is the date in the Start Date box of the Summary Info dialog box.

The Header tab looks like the following illustration.

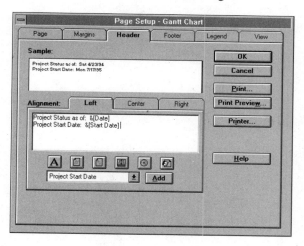

9   Click the Right alignment tab.

The information you enter on this tab will appear at the right edge of the project when you print it.

10   Click the down arrow below the buttons and select Project Title.

11   Click the Add button.

The code for the project title appears in the Right Alignment text box. The actual project title, as it will appear when you print, appears in the Sample text box. This is the text in the Title box of the Summary Info dialog box on the Document tab.

Change the Gantt Chart footer

In the same way you specify header information, you can also specify the information you want to appear as a footer on the bottom of every page.

1 Click the Footer tab.

The Footer tab appears in the dialog box. It looks similar to the Header tab, except that, by default, the page number code appears in the Center Alignment text box.

2 Place the insertion point at the end of the page number code in the Center Alignment text box.

3 Type a space followed by **of** and then type another space.

This text will appear after the page number.

Total Page Count

4 Click the Total Page Count button.

This selection will print the total number of pages in the project as part of the footer.

The Footer tab looks like the following illustration.

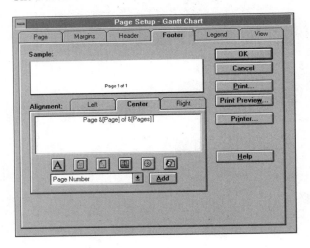

Previewing and Printing Views

Although you can use the Print button to print your view right away, it is a good idea to preview the project first with the Print Preview command. If you decide you want to make additional adjustments, you can return to the Page Setup dialog box. If you are satisfied with the appearance of the view, you can print it.

Preview the Gantt Chart view

If you are not already in the Page Setup dialog box, you can click the Preview button on the Standard toolbar to preview a project view or report.

Use the following steps to examine how the printed pages of the Gantt Chart will look before you print the view. You can complete these steps even if your computer is not connected to a printer.

1   In the Page Setup dialog box, click the Print Preview button.

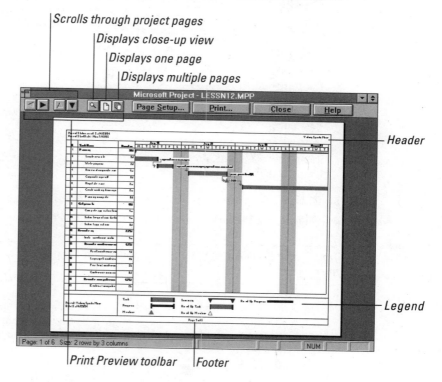

Scrolls through project pages

Displays close-up view

Displays one page

Displays multiple pages

Header

Legend

Print Preview toolbar   Footer

2   To get a close-up view of the task list, click on the left side of the page.

You see a close-up view of the area where you clicked. When you click the page, your project looks similar to the following illustration.

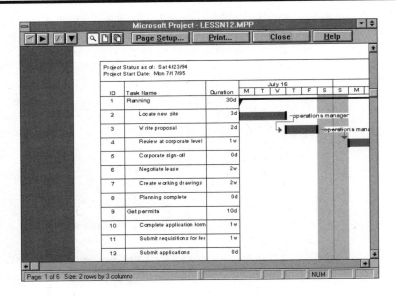

Multiple Pages

3 Click the page again to preview the entire page.

4 On the Print Preview toolbar, click the Multiple Pages button.

Tip You can also click the gray area outside of the page to display multiple pages of the project.

Now you can see all the pages in the Gantt Chart at the same time, as shown in the following illustration. Your screen might vary slightly from the following illustration, depending on the type of printer you have installed.

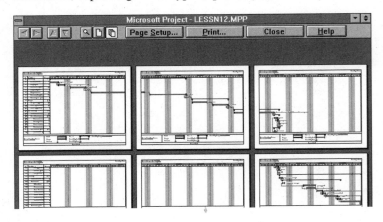

If you decide you want to make additional changes to your margins, header, footer, page orientation, or borders, you can click the Page Setup button to return to the Page Setup dialog box.

Printing Views

A printed view shows only what you see on your screen. You print a view with the Print command on the File menu. You can also use the Print button on the Standard toolbar. If you are in the Print Preview window, you can click the Print button on the Print Preview toolbar.

You can print all views except forms and the Task PERT Chart. If you have a combination view displayed on your screen, only the active section of the view is printed.

Print the Gantt Chart view

1   On the Print Preview toolbar, click the Print button.

The Print dialog box appears.

2   If your computer is connected to a printer, choose the OK button. If it is not connected to a printer, click the Cancel button.

3   If you chose the Cancel button, click the Close button to return to your project.

If you clicked the Print button, your project prints on the selected printer or plotter, and then you return to your project in the Gantt Chart view. If the printer or plotter prints only one color, Microsoft Project substitutes patterns for colors.

Tip   You can adjust the patterns with the Bar Styles command on the Format menu.

Previewing and Printing Reports

In a *report*, project information is summarized and organized for you in a way that best communicates about a specific aspect of the project. Print a report rather than a view when you want to convey more detail than what you see in a view. Microsoft Project provides five categories of reports. Each category contains several types of reports from which you can choose.

Report category	Description	Report type
Overview	Presents selected information over the entire project duration, such as summary and critical tasks, milestones, and scheduling.	Project Summary Top-Level Tasks Critical Tasks Milestones Working Days

Report category	Description	Report type
Current Activities	Presents selected task information, such as unstarted, in progress and finished tasks; tasks that are behind schedule or should start soon.	Unstarted Tasks Tasks Starting Soon Tasks in Progress Completed Tasks Should-Have-Started Tasks Slipping Tasks
Costs	Presents selected cost information, such as budgets for all tasks over the entire project duration, tasks and resources that are overbudget, and costs per task displayed in one-week periods.	Weekly Cash Flow Budget Overbudget Tasks Overbudget Resources Earned Value
Assignments	Presents selected resource assignment information, such as task schedules for all resources over the entire project duration, tasks for specified resources, and overallocated resources.	Who Does What Who Does What When Weekly To-do List Overallocated Resources
Workload	Crosstab reports that present task usage and resource usage information.	Task Usage Resource Usage

With the Reports command on the View menu, you can preview and print your reports. It is a good idea to preview your report before you print it. If you decide to make additional adjustments, you can return to the Page Setup dialog box and adjust the orientation, margins, headers, and footers just as you do when printing views. If you are satisfied with the appearance of the report, you can print it. You can also create custom reports based on your specific needs. In Part 5 of this book, you will learn how to create custom reports.

Print the summary report

In addition to the Gantt Chart, you want to give the vice president an overview of the top-level tasks in the project. This report provides a one-page overview of the tasks and their durations, start and finish dates, and their cost. As the project progresses, this report also displays how much of each top-level task is complete. You cannot change the contents of the Top-Level Tasks report. Print this report to accompany the printed Gantt Chart view.

1   From the <u>V</u>iew menu, choose <u>R</u>eports.

The Reports dialog box displays buttons that correspond to the general categories of reports provided with Microsoft Project.

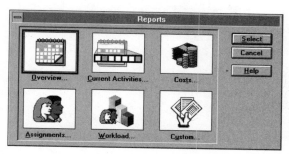

2   Click the Select button to view the selection of Overview reports.

Tip   You can also double-click a button to open the next dialog box.

Overview is the default in the Reports dialog box. The Overview Reports dialog box appears.

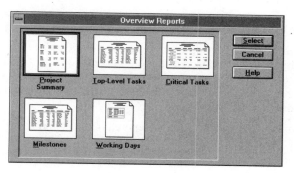

3   Click the Top-Level Tasks button, and then click the Select button.

A preview of the Top-Level Tasks report appears. It looks like the following illustration.

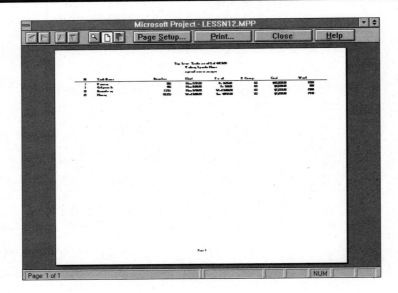

4   If your computer is connected to a printer, click the Print button and then choose the OK button.

Click the Close button if you are not able to print the report.

Print a weekly to-do list

Although management appreciates the concise nature of the top-level tasks report, your project team members need more information about what is expected of them. In the Assignments category of reports, you can print a weekly "to-do" list of project tasks for individual resources. Use the Weekly To-do List report to create a "to-do" list for the day warehouse workers.

1   From the View menu, choose Reports, if the Reports dialog box is not already displayed.

2   Click the Assignments button.

3   Click the Select button to view the selection of Assignment reports.

The Assignment Reports dialog box appears.

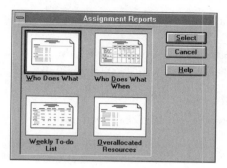

4   Click the Weekly To-do List button, and then click the Select button.

The Using Resource dialog box appears.

5   Click the down arrow and scroll through the list of resources, and then select "day warehouse workers."

6   Choose the OK button.

A preview of the report appears.

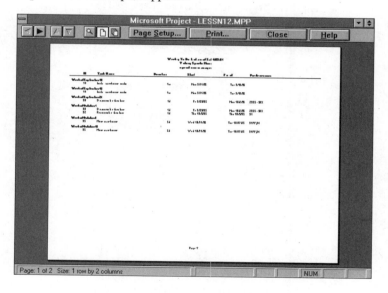

7   If your computer is connected to a printer, click the Print button, and then choose
the OK button.

Click the Close button if you are not able to print the report, then click the Cancel
button to close the Reports dialog box and return to the Gantt Chart view.

Save

Save your project

▶   On the Standard toolbar, click the Save button.

One Step Further

You can also change the font family and size to make information in the header,
footer, and legend stand out better. To emphasize the text in the footer, you can apply
special formatting to it.

1   From the File menu, choose Page Setup.

2   Click the Footer tab if it is not already active.

Text

3   Click the Text button.

The Text Styles dialog box appears.

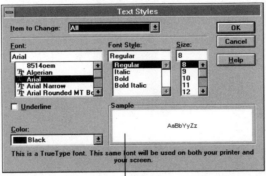

|Previews formatting changes

4   In the Font Style list box, select Bold Italic.

5   Choose the OK button.

The text of the Gantt Chart footer now appears in bold italic.

6   Click the Print Preview button.

7   If your computer is connected to a printer, click the Print button, and then choose
the OK button.

Click the Close button if you are not able to print the report.

If You Want to Continue to the Next Lesson

1 From the File menu, choose Close to close the project file.

2 Choose the Yes button if you see the message box asking whether you want to save your work. Leave the baseline unchanged.

If You Want to Quit Microsoft Project for Now

1 From the File menu, choose Exit.

2 Choose the Yes button if you see the message box asking whether you want to save your work. Leave the baseline unchanged.

Lesson Summary

To	Do this	Button
Have Microsoft Project enhance the appearance of the project	On the Standard toolbar, click the GanttChartWizard button and specify the formatting options you want.	
Select a printer	Click the Page Setup command (or the Print command) from the File menu. Click the Printer button. Select a printer from the list of printers installed on your computer.	
Change the headers, footers, and legends for views and reports	Click the Page Setup command from the File menu. Click the appropriate tab for the object you want to format. Use the tabs, buttons, and drop-down lists to specify the information and formatting you want to appear for the object.	
Preview and print a view	Click the Print Preview button on the Standard toolbar. *or* In the Page Setup dialog box, click the Print Preview button. Use the Print button on the Print Preview toolbar to print.	
Preview and print a report	Choose Reports from the View menu. In the Reports dialog box, select the general category from which you want to choose a report. Then select from the list of reports the one you want to print. In Print Preview, click the Print button.	

For more information on	See in *Microsoft Project User's Guide*
Adjusting page information	Chapter 8, "Printing and Reporting"
Printing views and reports	Chapter 8, "Printing and Reporting"
Descriptions of reports	Chapter 8, "Printing and Reporting"

For online information about	From the <u>H</u>elp menu, choose <u>S</u>earch and then type
Selecting a printer	printers
Changing page setup	page setup
Printing reports	reports: printing
Printing views	views: printing

Preview of the Next Lessons

In the next part of the book, you will learn about controlling project costs and deadlines. You will also track project progress and adjust the plan as needed. In the next lesson, you will learn how to adjust project costs to keep the project within budgeted amounts.

Review & Practice

In the lessons in Part 3, "Viewing the Plan," you learned skills to help you arrange and organize project information. If you want to practice these skills and test your knowledge before you proceed with the lessons in Part 4, you can work through the Review & Practice following this lesson.

Part 3   Review & Practice

Before you begin planning a project of your own, practice the skills you learned in Part 3 by working through the project organizing and reporting activities in this Review & Practice section. Based on the plan you created in the Part 2 Review & Practice, you will filter and sort tasks and resources. You will also combine information from another project, and then print a view and a report to obtain a hard copy of project information.

Scenario

With the project plan for the development of the Victory Sports Summit Boots completed, you are now ready to focus on specific parts of the plan. Use filters and sorting to focus on different kinds of tasks and resources as they become important to you. To help you understand the process involved in the promotion and advertising tasks of the project, you will also combine project information entered by the marketing company you are using to handle that part of the project. Finally, because your management wants to see information related to contractors as well as the overall schedule, you need to print views and reports.

You will review and practice how to:

- Use filtering and sorting to organize and rearrange lists of tasks and resources.
- Specify a subtask to combine information from another project.
- Print views and reports to obtain a hard copy of project information.

Estimated practice time: 25 minutes

Before You Begin

▶ Open the scenario project file called P3REVIEW.MPP. Before you make any changes in this project, save it with the new name REVIEWP3.MPP.

This project file should look similar to the file you saved after completing the steps in the Part 2 Review & Practice. This file already has a baseline.

Step 1: Filter Tasks Assigned to a Resource

Your management wants to compare the number of tasks assigned to staff resources versus contractor resources. You can determine this quickly with the Resource Group filter.

1 Use the Filter list box on the Formatting toolbar to select the Resource Group filter, and specify that you want to see only those tasks assigned to the "staff" resource group.

2   Use the Filter list box to select the Resource Group filter and specify that you want to see only those tasks assigned to the "contractor" resource group.

For more information on	See
Using a filter	Lesson 10

Step 2: Sort and Rearrange a List of Resources

Next you want to focus on resources. The number of resources Morton Marketing has assigned to your project has increased. After displaying the project in the Resource Sheet view, sort and renumber the resource IDs. While you are in this view, change the number of the maximum units of this resource.

1   You want to focus on resource information, so switch to the Resource Sheet view.

2   To make the list of resources easier to read, sort the resources first by Group and then by Name. Use the default ascending order. Be sure the Permanently Renumber Resources check box is selected to renumber the resources in the order in which you sort them.

3   Add two more units to the Max. Units field for Morton Marketing.

For more information on	See
Sorting by multiple fields	Lesson 10

Step 3: Combine Information from Other Projects

Your counterpart at the outside marketing resource, Morton Marketing, has followed your example and created a project plan for the promotion and advertising part of the project. He has also prepared a plan to conduct a survey for a future line of sporting gear at Victory Sports. Because you want to consider information about these projects along with your Summit Boots project, use multiple project techniques to work with all these project files.

1   Return to the Gantt Chart view, and create a workspace that includes the project files REVIEWP3.MPP, P3REVSUB.MPP, and P3SURVEY.MPP. Save the workspace with the name REVIEWP3.MPW.

2   Consolidate the three projects so that the consolidated file is attached to the source files. Because you want to arrange the projects so that the REVIEWP3.MPP file appears first, and the P3SURVEY.MPP project appears last, use the Multiple Projects command from the Tools menu. Use the Move buttons to arrange the projects in this order.

3   Adjust the timescale to quarters over months, so that you can see more of the tasks related to new product development at Victory Sports.

4 Close the consolidated file, and save it with the name REVMLTP3.MPP. Close the P3REVSUB.MPP and P3SURVEY.MPP files. Keep the project file REVIEWP3.MPP open for now.

5 So that you can quickly examine the detailed tasks of the Promotion and Advertising task, double-click task 21 and specify the subproject P3REVSUB.MPP on the Advanced tab.

6 Take another look at the subproject information by double-clicking task 21. Then switch back to the main project, REVIEWP3.MPP.

For more information on	See
Working with multiple projects	Lesson 11

Step 4: Print Views and Reports

Now that you have examined the project information, you are ready to print it. First use the GanttChartWizard to improve the appearance of the Gantt Chart. Then print the view and a "to do" list for yourself.

1 Use the GanttChartWizard to enhance the appearance of the Gantt Chart. In the second wizard window, select Standard 3 from the Other option. In all the other windows, use the default settings.

2 Preview all pages of the view and, if you have a printer connected to your computer, print the view.

3 From the Assignments category of reports, select the Weekly To-do List and specify yourself, as product manager, in the Using Resource dialog box.

4 Before you print the report, use the Page Setup command to specify the project filename in the footer. Align this information on the right edge of the page. If your computer is connected to a printer, review the report and print it.

For more information on	See
Printing views and reports	Lesson 12

If You Want to Continue to the Next Lesson

▶ From the File menu, choose Close to close and save your project without changing the baseline.

If You Want to Quit Microsoft Project for Now

▶ From the File menu, choose Exit.

4 Controlling the Project

Adjusting Project Costs

If detailed cost management is not one of your usual project responsibilities, feel free to skip this lesson for now, and return to it later when it's needed.

At the end of Part 2, you saved a "snapshot" of your original project plan as a baseline. The baseline included the project budget with the resource costs you entered in Lesson 6. After the project progresses and you adjust the plan, you can compare the working plan to the baseline and, if necessary, make adjustments to the plan. In this lesson, you'll learn how to identify tasks that are over budget and how to use different strategies for reducing costs to meet your original plan of expenditures that you projected in the baseline.

You will learn how to:

- Change the current date.
- Identify tasks that are over budget.
- Reduce costs to meet the budget.

Estimated lesson time: 25 minutes

Start Microsoft Project

If you closed Microsoft Project in the last lesson, you need to restart the application before you can continue.

▶ Double-click the Microsoft Project icon.

Start the lesson

If you see the Welcome dialog box, click the Close button. If you see the Tip Of The Day dialog box, read the tip, and then click OK.

Open the project file called 13LESSN.MPP, and save it as LESSN13.MPP.

1 From the File menu, choose Open.
2 In the Directories box, double-click PRACTICE.
3 In the File Name box, double-click 13LESSN.MPP.
4 From the File menu, choose Save As.
5 In the File Name box, type **lessn13.mpp**
6 Choose the OK button.

Microsoft Project stores your project on your hard disk with the filename LESSN13.MPP. This file is similar to the project file you worked with in the previous lesson.

Change the current date

The following steps set the current date in Microsoft Project to reflect the passage of time to just before the project is scheduled to begin. With new information you have determined since you set the plan, you can update the schedule and compare this information with what you planned originally.

1 From the File menu, choose Summary Info.

2 Click the Project tab, if it is not already active.

3 In the Current Date box, select the existing date, and then type **6/26/95 10:00 am**

  Leave the dialog box open for now.

Tip A fast way to see a specific date in the Gantt Chart is to use the Go To command on the Edit menu. (You can also press F5 to display the Go To dialog box.) In the Date box, enter the date to which you want to go.

Computing Costs

The cost of a task is the sum of the fixed cost, if any, plus the cost of its resource assignments. The resource cost is calculated from the resource unit cost information—standard rate, overtime rate, cost per use, and accrual method—that you enter for the resource.

For example, a task with one resource that is assigned to do 40 hours of work at a standard rate of $10 per hour has a resource cost of $400. A task with two resources assigned, each incurring a cost of $400, has a resource cost of $800. You view the resource costs in the Cost table.

Viewing Project Statistics

It is now June 26, 1995, and the project start is only three weeks away. Since you established the baseline earlier in this book, the project has been updated to reflect changes in tasks, durations, and resources. These new estimates reflect the current schedule. To see how the changes have affected the cost of the move, you can click the Statistics button in the Summary Info dialog box. This button is on both tabs in the dialog box.

View the current budget and the baseline

With the Tracking toolbar displayed, you can click the Statistics button to display the Project Statistics dialog box.

Check to see how the current estimate compares to the original budget by comparing the current cost to the baseline cost.

1 In the Summary Info dialog box, click the Statistics button.

  The Project Statistics dialog box for this project appears.

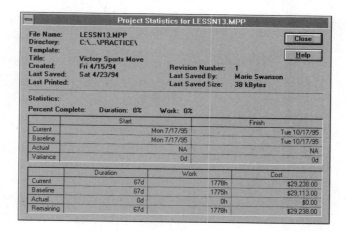

In the Cost column in the lower right corner of the dialog box, you can see that the current cost is somewhat more than the baseline cost.

2   Click the Close button.

Comparing Costs Using the Cost Table

While the Project Statistics dialog box displays total cost, displaying your project using the Cost table provides detailed cost information for each task. The Cost table displays columns of cost information that make it easy to compare the current, baseline, and actual costs. You apply the Cost table in a resource view to see resource costs. To see task costs, you apply the Cost table in a task view.

View task cost information with the Cost table

To find a way to lower the project costs, look at the costs for individual tasks. First display the Task Sheet, and then apply the Cost table.

1   From the View menu, choose More Views.

2   In the Views list, scroll to and select Task Sheet.

3   Click the Apply button.

The Task Sheet view appears.

4   From the View menu, choose Table: Entry, and then choose Cost.

Your screen looks like the following illustration.

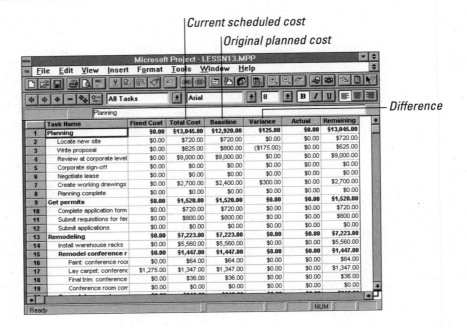

Current scheduled cost

Original planned cost

Difference

Task Name	Fixed Cost	Total Cost	Baseline	Variance	Actual	Remaining
1	Planning	$0.00	$13,045.00	$12,920.00	$125.00	$0.00	$13,045.00
2	Locate new site	$0.00	$720.00	$720.00	$0.00	$0.00	$720.00
3	Write proposal	$0.00	$625.00	$800.00	($175.00)	$0.00	$625.00
4	Review at corporate level	$0.00	$9,000.00	$9,000.00	$0.00	$0.00	$9,000.00
5	Corporate sign-off	$0.00	$0.00	$0.00	$0.00	$0.00	$0.00
6	Negotiate lease	$0.00	$0.00	$0.00	$0.00	$0.00	$0.00
7	Create working drawings	$0.00	$2,700.00	$2,400.00	$300.00	$0.00	$2,700.00
8	Planning complete	$0.00	$0.00	$0.00	$0.00	$0.00	$0.00
9	Get permits	$0.00	$1,520.00	$1,520.00	$0.00	$0.00	$1,520.00
10	Complete application form	$0.00	$720.00	$720.00	$0.00	$0.00	$720.00
11	Submit requisitions for fee	$0.00	$800.00	$800.00	$0.00	$0.00	$800.00
12	Submit applications	$0.00	$0.00	$0.00	$0.00	$0.00	$0.00
13	Remodeling	$0.00	$7,223.00	$7,223.00	$0.00	$0.00	$7,223.00
14	Install warehouse racks	$0.00	$5,560.00	$5,560.00	$0.00	$0.00	$5,560.00
15	Remodel conference r	$0.00	$1,447.00	$1,447.00	$0.00	$0.00	$1,447.00
16	Paint: conference roo	$0.00	$64.00	$64.00	$0.00	$0.00	$64.00
17	Lay carpet: conferenc	$1,275.00	$1,347.00	$1,347.00	$0.00	$0.00	$1,347.00
18	Final trim: conference	$0.00	$36.00	$36.00	$0.00	$0.00	$36.00
19	Conference room corr	$0.00	$0.00	$0.00	$0.00	$0.00	$0.00

Reducing Costs

You can use filters supplied with Microsoft Project to focus on tasks and resources that exceed the budget. When you are in a task view (such as the Task Sheet), the Cost Overbudget filter displays tasks whose scheduled costs exceed planned costs. If you are in a resource view, this filter displays resources whose scheduled costs exceed planned costs. You can reduce task costs in many ways. Use the filters to identify the method that is best for your project.

Substitute higher-cost, more efficient resources. For example, an experienced engineer might cost more, but might work much faster than a less-experienced engineer. Because a more efficient resource works fewer hours on a task, you can pay a higher rate and still reduce the cost of the resource assignment.

Trade equipment expenses for labor costs. If adding equipment lets your employees work faster, you might save more in labor than you spend on the extra equipment. For example, if you are renting only one scaffold, you might consider renting a second to speed the task.

Substitute a lower-cost resource. As illustrated in the following steps, another way to reduce costs is to assign a less-expensive, but equally effective, resource. For example, a $20-per hour draftsman might be able to do some of a $30-per hour architect's work.

Display the tasks that are over budget

You want to focus on tasks that are over budget. Applying the Cost Overbudget filter is a quick way to find out which tasks exceed the budget.

▶ On the Formatting toolbar, from the Filter list box, select Cost Overbudget.

The "Create working drawings" task is the only task that is over budget, as shown in the following illustration.

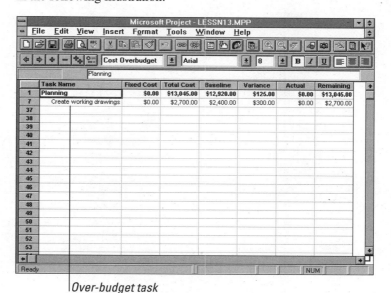

Over-budget task

The "Planning" phase is over budget because the "Create working drawings" task under it is over budget. The Variance column shows that the task is over budget by $300.

Examine resource assignments

You need to find out why the costs for the task have increased before you can find a way to lower the costs. By applying the Work table to the Task Sheet, you can examine the work assignment for this task.

▶ From the View menu, choose Table: Cost, and then choose Work.

Work information now appears in the Task Sheet, as shown in the following illustration.

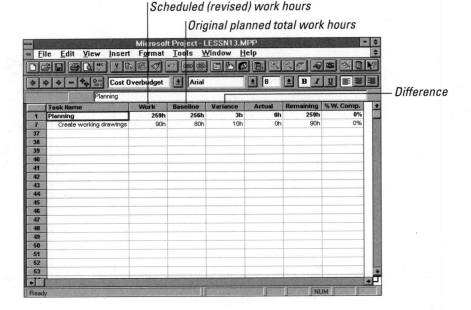

Scheduled (revised) work hours

Original planned total work hours

Difference

You can see in the Work field that the work estimate for the architect increased from the planned work of 80 hours to the currently scheduled work of 90 hours.

Reducing a Task Cost

Since the original estimate was made for the "Create working drawings" task, an additional draftsman has been hired to do some of the work on the task. The draftsman's standard rate is $20 per hour as opposed to the architect's standard rate of $30 per hour. To reduce costs, you can add the draftsman to the task and transfer 30 hours of work to the draftsman.

Display the Task Form view

You can adjust the amount of work assigned to resources for a specific task in the Task Form. You can also add a new resource to the resource pools in this view as well.

1 Select task 7, "Create working drawings."

2 From the View menu, choose More Views.

3 In the Views list, select Task Form.

4 Click the Apply button.

The Task Form view appears, as shown in the following illustration.

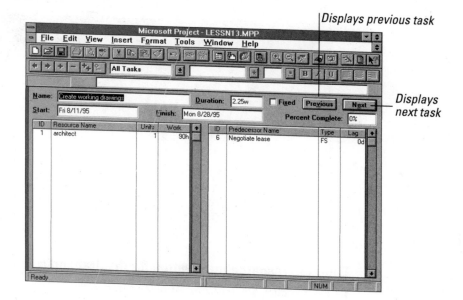

Displays previous task

Displays next task

Transfer work to a new, less expensive resource

1 In the Task Form, select the blank Resource Name field below architect.

2 Type **draftsman**

3 In the Work field for the draftsman, type **30h**, and click the enter button on the entry bar, or press ENTER.

4 In the Work field for the architect, type **60h**, and click the enter button on the entry bar, or press ENTER.

5 Choose the OK button.

Your completed Task Form looks like the following illustration.

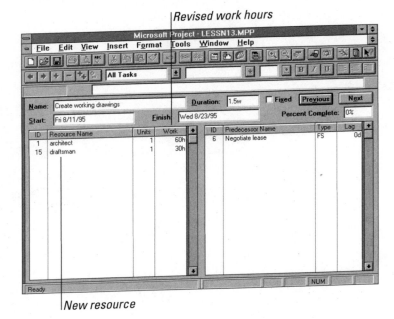

Revised work hours

New resource

Enter the resource information for the draftsman

1 Double-click the draftsman resource name.

The Resource Information dialog box appears.

2 Select entry in the Std Rate box, and then type **$20/h**

3 In the Accrue At box, select End.

Both the architect and the draftsman are paid upon completion of the work, so the cost does not accrue until the end of a task.

4 In the Group box, type **contractor**

5 In the Code box, type **501-110**

This code is the Victory Sports accounting code for this kind of contractor.

6 Choose the OK button.

Microsoft Project recalculates the cost of the resources for this task.

Compare updated costs

To compare the revised costs to the original baseline, return to the Task Sheet view and apply the Cost table.

1 From the View menu, choose More Views.

2 In the Views list, select Task Sheet.

3 Click the Apply button.

The Task Sheet view appears.

4 From the View menu, choose Table: Work, and then choose Cost.

The cost for task 7 is once again $2,400, so your project is back within budget. The Variance field for the "Create working drawings" task contains 0 (zero) because the scheduled cost and the planned cost are now the same.

Save

Save your project

▶ On the Standard toolbar, click the Save button.

One Step Further

An "underbudget" filter can be used to locate extra funds in case other tasks are overbudget. Follow these steps to create and apply a filter that looks for tasks that are underbudget.

Create a custom filter for underbudget tasks

1 From the Tools menu, choose Filtered For: All Tasks, and then choose More Filters.

2 Click the New button.

3 In the Name box, type **Underbudget**

4 In the Field Name column, click the down arrow in the entry bar and select Cost Variance.

5 In the Test column, click the down arrow in the entry bar and select Less.

6 In the Value(s) column, type **0**, and click the enter button on the entry bar, or press ENTER.

7 Choose the OK button.

8 Click the Apply button to apply the new filter.

After viewing only the underbudget tasks, you'll want to reset the view to display all tasks.

9 From the Filter list box on the Formatting toolbar, choose All Tasks.

If You Want to Continue to the Next Lesson

1 From the File menu, choose Close to save your project file.

2 Choose the Yes button if you see the message box asking whether you want to save your work. Leave the baseline unchanged.

If You Want to Quit Microsoft Project for Now

1   From the File menu, choose Exit.

2   Choose the Yes button if you see the message box asking whether you want to save your work. Leave the baseline unchanged.

Lesson Summary

To	Do this
View task costs	From the View menu, choose More Views. Then select Task Sheet and click Apply. On the View menu, choose Cost from the Table submenu.
Identify tasks that are over budget	In the Task Sheet view, display the Cost table. On the Formatting toolbar, from the Filter box, select the Cost Overbudget filter.
Reduce costs to meet the budget	From Task Sheet view, choose Work from the Table submenu (on the View menu). Examine resource assignments, and determine whether you should substitute lower-cost, equally effective resources; substitute higher-cost, more efficient resources; or add equipment to reduce labor time. Make any adjustments in the Task Form view.

For more information on	See in *Microsoft Project User's Guide*
Viewing task costs	Chapter 7, "Evaluating and Adjusting Your Schedule"
Viewing resource costs	Chapter 7, "Evaluating and Adjusting Your Schedule"

For online information about	From the Help menu, choose Search and then type
Viewing project costs	Cost table costs: viewing
Reducing costs	Cost Overbudget command costs: determining costs: reducing

Preview of the Next Lesson

In the next lesson, "Managing the Schedule," you specify constraints for task start and finish dates. You also learn how to track the progress of the project after it has started.

Scheduling Task Constraints

When you use Microsoft Project to schedule tasks and level overallocated resources, the tasks are scheduled to start as soon as possible. However, sometimes "as soon as possible" does not really meet your project's requirements. In this lesson, you'll learn to apply task constraints to restrict how Microsoft Project schedules tasks. You'll also learn how to resolve scheduling conflicts that might result when you apply task constraints in the schedule.

You will learn how to:

- Use constraints to set time limitations.
- Resolve constraint conflicts.

Estimated lesson time: 20 minutes

Start Microsoft Project

If you closed Microsoft Project in the last lesson, you need to restart the application before you can continue.

▶ Double-click the Microsoft Project icon.

Start the lesson

If you see the Welcome dialog box, click the Close button. If you see the Tip Of The Day dialog box, read the tip, and then click OK.

Open the project file called 14LESSN.MPP, and save it as LESSN14.MPP.

1 From the File menu, choose Open.
2 In the Directories box, double-click PRACTICE.
3 In the File Name box, double-click 14LESSN.MPP.
4 From the File menu, choose Save As.
5 In the File Name box, type **lessn14.mpp**
6 Choose the OK button.

Microsoft Project stores your project on your hard disk with the filename LESSN14.MPP. This file is similar to the project file you worked with in the previous lesson.

Display date columns

Because you will be focusing on task start and finish dates, you want to display the Start and Finish columns in the Gantt table.

▶ Drag the divider between the Gantt table and the Gantt Chart to the right until you can see the Finish column in the Gantt table.

Restricting Task Start and Finish Dates

In general, you should allow Microsoft Project to schedule project tasks for you. Use task constraints only when necessary to limit the schedule for a task.

Constraints are schedule restrictions that you place on individual tasks to affect task start and finish dates. All constraints (except As Soon As Possible and As Late As Possible) are based on a date you specify. Use constraint dates to reflect deadlines and availability of resources. For example, if some essential materials won't be available until after a specific date, you can schedule the task with the constraint "Start No Earlier Than" and then specify a date. Constraint dates do not vary with other changes in the schedule; other tasks are scheduled to accommodate the constraint dates. With such constraints applied to tasks, Microsoft Project creates a project schedule that meets the realities of your project.

In the Task Information dialog box, use the Constrain Task box on the Advanced tab to set constraints for individual tasks or groups of tasks. You can apply any one of these eight constraints to individual tasks:

- As Late As Possible
- As Soon As Possible
- Finish No Earlier Than
- Finish No Later Than
- Must Finish On
- Must Start On
- Start No Earlier Than
- Start No Later Than

In a project that is scheduled from start to finish (as specified in the Summary Info dialog box), the default task constraint is As Soon As Possible. In a project that is scheduled from finish to start, the default constraint is As Late As Possible.

Schedule tasks as late as possible

The computers and office furniture are essential to the operation of Victory Sports. To minimize the disruption the move will have on the office workers, schedule the tasks "Disconnect computers" and "Disassemble furniture" to start as late as possible, without delaying any other tasks. Use the Multiple Task Information dialog box to schedule this.

1 Select task 29, "Disconnect computers," and task 30, "Disassemble furniture."

Goto Selected Task

2 On the Standard toolbar, click the Goto Selected Task button to display the Gantt bars for these tasks in the Gantt Chart.

3 On the Standard toolbar, click the Information button to display the Multiple Task Information dialog box.

Information

4 Click the Advanced tab to display it in the dialog box.

5 Next to the Constrain Task Type list box, click the down arrow to display the list of scheduling constraints from which you can choose.

6 Select As Late As Possible from the list.

Watch the Gantt bars for these tasks as you complete the next step. If the dialog box is covering the Gantt bars for these tasks, drag the dialog box away from the Gantt bars. You can also observe the effects of changing the constraints as the dates in the Start and Finish column change.

7 Choose the OK button.

The tasks shift within their slack to the latest possible start dates. Notice that none of the start dates for the other tasks changed. Your Gantt Chart view looks like the following illustration.

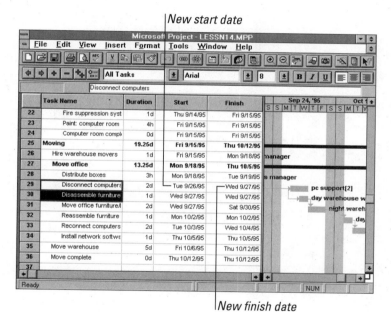

New start date

New finish date

Resolving Constraint Conflicts

Constraints can affect the project finish date or conflict with other scheduling requirements. If there is a conflict, a message from the Microsoft Project PlanningWizard appears, informing you of the conflict (or potential conflict) this constraint could have in your project. In the PlanningWizard, you can follow the wizard's advice and not make the constraint change, or you can continue with the change despite the conflict and adjust the schedule yourself. To get more information about how to resolve the conflict, you can also click the Help button in the PlanningWizard.

Verify the PlanningWizard for scheduling is on

1   From the Tools menu, choose Options.

The Options dialog box appears.

2   Click the General tab to make it active.

3   In the PlanningWizard area, be sure the Advice About Errors check box is selected.

Your dialog box should look like the following illustration.

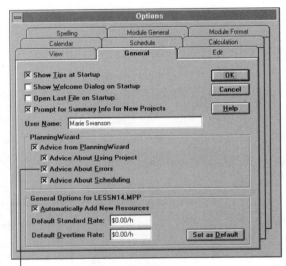

Displays Planning Wizard for errors

4   Choose the OK button.

Schedule tasks to finish before a set date

The president has arranged for a sports celebrity to come to Victory Sports to endorse a new high-tech athletic shoe on September 23, 1995. The marketing department wants to use the conference room for the event. Schedule the milestone "Conference room complete" to finish no later than September 19, 1995. This allows several days to address any problems before the publicity session is held.

1   Double-click task 19, "Conference room complete."

The Task Information dialog box appears.

2   Click the Advanced tab to make it active.

3   Click the Constrain Task Type down arrow to display the list, and then select Finish No Later Than.

4   In the Date box, type **9/19/95**

The task is scheduled to finish no later than September 19, 1995.

5 Choose the OK button.

You see the PlanningWizard informing you of a potential conflict by using this task constraint.

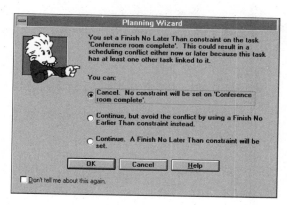

6 Click the third option button to use this constraint.

7 Choose the OK button.

The milestone "Conference room complete" is not affected by this constraint because it was already scheduled to finish before September 19, 1995. Nevertheless, this constraint ensures that future scheduling changes do not cause the task to finish beyond September 19, 1995.

Schedule tasks to start after a set date

You've just been informed that the custom paint you've wanted for the conference room won't be available until September 19, 1995. The painting supervisor wants to know whether he should place the order for custom paint or substitute your second choice, which is available right away. What effect does this new constraint have on the schedule? Enter the constraint Start No Earlier Than September 19 for task 16, "Paint: conference room," because the custom paint won't be ready until then.

1 Double-click task 16, "Paint: conference room," to display the Task Information dialog box.

2 Click the Advanced tab to make it active.

3 Click the Constrain Task Type arrow to display the list, and then select Start No Earlier Than.

4 In the Date box, type **9/19/95**

The task is scheduled to start no earlier than September 19, 1995.

5 Choose the OK button.

Microsoft Project displays a PlanningWizard message indicating that this task constraint creates a scheduling conflict with task 18.

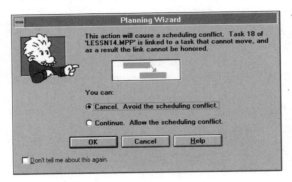

Because you just put a constraint on when the room had to be ready, Microsoft Project warns you that if you cannot start painting until September 19, other tasks cannot be completed on schedule.

Display the Help message

Microsoft Project Help gives you a more detailed message about the conflict.

1   Click the Help button to display Help about the message.

You can also press F1. You see the following Help window.

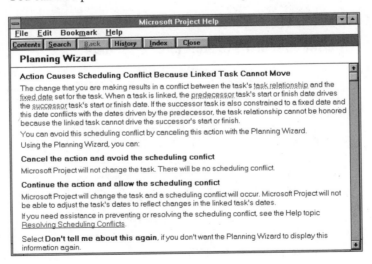

To summarize, the Help window explains that the predecessor task must be completed early enough to accommodate a fixed-date successor (in this project, task 19, "Conference room complete"). Or, depending on your project, you must remove the fixed-date constraint in a predecessor task to correct the conflict.

2 From the File menu in the Help window, choose Exit to close the Help window.

3 Choose the OK button to cancel the task constraint.

The PlanningWizard closes without making any changes to the schedule. You will need to tell the painting supervisor not to order the custom paint and to use your second choice that is in stock.

Save your project

Save

▶ On the Standard toolbar, click the Save button.

Note As you learned in Lesson 9, you can specify that you want Microsoft Project to level overallocated resources for you. If the tasks to which the overallocated resources are assigned use conflicting task constraints, Microsoft Project might not be able to resolve the resource conflict.

One Step Further

You can display all constraints in your project by changing to a Task Sheet view of your task information and by applying the Constraint Dates table. Because Microsoft Project can contain many columns of information, tables are a fast way to display a set of useful, related columns. Combined with a filter to display only those tasks that do not use the default constraint, you can quickly locate, and adjust if necessary, those tasks that constrain the schedule.

Tip The Constraint Dates table is also useful when you want to enter the same constraint for a number of tasks.

View constraint dates

1 From the View menu, choose More Views.

2 In the Views list, select Task Sheet.

3 Click the Apply button.

4 From the View menu, choose Table: Entry, and then choose More Tables.

5 In the Tables list box, select Constraint Dates.

6 Click the Apply button.

Your screen displays columns containing constraint information for each task in the project.

7 From the Filter list box on the Formatting toolbar, choose Tasks With Fixed Dates.

Your Task Sheet view looks like the following illustration.

Tasks with task constraints

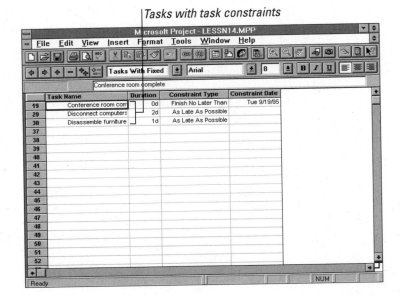

If you are having difficulty resolving resource conflicts, it could be because there are too many tasks with task constraints. Using the Constraint Dates table and the Tasks With Fixed Dates filter in the Task Sheet view is a great way to locate the task constraints in the project.

If You Want to Continue to the Next Lesson

1   From the File menu, choose Close to close your project.

2   Choose the Yes button if you see the message box asking whether you want to save your work. Leave the baseline unchanged.

If You Want to Quit Microsoft Project for Now

1   From the File menu, choose Exit.

2   Choose the Yes button if you see the message box asking whether you want to save your work. Leave the baseline unchanged.

Lesson Summary

To	Do this
Set task constraints	Double-click the task to display the Task Information dialog box. Click the Advanced tab. Click the Constrain Task Type down arrow to display the list of scheduling constraints from which you can choose. Select the constraint to apply to the task.
Turn the PlanningWizard on	From the Tools menu, choose Options. Click the General tab. In the PlanningWizards area, be sure the Advice About Errors check box is selected.
Resolve constraint conflicts	In the PlanningWizard dialog box, click the Help button to display suggestions for resolving constraint conflicts. Add resources to constrained tasks or remove conflicting constraints.

For more information on	See in *Microsoft Project User's Guide*
Constraints	Chapter 4, "Scheduling Tasks"

For online information about	From the <u>H</u>elp menu, choose <u>S</u>earch and then type
Examining task constraints	constraints
Setting task constraints	constraining tasks constraints

Preview of the Next Lesson

In the next lesson, you'll learn how to change the schedule to reflect the actual status of the project tasks. You'll learn several ways to indicate when tasks have occurred exactly as planned, experienced delays or slowdowns, or even finished early.

Tracking Project Progress

Even with the best plan, the schedule is likely to deviate from the original one you lay out. By tracking progress, you can discover which tasks need extra attention in time to make adjustments for your project to continue smoothly. In this lesson, you'll learn how to track the progress of your project's performance after the project is under way. You will learn to compare the current schedule and actual data to the original.

You will learn how to:

- Update the current schedule with actual data.
- Compare the current schedule to the baseline.
- Compare actual data to the baseline.

Estimated lesson time: 30 minutes

Start Microsoft Project

If you closed Microsoft Project in the last lesson, you need to restart the application before you can continue.

If you see the Welcome dialog box, click the Close button. If you see the Tip Of The Day dialog box, read the tip, and then click OK.

▶ Double-click the Microsoft Project icon.

Start the lesson

Open the project file called 15LESSN.MPP and save it as LESSN15.MPP.

1 From the File menu, choose Open.

2 In the Directories box, double-click PRACTICE.

3 In the File Name box, double-click 15LESSN.MPP.

4 From the File menu, choose Save As.

5 In the File Name box, type **lessn15.mpp**

6 Choose the OK button.

Microsoft Project stores your project on your hard disk with the filename LESSN15.MPP. This file is similar to the project file you worked with in the previous lesson, except that the timescale has been adjusted to allow you to see more of the project.

Change the current date

Assume it's now September 11, and the office move is well under way. The following steps set the current date in Microsoft Project to reflect the passage of time to after the project has begun, 9/11/95.

1   From the File menu, choose Summary Info.

2   Click the Project tab, if it is not already active.

3   In the Current Date box, select the existing date, and then type **9/11/95**

4   Choose the OK button.

5   In the Gantt table, select task 10, "Complete application forms."

Goto Selected Task

6   On the Standard toolbar, click the Goto Selected Task button.

Tracking Progress

Tracking progress means updating and analyzing your project's performance once the project is under way. Before the project starts, you create a baseline, which is a copy of the original schedule that does not change. During the project, you compare the current schedule to the baseline.

To track progress, start by using the Save Baseline command on the Tools menu (or in the PlanningWizard when you save a project file you changed). This command freezes the data that becomes a baseline, against which you can compare your constantly changing schedule. In the move project for Victory Sports, you already created a baseline in Lesson 9, "Managing Resource Workloads."

When tracking progress, you work with three types of information: baseline, current, and actual.

Baseline. This is your fixed model for how the project should proceed. This is also known as *planned* information. This information does not change unless you specify you want to modify the baseline. For example, in the original schedule, you might plan on obtaining waste barrels beginning on September 27, with a duration of two days and a fixed cost of $400. This information is the task's baseline data, as set when you saved the baseline.

Current. This is a changing, working model for upcoming tasks after the project is under way. The schedule might change as you receive new information and make adjustments. For example, before you begin purchasing waste barrels, you might discover you can't begin until September 28 and the barrels will then cost $500. This revised information is the task's current data.

Actual. These are tasks already in progress or are finished. As you enter actual dates for completed tasks, the start and finish dates for the remaining scheduled tasks are updated. For example, after the acquisition of the waste barrels is completed, you realize that the task took three days rather than two. The start and finish dates of the subsequent tasks are updated to reflect the longer duration.

Updating the Schedule with Actual Information

Updating your project is an ongoing process of modifying the current schedule (for upcoming tasks) and entering actual information (for tasks that have started). To the extent that previous tasks affect the start and finish dates of future tasks, Microsoft Project incorporates this information and recalculates the schedule for future tasks. Your schedule changes, but your baseline remains unaffected.

Entering Actual Information

You enter actual information as tasks happen. How often you update the schedule depends on how closely you want to track progress. The Tracking submenu on the Tools menu contains the commands you need to enter the progress or status of a task, selected tasks, or the entire project.

You can also use a Tracking toolbar that contains the buttons for updating the project. In addition, it contains buttons that display the same dialog boxes you see when you choose the Update Tasks command for a range of tasks you specify.

Display the Tracking toolbar

▶ With the right mouse button, click a toolbar to display the Toolbars shortcut menu, and then choose Tracking.

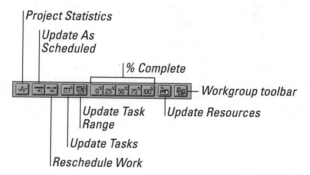

Update the schedule

All the tasks scheduled to begin before today are proceeding according to plan. To update the schedule to reflect this progress, select all the tasks and click the Update As Scheduled button on the Tracking toolbar.

1   Click the Task Name column heading to select all the tasks in the project.

2   On the Tracking toolbar, click the Update As Scheduled button.

The tasks are updated and progress bars appear inside the Gantt bars.

*Update As
Scheduled*

3   Click the task name for task 1, "Planning."

Viewing the Schedule

*You can also change
actual data directly
on the Gantt Chart by
dragging the
progress bars inside
the Gantt bars.*

The vertical dashed gridline on the Gantt Chart marks today's date on the timescale. Tasks with Gantt bars completely to the left of the date line should be complete. For example, in the following illustration, task 7, "Create working drawings," should be 100% complete. Tasks whose Gantt bars intersect the date line should be partially complete. For example, task 14, "Install warehouse racks," has already started and should be about 50% complete. Tasks to the right of the date line are scheduled to begin later. In addition, progress bars within the Gantt bars provide a graphical indication of the progress of the tasks.

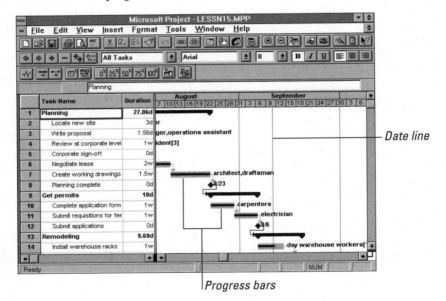

— *Date line*

|*Progress bars*

Updating Specific Tasks

When tasks are not completed as scheduled, you must enter their actual progress. You can select a single task, multiple tasks, or a group of tasks within a date range. To make it easier to update tasks and see progress, you can change a viewing option to display times as well as dates in the project. In addition, you can change the timescale to see these tasks in greater detail.

Change the date format

The tasks you will update in the next exercise have durations of less than one day. To see the start and finish times, as well as the dates, you need to change the format of the date. You can change the date format in the Options dialog box.

1 From the Tools menu, choose Options.

2 Click the View tab, if it is not already active.

3 Click the Date Format down arrow, and select 1/31/94 12:33 PM, if it is not already selected.

Depending on your computer's system date, the year you see in the format settings might be different.

4 Choose the OK button.

Change the current date

By selecting a date format that includes the time, you can specify the current time (as well as the date) when you update tasks. Assume that it's now September 19, 1995, 12:00 P.M., and you need to update the progress of additional tasks in the project. Change the current date to reflect the new date and time.

1 From the File menu, choose Summary Info.

2 Click the Project tab, if it is not already active.

3 In the Current Date box, select the date and time and type **9/19/95 12:00 pm**

4 Choose the OK button.

The date line moves to reflect the new current date and time.

Adjust the timescale

To see tasks that have shorter durations in greater detail, you need to zoom in the timescale.

Zoom In

1 On the Standard toolbar, click the Zoom In button twice.

The timescale now displays days over hours (in 6-hour increments).

Goto Selected Task

2 Select task 16, "Paint: Conference room," and, on the Standard toolbar, click the Goto Selected Task button.

Your project looks like the following illustration.

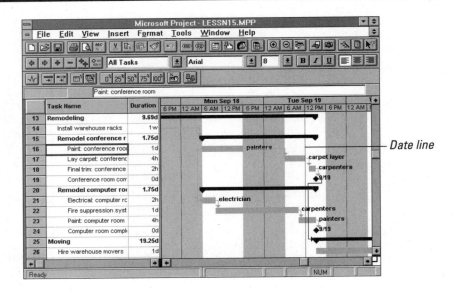

— Date line

Enter actual data for on-time tasks

The remodeling tasks 14, 16, and 21 started and finished on schedule. You can update these tasks quickly by selecting them and then clicking the Update As Scheduled button on the Tracking toolbar.

1   With task 16 still selected, hold down CTRL and select task 14, " Install warehouse racks," and then task 21, "Electrical: computer room."

2   On the Tracking toolbar, click the Update As Scheduled button.

Progress bars appear in the Gantt bars for these tasks, reflecting the fact that they are completed as scheduled. You might have to scroll to see the Gantt bar for task 14.

Update As
Scheduled

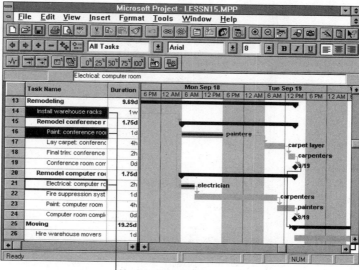

Updated tasks

Update a task that started late

When tasks don't go as scheduled, you need to enter actual data manually. Enter actual data for the "Lay carpet: conference room" task to show that it started two hours late, but is 50 percent complete.

1 Select task 17, "Lay carpet conference room."

Update Tasks

2 On the Tracking toolbar, click the Update Tasks button.

The Update Tasks dialog box appears. In this dialog box, you can specify actual start and finish information, as well as actual percent completion.

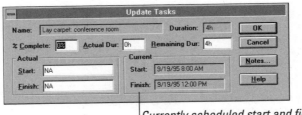

Currently scheduled start and finish

3 In the Actual area, select the existing text in the Start box, and then type **9/19/95 10:00 am**

4 In the % Complete box, type **50%**

Despite the late start, this task is still 50% complete.

5 Choose the OK button.

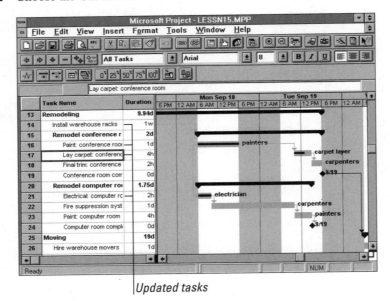

Updated tasks

Note If you have several tasks you need to update, you can use the Update Task Range button on the Tracking toolbar. This button filters tasks within a date range you specify, and then displays the Update Task dialog box for each task in the range. Using this button saves you time, because you don't need to filter the tasks yourself and open the Update Task dialog box for each task individually.

Update a task in progress

You originally estimated the "Fire suppression system: computer room" task to take one day. The task started on time, but is running somewhat ahead of schedule. With the % Complete buttons on the Tracking toolbar, you can specify how much of the task is complete.

1 Select task 22, "Fire suppression system: computer room."

2 On the Tracking toolbar, click the 75% Complete button.

75% Complete

Apply the Tracking table to view actual data

Microsoft Project's Tracking table is a convenient way to view and update data in the actual fields. Use the Tracking table to update the office move schedule with tasks that have finished or are happening now.

1 From the View menu, choose Table: Entry, and then choose Tracking.

The Gantt table now contains tracking information. The #s in the columns mean that the columns are not wide enough to display the date and time used in the new date format you set earlier.

2 Drag the divider to the right until you can see about half of the Act. Dur. column in the Gantt table.

3 Double-click the right border of each of the Act. Start and Act. Finish columns to make each column wider so that the #s no longer appear.

The actual fields appear in the Gantt table. "NA" means no actual data has been entered. Your project looks like the following illustration.

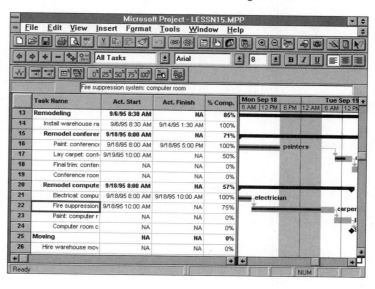

Comparing Results

Microsoft Project provides many ways for you to compare your current schedule and actual data to the baseline. You can choose the most convenient method to find out what you need to know.

Apply the Variance table to view the baseline

When you save the baseline, Microsoft Project copies data from currently scheduled fields into baseline fields. If you need to see by how many days the schedule is off from the original plan, you can display the Task Sheet view and apply the Variance table. This view and table displays baseline start and finish dates along with the scheduled start and finish dates. Microsoft Project also calculates the difference between the baseline and scheduled dates.

1   From the View menu, choose More Views.

2   In the Views list, select Task Sheet.

3   Click the Apply button.

Your project is displayed in the Task Sheet view.

4   From the View menu, choose Table: Entry, and then choose Variance. Double-click the column borders, if necessary, to adjust the column widths.

Microsoft Project displays the scheduled and baseline dates in the Task Sheet. The Start Var. and Finish Var. columns display the difference (in days) between the original dates stored in the baseline and the currently scheduled dates. For many tasks, the project is ahead of schedule.

Note   Depending on the resolution of your monitor, you might need to scroll horizontally to see the last column, Finish Var.

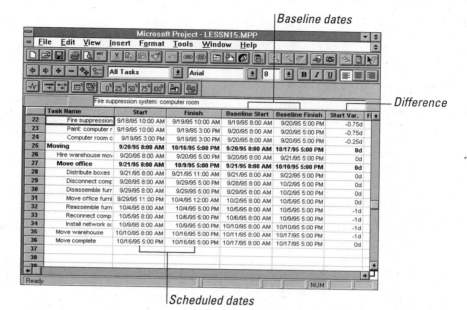

Baseline dates

Difference

Scheduled dates

Comparing Baseline vs. Actual Data

After the actual data is entered, your schedule is changed significantly. You now need to compare the current schedule to your plan to see the project's performance. In addition to the Variance table, which you applied earlier in this lesson, the Tracking Gantt view allows you to visually compare planned to scheduled progress by displaying Gantt bars for both the baseline and actual schedules.

Display the Tracking Gantt view

1   From the View menu, choose More Views.

The More Views dialog box appears.

2   In the Views list, select Tracking Gantt.

3   Click the Apply button.

The Tracking Gantt view appears. Adjust the divider to the right to see the Start and Finish columns.

4   Widen the Start and Finish column borders as necessary, so they are wide enough to display the dates.

Goto Selected Task

5   Select task 15, "Remodel conference room," and click the Goto Selected Task button on the Standard toolbar.

The Gantt Chart in the Tracking Gantt view displays another Gantt bar for each task. The top bar represents actual information, while the bottom bar represents baseline information.

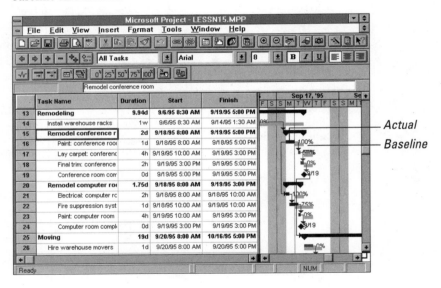

Display the Work table

Use the Work table and Cost table applied to the Task Sheet to compare actual costs and work to what you originally planned.

1 From the View menu, choose Table: Entry, and then choose Work.

The Work table shows scheduled, planned, and actual work.

2 If necessary, adjust the divider to the right to display the Actual column.

Your screen looks like the following illustration.

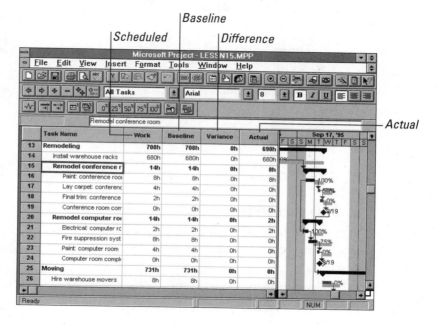

Display the Cost table

The Cost table shows actual costs and baseline costs.

1 From the View menu, choose Table:Work, and then choose Cost.

2 Adjust the divider to the right to display the Actual column.

Your screen looks like the following illustration.

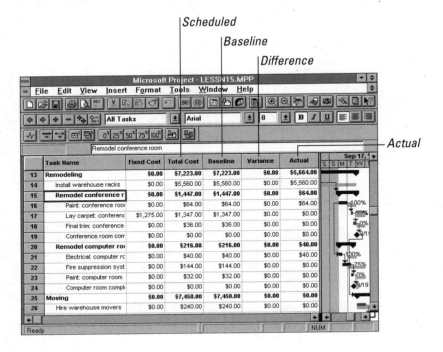

Scheduled

Baseline

Difference

Actual

Save your project and return to the Gantt Chart view

1 From the <u>V</u>iew menu, choose <u>G</u>antt Chart.

2 From the <u>V</u>iew menu, choose Ta<u>b</u>le: Tracking, and then choose <u>E</u>ntry.

3 With the right mouse button, click a toolbar to display the Toolbar shortcut menu, and then choose Tracking to hide the Tracking toolbar.

Save

4 On the Standard toolbar, click the Save button.

One Step Further

With the mouse, you can get fast information about a task by clicking the Gantt bar for the task. In addition, dragging the end of the progress bar allows you to change the percent complete. Dragging the end of the Gantt bar allows you to change the duration. Dragging in the center of the Gantt bar itself lets you change the start date of the task. Try these techniques to change task information.

1 Point to the Gantt bar for task 22, "Fire suppression system: computer room," and hold down the mouse button.

A pop-up window displays information about the task.

2 Point to the right end of the progress bar and hold down the mouse button while you drag to the right until the Complete Through value indicates the task is completed through 9:00 A.M.

When you move to the right end of the progress bar, the pointer looks like the percent arrow in the following table. The Complete Through value represents the date or time through which the task is complete. For example, if the task is ahead of schedule and the amount of work completed is what you expected to finish by the end of the day, drag the end of the progress bar to that point in the schedule.

3 Point to the right end of the Gantt bar and hold down the mouse button while you drag to the right until the duration becomes 2 days.

When you move to the right end of the Gantt bar, the pointer looks like the right arrow below.

Pointer	Pointer name
%▸	Percent arrow
▸	Right arrow
◈	Four-sided arrow
◂	Left arrow

You are not going to save these changes, so feel free to experiment with clicking and dragging on the Gantt bars to see the effect on durations, percent complete, and scheduled start dates.

If You Want to Continue to the Next Lesson

1 From the File menu, choose Close to close your project.

2 Choose the No button if you see the message box asking whether you want to save your work.

If You Want to Quit Microsoft Project for Now

1 From the File menu, choose Exit.

2 Choose the No button if you see the message box asking whether you want to save your work.

Lesson Summary

To	Do this	Button
Display the Tracking toolbar	With the right mouse button, click a toolbar to display the shortcut menu, and then choose Tracking.	
Update the current schedule with actual data as scheduled	Select the task to be updated. On the Tracking toolbar, click the Update As Scheduled button.	
Update the current schedule with actual data when a task does not proceed as scheduled	Select the task to be updated. On the Tracking toolbar, click the Update Tasks button to display the Update Task dialog box. Enter actual information in the Actual boxes.	
Update a task with a specific % complete	Select the task to be updated. On the Tracking toolbar, click the % Complete button that matches the amount completed, such as the button shown here.	
Compare the current schedule to the baseline	In the Task Sheet view, from the View menu, choose the Variance table on the Table submenu.	
Compare actual data to the baseline	In the Tracking Gantt view, from the View menu, choose the Work and Cost tables on the Table submenu.	

For more information on	See in *Microsoft Project User's Guide*
Tracking progress	Chapter 10, "Tracking the Progress of Your Project"

For online information about	From the **H**elp menu, choose **S**earch and then type
Tracking progress	tracking progress

Preview of the Next Lesson

In the next lesson, you'll learn how to reschedule tasks to meet a deadline. You'll also learn how to recognize critical tasks and use three strategies for shortening the critical path to meet a deadline.

Working with the Critical Path

Meeting the project goals on time is essential to the success of many projects. Unexpected delays or the addition of new tasks can cause projects to finish later than planned. In this lesson, you'll learn three ways to shorten the critical path so that you can complete a project faster. You'll change the task relationships of, and add resources to, critical tasks. You'll also learn to adjust the work schedule of resources assigned to critical tasks.

You will learn how to:

- Change task relationships to shorten the critical path.
- Add resources to shorten the critical path.
- Extend workdays to shorten the critical path.

Estimated lesson time: 20 minutes

Start Microsoft Project

If you closed Microsoft Project in the last lesson, you need to restart the application before you can continue.

▶ Double-click the Microsoft Project icon.

Start the lesson

If you see the Welcome dialog box, click the Close button. If you see the Tip Of The Day dialog box, read the tip, and then click OK.

Open the project file called 16LESSN.MPP, and save it as LESSN16.MPP.

1 From the File menu, choose Open.

2 In the Directories box, double-click PRACTICE.

3 In the File Name box, double-click 16LESSN.MPP.

4 From the File menu, choose Save As.

5 In the File Name box, type **lessn16.mpp**

6 Choose the OK button.

Microsoft Project stores your project on your hard disk with the filename LESSN16.MPP. This file is similar to the project file you worked with in the previous lesson, except that the timescale has been adjusted to allow you to see the Gantt bar in detail.

Change the current date

Assume it's now September 24, 1995, and the office move is entering its final phases. Set the current date in Microsoft Project to reflect the passage of time to a date further into the project, 9/24/95.

1 From the File menu, choose Summary Info.

2 Click the Project tab, if it is not already active.

3 In the Current Date box, select the existing text and type **9/24/95**

4 Choose the OK button.

Change the date format

To see the start and finish times, as well as dates, you might need to change the format of the date.

1 From the Tools menu, choose Options.

2 Click the View tab, if it is not already active.

3 Click the Date Format arrow, and select 1/31/94 12:33 PM, if it is not already selected.

4 Choose the OK button.

Crashing the Critical Path

Tasks that cause the project finish date to be delayed if they are not completed as scheduled are said to be on the *critical path*. Tasks on the critical path are called *critical tasks*. When you increase the duration of a critical task, the project is delayed. Similarly, shortening the duration of a critical task causes your project to finish sooner.

Reducing the duration of the critical path is often referred to as *crashing* the critical path. Because critical tasks directly affect the project's finish date, the following strategies for crashing the critical path focus on reducing task duration.

Changing the relationship between tasks. This strategy shortens the critical path without adding resources or extending work hours.

Scheduling overtime. This strategy shortens the duration.

Adding more resources. This strategy shortens the duration of resource-driven tasks.

Removing unnecessary predecessors. This strategy eliminates delays caused by predecessors that do not affect the task. Be sure all predecessors to critical tasks are essential.

Dealing with the Unexpected

The Victory Sports move is scheduled to finish at the end of business on October 16. You've just learned that the company president wants to celebrate with a company-wide party at the new site on October 13.

You have to speed up the move by shortening the critical path. First, you display the tasks on the critical path, and then you try changing the relationships of some tasks.

Filter critical tasks

See which tasks are critical to the project finishing on time.

1   On the Formatting toolbar, from the Filter box, select Critical.

Critical tasks are displayed.

Goto Selected Task

2   With task 32, "Reassemble furniture," selected, click the Goto Selected Task button on the Standard toolbar.

With only the critical tasks displayed, your project looks like the following illustration.

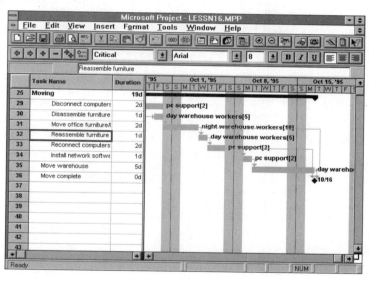

Changing Task Relationships

Defining task relationships more realistically can be the most economical way to shorten the critical path. You might not need to add resources or increase the working hours. Try this strategy first.

Change the relationship of two tasks

Task 33, "Reconnect computers," is not scheduled to begin until the "Reassemble furniture" task is completely finished. In fact, the two tasks can overlap, because the computers can be reconnected for those workers whose furniture has been assembled. Change the relationship of these tasks so that task 33 begins after 50% of the "Reassemble furniture" task is complete.

1   Double-click task 33, "Reconnect computers."

The Task Information dialog box appears.

2   Click the Predecessors tab to make it active in the dialog box.

3   In the Lag field for "Reassemble furniture," type **-50%**

This indicates task 33 starts halfway through the scheduled start of task 32.

4   Choose the OK button.

Look at the Gantt bars to see how the tasks are scheduled now.

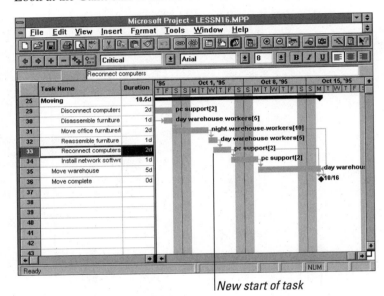

New start of task

The finish date is still October 16. You need to try additional strategies to shorten the schedule.

Save

Save your work

▶   On the Standard toolbar, click the Save button.

Adding Resources to Shorten the Critical Path

Despite your best efforts to simplify task relationships, a project might still require that you add resources to a critical task to meet your deadline. However, be prepared to deal with resource overallocation conflicts when you assign more resources to a task.

Add resources to a task

Because moving the office furniture is a resource-driven task, you can shorten the duration by adding two workers to the task.

1 Double-click task 31, "Move office furniture."

The Task Information dialog box appears.

2 Click the Resources tab to make it active in the dialog box.

3 In the Units column, type **12**

4 Choose the OK button.

Microsoft Project adjusts the duration of the task to include the new resources. Notice how the Gantt bars reflect the change.

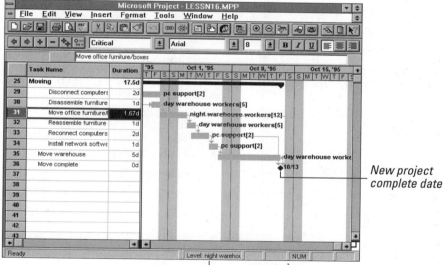

New project complete date

Overallocation message

Level overallocated resources

Notice that the message "Level: night warehouse workers" appears in the status bar. Because there are only 10 night warehouse workers employed at Victory Sports, they became overallocated when you added the additional workers in the previous step. If you use automatic leveling or the Level Now leveling feature, you will introduce delays in the schedule. As a result, Microsoft Project will not be able to calculate an accurate critical path. Because you cannot add more night warehouse workers, change the units back to 10 for this task.

1 Double-click task 31, "Move office furniture."

The Task Information dialog box appears.

2 Click the Resources tab to make it active in the dialog box.

3 In the Units column, type **10**

4 Choose the OK button.

The project finish date returns to October 16. You need to try a different strategy to shorten the project.

Changing the Calendar

When adding more resources is not an option for your project, another way to shorten the critical path is to extend the work day or work week in the resource calendar for the resource assigned to the task, or in the base calendar if several resources are assigned to the tasks whose duration you wish to shorten.

Increase the working hours

Another task, "Move warehouse," is also on the critical path. Because the other six day warehouse workers are busy on another project, you need to shorten this critical task by increasing their working hours. Try shortening this task by increasing the work day for the week this task is scheduled. For this week only, change the start time of 8:00 A.M. to 6:00 A.M. To compensate for the extra hours worked, shorten the work day for the following week after the project is complete.

1 Select task 35, "Move warehouse."

2 From the Tools menu, choose Change Working Time.

The Change Working Time dialog box appears.

3 In the For box, click the down arrow and select "day warehouse workers."

4 In the calendar, scroll to October 1995.

5 Select the days October 9 through October 13.

6 Under Working Time, in the first From box, select the "8," and then type **6**

7 Select the days October 16 through October 20.

8 Under Working Time, in the second To box, select the "5," and then type **3**

9 Choose the OK button.

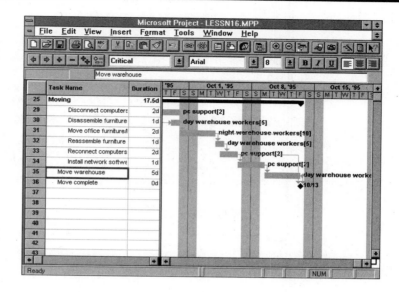

The project finish date is now scheduled for October 13. It's close, but you can finish in time for the party.

Save

Save your work

▶ On the Standard toolbar, click the Save button.

One Step Further

Understanding the relationship between tasks is important when crashing the critical path. Another way to view task relationships is to display the project in the PERT Chart view. In this view, you get a visual representation of the flow of tasks in the project. Appendix A, "Using PERT Charts," provides more information about PERT Charts, but for now you can view your project in this view.

Display the PERT Chart view

1 From the View menu, choose PERT Chart.

Your project appears in the PERT Chart view.

2 From the View menu, choose Zoom.

The Zoom dialog box appears. In this dialog box, you can adjust the magnification of the view. Unlike the Zoom In and Zoom Out buttons on the Standard toolbar, you can specify an exact magnification setting.

3 Select the Entire Project option button, and then choose the OK button.

Depending on the capabilities of your monitor, you can see most, if not all, of the tasks of the project in the PERT Chart. You might need to scroll downward to match the following illustration.

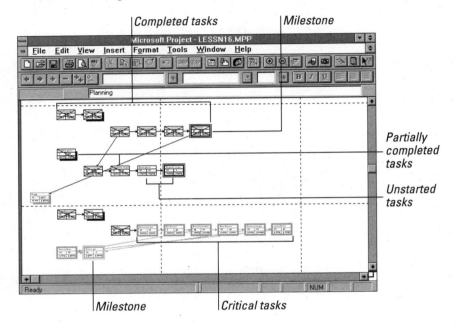

4 On the Standard toolbar, click the Zoom In button three times.

Zoom In

5 Scroll downward until you see the "Move complete" task.

6 Below the "Move complete" task, drag to create a box that is about the same size as the box above it.

You have just created a new task in the project.

7 Type **Party!** and then click the enter button on the entry bar, or press ENTER.

This is the last task in the project and should follow the "Move complete" task.

8 Drag a line from inside the "Move complete" task to the "Party!" task.

Drawing lines from one task to another links the tasks in a PERT Chart view.

If You Want to Continue to the Next Lesson

1 From the File menu, choose Close to close your project.

2 Choose the Yes button if you see the message box asking whether you want to save your work. Leave the baseline unchanged.

If You Want to Quit Microsoft Project for Now

1 From the File menu, choose Exit.

2 Choose the Yes button if you see the message box asking whether you want to save your work. Leave the baseline unchanged.

Lesson Summary

To	Do this
View tasks on the critical path	On the Formatting toolbar in the Filters list box, select Critical.
Shorten the critical path	Add resources, change the relationship of tasks, or change the base or resource calendar.

For more information on	See in *Microsoft Project User's Guide*
Critical path	Chapter 7, "Evaluating and Adjusting Your Schedule"
Scheduling methods	Chapter 4, "Scheduling Tasks"

For online information about	From the Help menu, choose Search and then type
Adjusting schedules	critical path critical tasks shortening the critical path
Analyzing the plan	Critical command critical path critical tasks

Preview of the Next Lessons

In the next part of the book, you will learn how to customize the Microsoft Project environment, including toolbars and templates. In the next lesson, you will learn how to customize project views, tables, and reports to communicate about the project with other team members and management.

Review & Practice

In the lessons in Part 4, "Controlling the Project," you learned skills to help you become familiar with managing a project. If you want to practice these skills and test your knowledge before you proceed with the lessons in Part 5, you can work through the Review & Practice section following this lesson.

Part 4   Review & Practice

Before you begin planning a project of your own, practice the skills you learned in Part 4 by working through the project management activities in this Review & Practice section. Here you'll respond to changes in the project before the project begins, as well as during the course of the project. You'll also use different views to make changes and evaluate progress.

Scenario

Despite your best efforts to plan every detail of the Summit Boots project, there have been inevitable changes. Some tasks will require more time and additional resources. Other tasks will require shorter durations and less time for some of the resources assigned. You will also need to add constraints to certain tasks to accommodate a more aggressive schedule. Use the skills you learned in Part 4 to update the plan and ensure that the schedule for the rest of the project takes these changes into account.

You will review and practice how to:

- Compare the schedule to the plan.
- Adjust costs.
- Constrain the schedule for specific tasks.
- Update actual data.
- Shorten the critical path.

Estimated practice time: 30 minutes

Before You Begin

1 Open the scenario project file called P4REVIEW.MPP. Before you make any changes in this project, save it with the new name REVIEWP4.MPP.

   This project file should look similar to the file you saved after completing the steps in the Part 3 Review & Practice. This project is not linked to the subproject and already has a baseline.

2 Display the Tracking toolbar for easy access to the update and tracking features you will need in this Review & Practice section.

   You can display the shortcut menu with the right mouse button.

Step 1: Compare and Adjust Project Costs

After saving the baseline, you have learned that the rate for the line workers has increased to $12 per hour, and the rate for the analyst has increased to $22 per hour. In addition, the task to assemble a project team is now an all-day meeting with the team leader from Morton Marketing. Your assistant has already entered this information into the schedule. Now you must try to adjust the current costs so the project is within the original budget despite these changes.

View project statistics and over-budget tasks

1 Display the Project Statistics dialog box to see the effect of these changes on the overall cost of the project.

2 Because the current cost exceeds the amount in the baseline, you need to adjust the costs of the tasks that are overbudget. Apply the Cost Overbudget filter to view these tasks in the Gantt Chart view.

Adjust costs

Several tasks are overbudget. Even though you won't be able to adjust the costs for all the tasks, you can adjust some of the tasks to reduce the overall cost of the current schedule. Reapply the Cost Overbudget filter after each adjustment to see whether the task is still overbudget. View the project statistics after each change to see its effect on the overall costs.

1 The analyst received a raise because of her ability to work quickly. As a result, reduce the duration of task 7, "Analyze distribution channels," from 1 week to 4 days (4d).

2 The project leader from Morton Marketing is only required for one half day for task 3. Display the Task Details Form view, and adjust the work hours for this resource from 8 to 4. (Hint: You can remain in this view for the next step; just click the Next button until you see the information for the "Produce prototype" task.)

3 The designer is not required for the entire task of producing the prototype (task 12). In the Task Details Form view, adjust the hours for this resource from 80 to 40.

4 You have been able to negotiate a more favorable rate with the Morton Marketing resource. Switch to the Resource Sheet view, and change the standard rate for this resource from $50 to $48.

5 Examine the project statistics to see the results. The current costs are now lower than the baseline costs. Then return to the Gantt Chart view and save the project.

For more information on	See
Adjusting costs	Lesson 13

Step 2: Specify Task Constraints

The product needs to be ready to ship before the Spring Sports Expo, so you must specify a task constraint for this milestone. You also need to specify constraint dates for other tasks that need to be taken into account in the schedule.

1 To have the product ready to ship in time for the product announcement at the Spring Sports Expo on May 17, you decide to constrain milestone task 20,

"Product ready to ship," so that it finishes no later than May 15, 1996. (Hint: double-click the task and enter the constraint on the Advanced tab). If the PlanningWizard displays a message about potential conflicts, click the third option button to apply this constraint.

2   You might need to call the designer to help you start testing the prototype. Because the designer will not be available after March 14, you need to start the task by March 13, so you can ask the questions while he is still available. Specify this constraint to start no later than 3/13/96 for task 15, "Test prototype."

3   Morton Marketing has indicated that task 21 must start on February 27, 1996. Specify a Must Start On constraint for task 21, "Coordinate promotion & advertising." When you see the PlanningWizard informing you that the links cannot be honored, choose the OK button to cancel the constraint.

Because this task is linked to the approval of the design of the product, this constraint is unnecessary.

4   An important task was left out of the original schedule. Before milestone task 11, "Design approved," insert a new task, "Design shoelaces." When you see the PlanningWizard informing you that the links cannot be honored, click the second option button. Then move the new task to before the milestone task, "Prototype ready to test," to resolve the scheduling conflict.

5   Save the project.

For more information on	See
Task constraints	Lesson 14

Step 3: Enter Actual Data as the Project Begins

It is now February 21, 1996, and your project is under way. Update the tasks that have been completed as scheduled, as well as those that did not go according to plan.

1   If the date format does not display the time, change the date format on the View tab in the Options dialog box (from the Tools menu) to use the format 1/31/94 12:33 PM.

2   To simulate the status of your project in progress, change the current date in the Summary Info dialog box to 2/21/96 10:00 AM.

3   Tasks 2 and 3 have been completed as scheduled. Update these tasks with the Update As Scheduled button on the Tracking toolbar.

4   Task 4, "Review plan," took only three days to complete. Use the Update Tasks command from the Tracking submenu (on the Tools menu) to change the percent complete to 100% and the actual duration to 3 days.

5   Task 5, "Revise plan," was started early and is now 100% complete. Click the appropriate % Complete button to update this task.

6   Task 7, "Analyze distribution channels," is 50% complete. Click the appropriate % Complete button to update this task.

Optional: Because you expected the analyst to be further along by this date, you can assign yourself (as product manager) to 16 hours of work to assist in completing this task.

7   Save the project.

For more information on	See
Updating the plan with actual data	Lesson 15

Step 4: Shorten the Critical Path

Currently the project is scheduled to finish on May 15, 1996. However, you have just learned that the Spring Sports Expo is not scheduled for 5/17/96, but is scheduled for Monday, 5/13/96. This means everything must be ready to go by Friday, May 10, 1996. Adjust critical tasks to meet this new deadline.

1   Apply the Critical filter to view critical tasks.

2   Assign one half of an additional line worker to task 19, "Coordinate production." (Hint: Click the Resource Assignment button on the Standard toolbar, and specify 4.5 units of this resource.)

3   Assign one half of an additional team member from the Morton Marketing resource to task 20, "Produce packaging."

4   Check the predecessor relationship for task 22, "Coordinate promotion and advertising." Because this task can actually begin after the completion of task 8, "Market analysis complete," change the predecessor from task 11 to task 8. (Hint: Double-click task 22, and make your changes on the Predecessors tab.)

5   Double-click the last milestone in the project to see that the entire project is scheduled to finish by 5/10/96, in time for the Spring Sports Expo.

6   Save your project.

7   Hide the Tracking toolbar, and then close the Resource Assignment dialog box (if it is still open).

For more information on	See
Shortening the critical path	Lesson 16

If You Want to Continue to the Next Lesson

▶ From the File menu, choose Close to close your project file.

If You Want to Quit Microsoft Project for Now

▶ From the File menu, choose Exit.

5 Customizing Microsoft Project 4

Customizing Tables, Views, and Reports

The tables and reports supplied with Microsoft Project are designed to meet most of your project information needs. If you have unique information requirements, you can modify existing reports and tables, or you can create entirely new ones. In this lesson, you'll learn how to create customized tables, views, and reports. First, you'll create a custom table based on an existing table and include this custom table in a custom view. Then you'll create a view that displays both the custom view and the Resource Sheet at the same time. Finally, you'll create an original custom report.

You will learn how to:

- Create a custom table.
- Create a custom view.
- Format text in a view.
- Create a custom report.

Estimated lesson time: 30 minutes

Start Microsoft Project

If you closed Microsoft Project in the last lesson, you need to restart the application before you can continue.

If you see the Welcome dialog box, click the Close button. If you see the Tip Of The Day dialog box, read the tip, and then click OK.

▶ Double-click the Microsoft Project icon.

Start the lesson

Open the project file called 17LESSN.MPP, and save it as LESSN17.MPP.

1 From the File menu, choose Open.

2 In the Directories box, double-click PRACTICE.

3 In the File Name box, double-click 17LESSN.MPP.

4 From the File menu, choose Save As.

5 In the File Name box, type **lessn17.mpp**

6 Choose the OK button.

Microsoft Project stores your project on your hard disk with the filename LESSN17.MPP. It appears in the Task Sheet view.

Change the current date

Assume it's now October 2, 1995, and the office move is entering its final phase. Set the current date in Microsoft Project to reflect the passage of time to this date.

1   From the File menu, choose Summary Info.

2   Click the Project tab, if it is not already active.

3   In the Current Date box, select the existing text, and then type **10/2/95 10:00 am**

4   Choose the OK button.

Creating a Custom Table

A table is a set of columns, or fields, that determines the information you see in a view. Throughout this book, you applied different tables to view the information you needed to enter project information, compare and assess project status, and display information about tasks or resources in specific views. When a table does not provide the information you need (or provides too much information), you can create a custom table that displays only the information you want.

The Summary table (along with the Task Sheet view) is especially useful for presenting an overview of the current schedule for each task: duration, start and finish dates, % complete, current costs, and work hours. At Victory Sports, you use the information in this table every week to produce your reports for senior management. Starting with this week's report, however, your management would like to see remaining duration instead of work hours and scheduled duration. They also would like to see the name of the resource group assigned to each task. Although you can modify the existing Summary table each time, you can save time in the future by creating a custom table. Then you can apply your custom table to quickly display only the information management requires.

Copy the existing Summary table

Because the table you want to create is similar to the existing Summary table, you can make your changes in a copy of the Summary table.

1   From the View menu, choose Table:Summary, and then choose More Tables from the submenu.

2   Be sure the Task option button is selected, so that the task-related tables appear in the dialog box.

3   In the Tables list box, select Summary if it is not already selected.

4   Click the Copy button.

Microsoft Project makes a copy of the Summary table and displays the Table Definition dialog box.

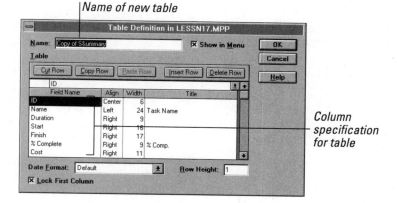

Name of new table

Column specification for table

5   In the Name text box, type **Management Summary**

This is the name of the new table you are creating.

Delete columns from the table

You can begin customizing your table by deleting the columns you don't need.

1   In the Field Name column, select Duration.

Use the Cut Row button when you want to move the selected row to another position in the table. The Paste Row button is enabled after you click the Cut Row or Copy Row button.

2   Click the Delete Row button.

3   In the Field Name column, select Finish, and then click the Delete Row button.

4   In the Field Name column, select Work, and then click the Delete Row button.

Add new columns

In place of the columns you deleted, add the columns that management wants to see instead.

1   In the Field Name column, select Start.

2   Click the Insert Row button to create a blank row above "Start."

The Table Definition dialog box looks like the following illustration.

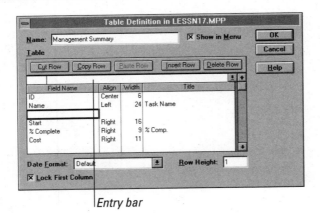

Entry bar

3 Click the down arrow in the entry bar, and then select Remaining Duration from the list box.

This list contains the field names from all the tables in Microsoft Project. By selecting fields from other tables, you can combine information from multiple tables.

4 Click in the Title column for this new row, and then type **Rem. Dur.**

Unless you specify otherwise, the name of the field will appear as the column heading when you apply the table. Using this abbreviation improves the appearance of the table.

5 Click in the blank row below Cost and, from the entry bar list, select Resource Group.

Resource Group appears in the last row.

6 Click in the Align column for this new row and, from the entry bar list, select Left.

In general, columns that contain text (rather than numbers) should be left-aligned.

7 Click in the Width column, and type **15**

By increasing the width of the column, you allow enough room for all the text "Resource Group" in the column heading.

8 Choose the OK button to return to the More Tables dialog box.

Apply the custom table

▶ Click the Apply button to apply your new table.

Your project looks like the following illustration.

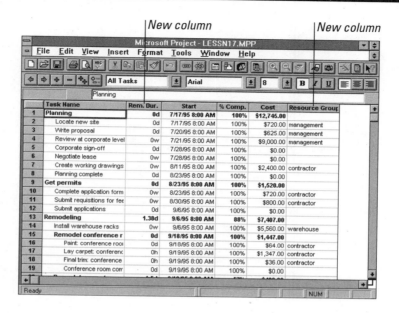

Save

Save your project

▶ On the Standard toolbar, click the Save button.

Creating a Custom View

A view contains a table and a filter (if any) already applied to your project. By creating a custom view, you can save time by displaying a table that is already formatted the way you want, with the filter you want already in effect. To increase the flexibility of your custom view, you can create a combination view that displays two views at once.

To facilitate your weekly reporting for the move project at Victory Sports, you will create a custom view that displays the Task Sheet view using the custom table you created earlier in this lesson. This view also uses the Summary Tasks filter so that the summary tasks are highlighted in the view. To make your view easier to read, you will also emphasize important information in the view by formatting it. After completing your custom view, you will then include it in a combination view.

Create a custom view

The formatting currently in effect will be saved in your custom view. Your custom view is a copy of the Task Sheet view using the Management Summary table and the Summary Tasks filter.

1   From the <u>V</u>iew menu, choose <u>M</u>ore Views.

The More Views dialog box appears.

2   Select Task Sheet, if it is not already selected, and then click the Copy button.

The View Definition dialog box appears. It looks like the following illustration.

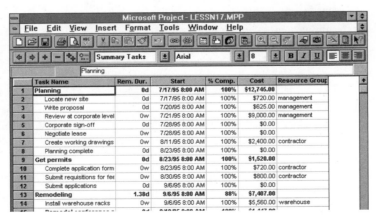

Name of new view

View Definition in LESSN17.MPP

<u>N</u>ame:	Copy of Task Sheet	OK
<u>S</u>creen:	Task Sheet	Cancel
<u>T</u>able:	Management Summary ±	<u>H</u>elp
<u>F</u>ilter:	All Tasks ±	

☐ Highlight Filte<u>r</u>
☐ Show in <u>M</u>enu

3   In the Name box, type **Management Task Sheet**

This is the name of your custom view.

4   In the Table box, be sure Management Summary is still selected.

The table that is already applied appears in the Table box.

5   In the Filter box, click the down arrow, and then scroll to and select Summary Tasks.

This filter displays only Summary Tasks.

6   Click the Highlight Filter check box, if it is not already selected.

Only the Summary Tasks will be highlighted.

7   Choose the OK button to return to the More Views dialog box.

8   Click the Apply button to apply this view to the project.

Your custom view looks like the following illustration.

Microsoft Project - LESSN17.MPP

<u>F</u>ile   <u>E</u>dit   <u>V</u>iew   <u>I</u>nsert   F<u>o</u>rmat   <u>T</u>ools   <u>W</u>indow   <u>H</u>elp

Summary Tasks   Arial   8   **B** *I* <u>U</u>

Planning

	Task Name	Rem. Dur.	Start	% Comp.	Cost	Resource Group
1	Planning	0d	7/17/95 8:00 AM	100%	$12,745.00	
2	Locate new site	0d	7/17/95 8:00 AM	100%	$720.00	management
3	Write proposal	0d	7/20/95 8:00 AM	100%	$625.00	management
4	Review at corporate level	0w	7/21/95 8:00 AM	100%	$9,000.00	management
5	Corporate sign-off	0d	7/28/95 8:00 AM	100%	$0.00	
6	Negotiate lease	0w	7/28/95 8:00 AM	100%	$0.00	
7	Create working drawings	0w	8/11/95 8:00 AM	100%	$2,400.00	contractor
8	Planning complete	0d	8/23/95 8:00 AM	100%	$0.00	
9	Get permits	0d	8/23/95 8:00 AM	100%	$1,520.00	
10	Complete application form	0w	8/23/95 8:00 AM	100%	$720.00	contractor
11	Submit requisitions for fee	0w	8/30/95 8:00 AM	100%	$800.00	contractor
12	Submit applications	0d	9/6/95 8:00 AM	100%	$0.00	
13	Remodeling	1.38d	9/6/95 8:00 AM	88%	$7,407.00	
14	Install warehouse racks	0w	9/6/95 8:00 AM	100%	$5,560.00	warehouse

Formatting a View

Earlier in this book, you learned how to use the GanttChartWizard to improve the appearance of the Gantt Chart view. Even without a wizard, you can add custom formatting to any view to make it more attractive and easier to read. You can specify the format for all the text in the view, or you can specify a unique format for specific information. For example, to draw attention to critical tasks, you can format them in bold and italic.

Format specific text

1 From the Format menu, choose Text Styles.

The Text Styles dialog box appears.

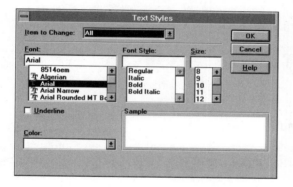

2 In the Item To Change box, click the down arrow, and then select Critical Tasks.

Your formatting will affect the tasks that are included in the critical path.

3 In the Font Style list box, select Bold Italic.

4 In the Size list box, select 10.

5 In the Item To Change box, click the down arrow, and then select Highlighted Tasks.

Your formatting will affect the tasks that are highlighted by the filter.

6 In the Font Style list box, select Bold.

7 Choose the OK button.

The custom view looks like the following illustration. You might need to scroll downward to see the critical tasks. If any column widths seem too narrow, you can adjust them as needed.

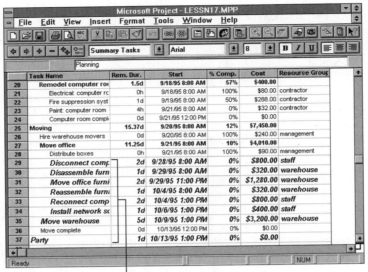

Formatted tasks

Create a new view

You frequently need to examine detailed resource information for selected tasks. To get the versatility you need when viewing data in the Management Task Sheet view, create a combination view that displays your custom Management Task Sheet view in the top half of the screen and the Resource Sheet in the bottom half.

1   So that you see data in the Resource Sheet part of the view, select task 32.

2   From the View menu, choose More Views.

3   In the More Views dialog box, click the New button.

The Define New View dialog box appears. Use this dialog box when you want to create a combination view or when the view you want to create is not based on a copy of an existing view.

4   Click the Combination View option button, and then choose the OK button.

The View Definition dialog box appears.

5   In the Name text box, type **Management Combo**

6   In the Top box, click the down arrow, and then select Management Task Sheet.

7   In the Bottom box, click the down arrow, and then scroll to and select Resource Sheet.

8   Select the Show In Menu check box, so that this view name appears on the View menu.

9 Choose the OK button to return to the More Views dialog box, and then click the Apply button to apply this view.

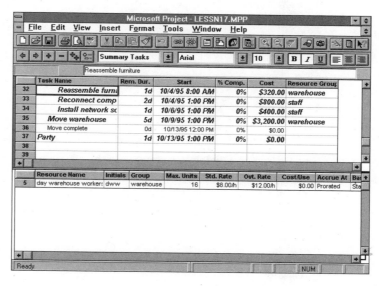

Save

Save your project

▶ On the Standard toolbar, click the Save button.

Creating a Custom Report

In this month's managers' meeting, you want to present the information in the Management Summary table as a report. Because you want to see the cost of the project, which is found in the Budget Report provided with Microsoft Project, you can base your custom report on a copy of the Budget Report.

Create and name a new report

Creating a report based on an existing report is easier than creating a report from scratch.

1 From the View menu, choose Reports.

The Reports dialog box appears.

2 Double-click the Custom button.

The Custom Reports dialog box appears. In this dialog box, you can select the report you want to copy. You can also edit an existing report or create an original report. The Custom Reports dialog box looks like the following illustration.

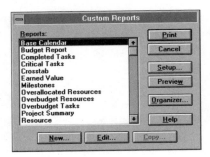

3   Select Budget Report, and then click the Copy button in the dialog box.

The Task Report dialog box appears. In this dialog box, you specify the settings for your new report.

4   Click the Definition tab, if it is not already active.

The dialog box looks like the following illustration.

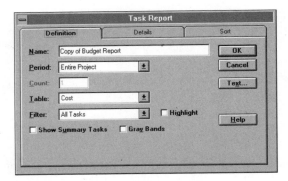

5   In the Name box, select the existing text, and then type **Management Budget Report**

Specify report settings

You can specify the table you want to use in your report. For your managers' meeting, you want to use the Management Summary table you created earlier.

1   In the Table box, click the down arrow, and then scroll to and select Management Summary.

This is the table you created earlier in this lesson.

2   In the Filter box, click the down arrow, and then select Cost Overbudget.

This filter displays tasks that are overbudget.

3   Click the Highlight check box so that the overbudget tasks are highlighted and the other tasks still appear in the report.

4 Click the Show Summary Tasks check box to include summary tasks in the report.

5 Click the Gray Bands check box.

Highlighted data will appear inside shaded gray bands in the report. The completed dialog box looks like the following illustration.

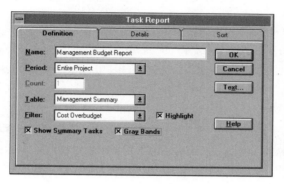

Specify report sorting options

By default, the information on a Budget Report is sorted by cost in descending order. Because the managers at Victory Sports prefer to see this information by the sequential order of the tasks, you need to change how the information is sorted in this report.

1 Click the Sort tab to make it active.

2 In the Sort By box, click the down arrow, and then select Start.

The tasks in the report will be sorted by their start date.

3 Click the Ascending option button to sort the dates from earliest to latest.

Adjust the text styles

To make the report easier to read, adjust the text style of highlighted text to be bold and italic. Also, change the text size of the summary tasks to 10 points and the size of the text in the column heading to 12 points.

1 In the Task Report dialog box, click the Text button.

The Text Styles dialog box appears.

2 In the Item To Change list box, click the down arrow, and then select Highlighted Tasks.

3 In the Font Style list box, select Bold Italic.

The highlighted text that appears in the gray bands will be formatted in bold and italic, making the text clearer.

4 In the Item To Change box, click the down arrow, and then select Summary Tasks.

5 In the Size list box, select 10.

6   In the Item To Change box, click the down arrow, and then select Column Titles.

7   In the Size box, select 12.

8   Choose the OK button to return to the Task Report dialog box.

9   Choose the OK button to return to the Custom Reports dialog box.

Preview the custom report

You can preview the report to check its appearance before printing it.

1   In the Custom Reports dialog box, click the Preview button to get a preview of the report.

   The preview of the report looks like the following illustration.

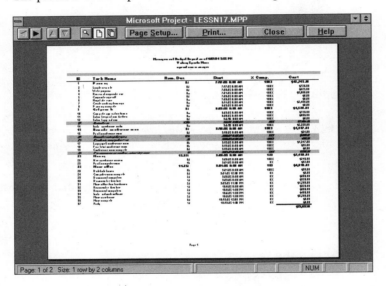

2   After previewing, click the Close button or, if your computer is connected to a printer, click the Print button and then choose the OK button.

3   If you closed the Preview window without printing, click the Close button in the Custom Reports dialog box.

4   When you return to the Reports dialog box, click the Cancel button.

Save your project

When you save your work, the tables, views, and reports you used and created in this lesson are also saved with the project file. If you share this project file with others, they will be able to use the same features, even the customized ones.

Save

▶ On the Standard toolbar, click the Save button.

One Step Further

The tables, views, and reports you create are only available in the project file in which you created them. To use these custom features in another project file, you can use the Organizer to copy individual tables, views, and reports from one file to another. The Organizer is available in the dialog boxes in which you create custom features, including the More Tables, More Views, and Custom Reports dialog boxes.

So that the data processing manager can take advantage of the table and report you created in this lesson, copy the Management Summary table and Management Budget Report to a project called 17MOVE.MPP. Begin by opening the other project file.

Open the original project file

Open

1   On the Standard toolbar, click the Open button.

2   In the Directories box, double-click PRACTICE.

3   In the File Name box, double-click 17MOVE.MPP.

4   From the File menu, choose Save As.

5   In the File Name box, type **move17.mpp**

6   Choose the OK button.

The currently active project is MOVE17.MPP.

Note   When you copy a customized report to another project file, be sure to copy any customized tables or filters that the report uses.

Copy a report to another project with the Organizer

You can copy features to and from any open project file using the Organizer.

1   From the View menu, choose Reports.

2   Double-click the Custom button.

3   Click the Organizer button.

4   Click the Reports tab, if it is not already active.

5   In the Reports Available In box (in the lower-*left* corner of the dialog box), click the down arrow, and then select LESSN17.MPP.

A list of reports used and created in this project file appears in the left side of the dialog box. You will copy a report from this list.

6   In the Reports Available In box (in the lower-*right* corner of the dialog box), click the down arrow, and then select MOVE17.MPP, if it is not already selected.

You will copy a report to this project.

7 In the list box on the left, select Management Budget Report.

8 Click the Copy button in the center of the dialog box.

The Management Budget Report appears in the list box on the right, and it is now available in this project.

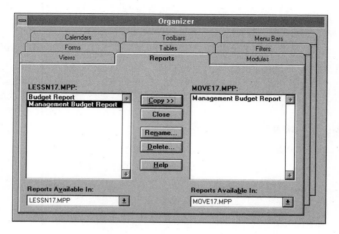

Copy a table to another project with the Organizer

Even though you started the Organizer from the Custom Reports dialog box, you can copy additional features by making another tab active.

1 Click the Tables tab to make it active.

2 In the list on the left, select Management Summary.

3 Click the Copy button in the center of the dialog box.

The Management Summary table appears in the list box on the right, and it is now available in this project.

4 Click the Close buttons in both the Organizer and the Custom Reports dialog boxes.

5 Click the Cancel button in the Reports dialog box to return to the project.

If You Want to Continue to the Next Lesson

1 From the File menu, choose Close to close the project MOVE17.MPP.

2 Choose the Yes button if you see the message box asking whether you want to save your work. Leave the baseline unchanged.

3 From the File menu, choose Close to close the project LESSN17.MPP.

4 Choose the Yes button if you see the message box asking whether you want to save your work.

If You Want to Quit Microsoft Project for Now

1   From the File menu, choose Exit.

2   Choose the Yes button each time you see the message box asking whether you want to save your work. Leave the baseline unchanged.

Lesson Summary

To	Do this
Create a custom table	From the View menu, choose the More Tables command from the Table submenu. To make a new table based on an existing table, select the existing table and click the Copy button. Click the Edit button to modify an existing table. Click the New button to create a new table not based on an existing table.
Create a custom view	From the View menu, choose the More Views command. To make a new view based on an existing view, select the existing view and click the Copy button. Click the Edit button to modify an existing view. Click the New button to create a new view not based on an existing view.
Format text	From the Format menu, choose the Text Styles command. Select the element you want to change from the Item To Change box. Then choose the font, font size, and style.
Create a custom report	From the View menu, choose the Reports command. Double-click the Custom button. To make a new report based on an existing report, select the existing report and click the Copy button. Click the Edit button to modify an existing report. Click the New button to create a new report not based on an existing report.

For more information on	See in *Microsoft Project User's Guide*
Customizing a view or report	Chapter 8, "Printing and Reporting"
Printing columns in a sheet view	Chapter 8, "Printing and Reporting"
Using views	Chapter 9, "Working with Views"
Organizing custom features	Chapter 13, "Customizing Microsoft Project"

For online information about	From the <u>H</u>elp menu, choose <u>S</u>earch and then type
Changing the look	Text Styles command text: formatting
Customizing tables, views, and reports	customizing reports customizing views customizing tables customizing views, tables, filters

Preview of the Next Lesson

In the next lesson, you will learn how to tailor Microsoft Project to your personal work style. You will create your own toolbar, and then assign frequently used commands to buttons on this toolbar. You will also create a macro to do multiple operations with a single command.

Customizing the Project Environment

In this lesson, you will learn how to customize the way you use the Microsoft Project program itself. First, you will record a sequence of commands as a macro and then assign the macro to a menu. Then you will create a project template so that you can have standard text and specific format settings—as well as tables, views, and reports—available in similar projects. After creating a project file based on this template, you will create your own customized toolbar with buttons you need for easy access to commonly used commands.

You will learn how to:

- Record a macro.
- Create a template.
- Create a custom toolbar.

Estimated lesson time: 30 minutes

Start Microsoft Project

If you closed Microsoft Project in the last lesson, you need to restart the application before you can continue.

If you see the Welcome dialog box, click the Close button. If you see the Tip Of The Day dialog box, read the tip, and then click OK.

▶ Double-click the Microsoft Project icon.

Start the lesson

Open the project file called 18LESSN.MPP, and save it as LESSN18.MPP.

1 From the File menu, choose Open.

2 In the Directories box, double-click PRACTICE.

3 In the File Name box, double-click 18LESSN.MPP.

4 From the File menu, choose Save As.

5 In the File Name box, type **lessn18.mpp**

6 Choose the OK button.

Microsoft Project stores your project on your hard disk with the filename LESSN18.MPP.

Understanding Macros

A *macro* is a series of commands performed in a sequence that you can initiate with a single command. When you find that you often repeat the same set of commands, such as when you create a month-end report, you can create a macro that carries out these commands. Then, at the end of the month, you can run the macro and have Microsoft Project create the report for you.

A macro can also be a single command that you wish to assign a keyboard shortcut or place on a toolbar as a button. For example, you can create a macro to display your project in the Gantt Chart view.

Creating a Macro

You create a macro with the Record Macro command. This command records every selection you make from menus or buttons until you stop the macro recorder with the Stop Recorder command. When you create a macro, you can give it a name that reflects the operation you want to perform, and that will appear in the Macro section of the Tools menu. You can also assign the macro to a key combination so that you can run the macro with a keyboard shortcut. You can specify whether a macro should be available in all project files (stored in the global template) or only in the currently open document.

Note   When you record a macro, each of the steps you perform and selections you make are stored as Microsoft Visual Basic code. You can use the Visual Basic programming language to enhance and extend the capabilities of the macro you record. See Chapter 16, "Automating Your Work," in the Microsoft Project User's Guide for more information. Use the Visual Basic toolbar for quick access to the Visual Basic Editor (for editing your macros) and other macro commands.

Start the macro recorder and name a macro

You can also record a macro using the buttons on the Visual Basic toolbar. To display the Visual Basic toolbar, click a toolbar with the right mouse button and select Visual Basic.

To make it easy to return to the Gantt Chart view with the Entry table applied, record a macro that contains the menu selections for this command. Begin by starting the macro recorder.

1   From the Tools menu, choose Record Macro.

The Record Macro dialog box appears. It looks like the following illustration.

2   In the Macro Name text box, type **ViewGanttChart**

A macro name cannot contain spaces.

3   In the Description list box, select the first line of existing text, and then type
ViewGanttChart displays the Gantt Chart view

Specify macro options

1   Click the Options button.

The dialog box changes to look like the following illustration.

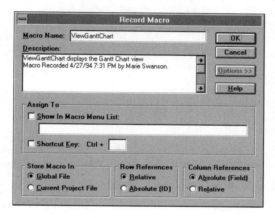

2   Click the Show In Macro Menu List check box.

Clicking this option displays the macro in the macro menu list of the Tools menu.
The text in the text box is selected when you click this check box. This is the text
that appears in the macro menu list.

3   Click the Shortcut Key check box.

4   Next to Ctrl +, type **G**

If you see a message indicating this keyboard shortcut is already assigned to
another command, choose another letter.

5   Under Store Macro In, click the Current Project File option button.

This option ensures that the global template is not changed. Your completed dialog
box should look like the following illustration.

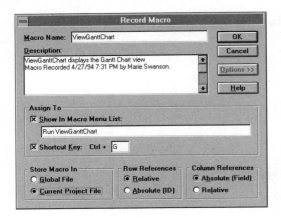

6   Choose the OK button.

Everything you do next will be recorded in the macro.

Perform macro operations

Even though your project is already in the Gantt Chart view with the Entry table, choose each of these commands anyway, so that they are recorded in the macro.

1   From the View menu, choose Gantt Chart.

2   From the View menu, choose Table: Entry, and then choose Entry.

You will see no change in the project file.

3   From the Tools menu, choose Stop Recorder.

4   Click the Tools menu.

The Tools menu looks like the following illustration. A command to run the new macro appears at the bottom of the menu.

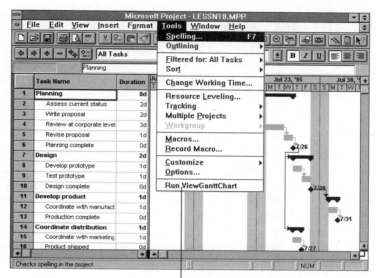

Macro command on menu

Run your macro

You can see your macro in action by first switching to another view and then applying a new table. Then run your macro.

1   From the View menu, choose Resource Sheet.

2   From the View menu, choose Table: Entry, and then choose Cost.

3   From the Tools menu, choose Run ViewGanttChart.

The project appears in the Gantt Chart view with the Entry table.

Using Project Templates

When you plan to create multiple projects that use the same set of project features, such as specific tables, views, and reports (as well as text formatting and page setup specifications), you can store all this information in a template. A *template* is a special kind of project file that contains all of the common or standard features you use in a specific kind of project. When you create a new project based on the template, the new project will already have the features and settings established for this project. A template can also contain macros, standard text and tasks, resources, and calendar information common to multiple project files you want to create.

For example, at Victory Sports, you have become the project management resource for other project managers. To make it easier for these managers to benefit from the Microsoft Project skills you've learned, and to ensure consistently high-quality results, you can create a template from which other project managers can create their own project files.

Creating a Project Template

The project file you opened at the start of this lesson contains many of the features, as well as customized tables, views, and reports, that you learned about throughout this book. It also contains the tasks of a planning phase that is now standard for all projects at Victory Sports. Other basic summary tasks and milestones are also included. By saving this project file as a template, you can save time when you want to use these features in future projects.

You can also use the Organizer to copy features such as tables, views, and reports from other project files.

Create a template

You can create a template based on an existing project, or you can create a new project file and specify the features you want to use.

1   From the File menu, choose Save As.

    The Save As dialog box appears.

2   In the File Name box, type **tmplat18**

    This is the name of the template based on the currently open project file.

3   In the Save File As Type list box, click the down arrow, and then select Template.

4   Choose the OK button.

Note   Microsoft Project automatically provides the extension MPT for template files.

---

5   From the File menu, choose Close.

Creating a Project From a Template

When you want to create a new project file based on a template, you first open the template. Then you save the template as a project file. You make your changes in the new project file, leaving the original project template unchanged.

Create a new project from a template

1 From the File menu, choose Open.

2 In the Directories box, double-click PRACTICE.

3 In the File Name box, double-click TMPLAT18.MPT.

4 From the File menu, choose Save As.

5 In the File Name box, type **lessn18a.mpp**

6 In the Save File As Type list box, select Project, if it is not already selected.

7 Choose the OK button.

The new project file you've created contains all the settings and features found in the template.

Creating a Custom Toolbar

As you worked through the lessons in this book, you frequently used buttons on the toolbars to perform most Microsoft Project operations. To customize Microsoft Project to match the way you work, you can add and rearrange the buttons on any of the toolbars. If you add too many buttons to a toolbar, you might run out of space. Instead of trying to decide which buttons to remove and which to keep, you can also create your own custom toolbars that contain the collections of buttons you use often.

Add the View list box to a toolbar

In the same way you have a Filters box from which you can select and apply filters, there is also a View box from which you can select and apply views. By adding this box to a toolbar, you can select and apply views quickly without using the More Views command and dialog box.

To display the Customize dialog box, you can also click a toolbar with the right mouse button, and then choose Customize from the shortcut menu.

1 From the Tools menu, choose Customize, and then choose Toolbars.

The Customize dialog box appears. Here you can copy buttons (and their corresponding commands) to a toolbar. The dialog box looks like the following illustration.

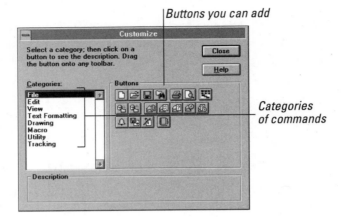

Buttons you can add

*Categories
of commands*

2 In the Categories list, select View.

A collection of buttons and boxes related to displaying views appears in the Buttons section.

Print Preview

3 In the Buttons area, drag the Views box from the dialog box to the Print Preview button on the Standard toolbar. Place the left edge of the box next to the right edge of the Print Preview button.

Your Standard toolbar looks like the following illustration.

Views list box

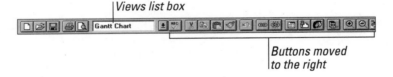

*Buttons moved
to the right*

Note Depending on the kind of monitor and display you are using, you might not be able to see some of the buttons on the right edge of the toolbar.

4 In the Customize dialog box, click the Close button.

Creating Your Own Toolbar

When you make a change to a toolbar (or a menu), you are changing a file called GLOBAL.MPT. This file affects the working environment for many aspects of Microsoft Project (including toolbars and menus) for all the projects on your computer. If you are sharing your computer with other Microsoft Project users (or the GLOBAL.MPT file is stored on a network), your customizations and preferences could confuse other users. Therefore, consider creating your own custom toolbar, that contains the special buttons you use often. Like other Microsoft Project toolbars, you can hide or display it whenever you wish, without affecting the environment for other users.

Even if you are not on a network, or you are the only one using Microsoft Project on your computer, you might still want to create specialized toolbars that contain buttons to meet a specific need or special purpose. By organizing buttons on separate toolbars, you can avoid overcrowding the existing toolbars and arrange buttons in a way that makes sense to you.

Create a toolbar

1　With the right mouse button, click a toolbar.

The Toolbars shortcut menu appears.

2　Choose Toolbars.

The Toolbars dialog box appears.

3　Click the New button to create a new toolbar.

The New Toolbar dialog box appears.

4　In the Name text box, type **Views and Editing**

This toolbar will contain buttons that help you quickly switch between different views and edit them.

5　Choose the OK button.

The Customize dialog box appears. Notice that a small empty toolbar appears next to the dialog box.

New toolbar

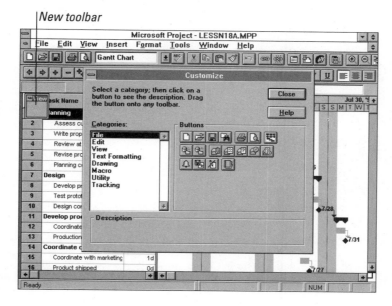

Add buttons to the toolbar

From the Edit and View categories, you can drag buttons to the new toolbar.

1   In the Categories list, select Edit.

A set of buttons related to editing appears in the Buttons area.

Delete Row

2   Drag the Delete Row button to the new toolbar.

The button appears in the new toolbar. This button deletes a selected row from the view.

Tip   When you click a button or box in the Buttons area, its description appears in the Description area.

Insert Row

3   Drag the Insert Row button to the new toolbar and drop it on top of the Delete Row button.

The toolbar expands to the right to make room for the new button. The Insert Row button inserts a blank row in the view.

Fill Down

4   Drag the Fill Down button to the new toolbar.

This button copies the contents of a cell downward to selected cells in a range.

Clear Formats

5   Drag the Clear Formats button to the new toolbar.

This button removes formatting in a cell.

Find

6   Drag the Find button to the new toolbar.

This button is the same as the Goto command on the Edit menu.

7   In the Categories list, select View.

A set of buttons and boxes related to using different views appears in the Button area.

8   Drag the Views box to the new toolbar.

This list box contains a list of all the views you can use to display project information.

You can also move the toolbar anywhere near one of the existing toolbars. Placing a toolbar in this area "docks" it. Double-click it when you want a floating toolbar.

9   Click the title bar of the custom toolbar to make it active.

Your custom toolbar looks like the following illustration.

Adjust the size of the toolbar

To accommodate the width of some of the longer view names, you can adjust the width of the Views list box.

1   In the new toolbar, position the pointer near the right edge of the Views list down arrow until the pointer changes shape to a four-headed arrow.

2   Drag to the right about one-half inch to increase the width of the box.

Notice that the size of the toolbar increases to accommodate the box.

3   Hold down SHIFT and drag the button next to the View list box a short distance (about half the width of a button) to the right to create a space to the left of the button.

The toolbar looks like the following illustration. Don't be concerned if the size of your Views box or the spacing and placement of buttons in your toolbar does not match the following illustration.

4   In the Customize dialog box, click the Close button.

Switch to the Resource Sheet view

Test your new toolbar by using the View box to switch to the Resource Sheet view.

1   From the Views And Editing toolbar, click the View list box down arrow, and then select Resource Sheet.

The project appears in the Resource Sheet view.

2   If you plan to work through the One Step Further activity, you can leave the custom toolbar displayed. Otherwise, click a toolbar with the right mouse button, and then choose Views And Editing to hide the custom toolbar.

One Step Further

You can customize a toolbar button to look the way you want. For example, to help you recall the purpose of the Insert Row button (on your custom Views and Editing toolbar), you can add a plus sign (+) to the button to make its purpose more obvious.

Customize a button

1   On the Views And Editing toolbar, click the Insert Row button with the right mouse button.

The Toolbars shortcut menu appears.

2   Choose Customize Tool.

The Customize Tool dialog box appears. In the Button Library, be sure the RowInsert button is selected.

3   Click the Edit Button button.

The Button Editor dialog box appears.

4   In the Picture area, to the right of the arrow part of the button, click the fifth box
from the bottom of the button.

The box you clicked is filled in black. If you click in the wrong place, just click the
same box again, so it turns back to gray.

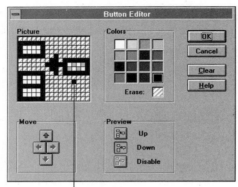

Click here.

5   Click each of the four boxes below the one you clicked in step 3, creating a vertical
line of five boxes.

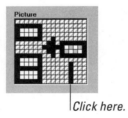

Click here.

You can see a preview of what your button will look like in the Preview area of the
dialog box.

6   Click the two boxes to the left of the middle of the vertical line.

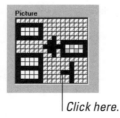

Click here.

7   Click the two boxes to the right of the middle of the vertical line.

Your customized button looks like the following illustration.

8   Choose the OK button to close each of the dialog boxes until you return to the project window.

Your custom button in the custom Views And Editing toolbar looks like the following illustration.

Modified button

9   Click a toolbar with the right mouse button, and then choose Views And Editing to hide the custom toolbar.

If You Want to Continue to the Review & Practice

1   From the File menu, choose Close to close the project LESSN18.MPP.

2   Choose the Yes button if you see the message box asking whether you want to save your work. Leave the baseline unchanged.

If You Want to Quit Microsoft Project for Now

1   From the File menu, choose Exit.

2   Choose the Yes button if you see the message box asking whether you want to save your work. Leave the baseline unchanged.

Lesson Summary

To	Do this
Record a macro	From the Tools menu, choose the Record Macro command. Click the Options button to add the macro to a menu or assign a keyboard shortcut. Perform the macro operations. From the Tools menu, choose the Stop Recorder command.

To	Do this
Create a template based on an existing project	Open the project file and, from the File menu, choose Save As. Select Template from the Save File As Type list box, and save the template with a new name.
Create a new project from a template	Open the template and, from the File menu, choose Save As. Select Project from the Save File As Type list box, and save the project with a new name.
Create a custom toolbar	Click any toolbar with the right mouse button. Choose Toolbars from the shortcut menu, and then click New. In the Customize dialog box, drag the buttons and boxes you want to the new toolbar.

For more information on	See in *Microsoft Project User's Guide*
Macros	Chapter 16, "Automating Your Work"
Toolbar	Chapter 13, "Customizing Microsoft Project"

For online information about	From the **Help** menu, choose **Search** and then type
Macros	macros: creating macros: customizing
Creating a template	templates
Creating a custom toolbar	toolbars: customizing

Review & Practice

In the lessons in Part 5, "Customizing Microsoft Project 4.0," you learned skills to help you work more effectively by customizing Microsoft Project. If you want to practice these skills and test your knowledge before you start working in projects of your own, you can work through the Review & Practice section following this lesson.

Part 5 Review & Practice

Before you begin planning a project of your own, practice the skills you learned in Part 5 by working through the customizing and automating activities in this Review & Practice section. In this practice exercise, you address the communication needs of your project.

Scenario

Now that the Summit Boots development project is under way and you have learned how to track its progress, many people are interested in getting information about the status of the project. As the project manager, you are expected to provide accurate and timely information to team members and management. Use Microsoft Project's ability to print views and reports to present the information you want in the way you want it. Use the customizing and automating features to make it easier to do your job.

You will review and practice how to:

- Create a custom table.
- Create a custom view.
- Create a custom report.
- Record a macro.
- Create a template.
- Create a custom toolbar.

Estimated practice time: 30 minutes

Before You Begin

▶ Open the scenario project file called P5REVIEW.MPP. Before you make any changes in this project, save it with the new name REVIEWP5.MPP.

This project file should look similar to the file you saved after completing the steps in the Part 4 Review & Practice. It appears in the Resource Sheet view.

Step 1: Customize a Table

To provide an overview of resource information in your project, you frequently use the Summary table in the Resource Sheet view. However, this table does not display the code for the resources. It also contains information that, for your presentation, you don't need right now.

1   Make a copy of the Summary table and name it Resource Overview. (Hint: From the View menu, choose Table, and then choose More Tables. Select the table you want to copy.)

2   In the Table Definition dialog box, delete the rows for Peak, Overtime Rate, and Work.

3   Above the Max Units row, insert a row and specify Code. Adjust the column width for this new row to 8.

4   Apply this table to the Resource Sheet view.

5   Save the project file.

For more information on	See
Customizing tables	Lesson 17

Step 2: Customize a View

To display the Resource Sheet view with the Resource Overview table already applied, create a custom view that specifies both the view and the table at the same time.

1   Make a copy of the Resource Sheet view and name it Resource Overview Sheet. (Hint: From the View menu, choose More Views. Then select the view you want to copy.)

2   In the View Definition dialog box, be sure Resource Overview is specified in the Table box and the All Resources filter is specified in the Filter box.

3   Apply this new view. Click the View menu to see the new view listed on the menu.

4   Save the project file.

For more information on	See
Customizing views	Lesson 17

Step 3: Customize a Report

After using the Resource Overview Sheet to prepare for meetings, you've discovered that it would be useful to include this information in the Who Does What report. Create a new report based on the Resource Overview table you created, and specify that you want to see resource information for each week (rather than for each month as specified in the default). You also want to improve the appearance of the report by formatting it.

1   Make a copy of the Who Does What report. (Hint: From the View menu, choose Reports. Double-click the Custom button, and then select the report you want to copy.)

2   In the Resource Report dialog box, name the new report "Weekly Who Does What." Specify a period of one week. Be sure the Resource Overview table is specified in the Table box and the All Resources filter is specified in the Filter box.

3 Click the Text button and specify that Resource Details appear in regular and 9 points rather than italic and 7 points. Also specify that Period is in bold italic and 10 points.

4 Click the Preview button in the Custom Reports dialog box to examine your report. If you have a printer connected to your computer, print the report. Exit all dialog boxes.

5 Save the project file.

For more information on	See
Customizing reports	Lesson 17

Step 4: Record a Macro

To make it easier to produce your report, record a macro that contains the commands for selecting this report and previewing it.

1 Start the macro recorder and name the new macro WeeklyWhoDoesWhatReport. (Remember not to use spaces in your macro name.) Be sure to enter a description of the macro.

2 Specify that this macro shows in the macro menu, and use "R" as the keyboard shortcut. Be sure to specify that this macro is stored in the currently open project file. (Hint: In the Record Macro dialog box, click Options to make these selections.)

3 Perform the selections to view the custom Weekly Who Does What report in Print Preview. Stop the recorder after leaving the Print Preview window and closing or canceling all open dialog boxes.

4 Run your macro. The macro will pause in the Print Preview window. Close the Print Preview window to complete the macro.

5 Save the project file.

For more information on	See
Creating a macro	Lesson 18
Viewing a report	Lesson 12

Step 5: Save Your Project as a Template

Other product managers throughout Victory Sports have heard about your new table, report, and macro that you used in the project. In fact, these elements are soon to become a corporate standard, as have the assignment of resources and scheduling you've developed. To share the customizations and features of your successful project plan with others, save the currently open document as a template.

1 In the Save As dialog box, specify that you want to save this project file as a template.

2   Name the new project template REVTMPP5.MPT. Click the Yes button if you see a message about OLE objects.

For more information on	See
Creating a template	Lesson 18

Step 6: Create a Custom Toolbar

You've been working with many different project files, with different features in each one. To help you manage your files and work with multiple files, create a file management toolbar that contains the buttons for working with project files.

1   Create a new toolbar and name it File Management. (Hint: Display the Toolbars dialog box by clicking a toolbar with the right mouse button, and then choosing Toolbars.)

Find File

2   In the Customize dialog box, drag the following three buttons from the File category to the new toolbar: Find File, Consolidate Projects, and Organizer. (Tip: Read the description of each button before you drag.)

Consolidate Projects

For more information on	See
Creating a toolbar	Lesson 18

Organizer

If You Want to Quit Microsoft Project for Now

▶   From the File menu, choose Exit. Do not save the file.

Appendixes

Using PERT Charts

This appendix is a lesson in which you'll learn how to use the PERT Chart. This chart provides a graphical view of the dependencies between tasks in your project. After you add a task on the PERT Chart, you will change the layout and format of the PERT Chart. In the new view, you will learn how to assign resources to tasks. Finally, using the Task PERT Chart, you will view task predecessors and successors.

You will learn how to:

- View a PERT Chart of the project.
- Add a task on the PERT Chart.
- Change the layout and format of the PERT Chart.
- Use the PERT Chart to assign resources to tasks.
- Display task predecessors and successors.

Estimated lesson time: 30 minutes

Start Microsoft Project

If you closed Microsoft Project in the last lesson, you need to restart the application before you can continue.

If you see the Welcome dialog box, click the Close button. If you see the Tip Of The Day dialog box, read the tip, and then click OK.

▶ Double-click the Microsoft Project icon.

Start the lesson

Open the project file called XALESSN.MPP, and save it as LESSNXA.MPP.

1 From the File menu, choose Open.

2 In the Directories box, double-click PRACTICE.

3 In the File Name box, double-click XALESSN.MPP.

4 From the File menu, choose Save As.

If you see the PlanningWizard, click the second option button, and then click OK. Continue with step 5.

5 In the File Name box, type **lessnxa.mpp**

6 Choose the OK button.

Microsoft Project stores your project on your hard disk with the filename LESSNXA.MPP. This project file is similar to the one you used in Lesson 6.

Understanding PERT Chart Basics

A PERT Chart represents each task as a box, called a *node*. In the node, you can see up to five fields of information. Although you can easily change the fields displayed in the nodes, the default node fields are task name, task ID number, duration, scheduled start date, and scheduled finish date. The lines connecting the nodes reflect the task relationships. You can view the PERT Chart by using the PERT Chart command from the View menu.

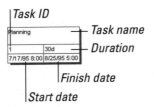

The *borders* around each node indicate whether the node is a summary task, a subtask, or a milestone, and whether it is on the critical path. By default, nodes on the critical path have a thick red or patterned border; noncritical nodes have a thin black border; summary tasks have a shadow box border; and milestones have a double or frame border. The following table displays the different borders for the different types of tasks in a PERT Chart.

Type of task	Critical	Noncritical
Task or subtask		
Summary task		
Milestone		

You use the scroll bars to move around the PERT Chart, and you click a node or node field to select it.

Entering Task Information in a PERT Chart

There are two ways in which you can enter task information in a PERT Chart. You can type directly in the node fields, or you can drag to create and move tasks directly in the PERT Chart. You can also double-click on a node to display the Task Information dialog box. Use this technique when you want to enter task information when you have zoomed out the view and the font size is too small.

View the PERT Chart

The plant manager wants an overview of the company move. Make a few last-minute changes, and then create a PERT Chart to show at the briefing. Because you need information on potential delays, take a moment to review the critical path of the project.

1   From the _V_iew menu, choose _P_ERT Chart.

The PERT Chart view appears. It looks like the following illustration.

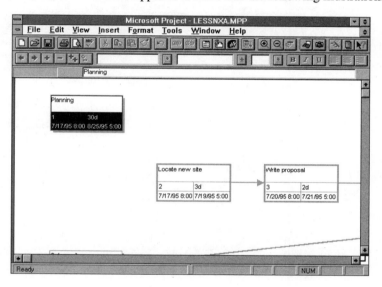

Tip   You can combine the PERT Chart view with the Task Form in a combination view to conveniently change task details.

---

2   Use the scroll arrows to move through the PERT Chart, looking for tasks on the critical path.

Adjust the magnification

In the Gantt Chart view, you used the Zoom In and Zoom Out buttons to change the timescale so that you could see your project in more or less detail. You can use these same buttons in the PERT Chart view to adjust the magnification so you can see the big picture or focus on the details.

The nodes on the PERT Chart are arranged so that summary tasks appear on the left. Subtasks are indented below their summary tasks. Detail tasks are placed in sequence to the right.

1   Press SHIFT+HOME to move to the first task in the PERT Chart.

2   On the Standard toolbar, click the Zoom Out button three times.

Zoom Out

Note the change in magnification with each click. Your PERT Chart view looks like the following illustration.

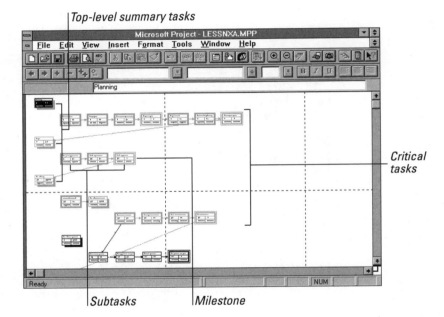

Top-level summary tasks

Critical tasks

Subtasks   *Milestone*

Zoom In

3   On the Standard toolbar, click the Zoom In button three times to better see individual task information in each node.

Note   Depending on your monitor, you might prefer to increase the magnification even more.

Adding and Deleting Nodes

You can create a new node by dragging the mouse on a blank area of the PERT Chart. The ID of the new task will be one greater than the currently selected task. The subsequent tasks are automatically renumbered.

You can also use the Insert Task command on the Insert menu. When you use this command, a new node appears to the right of the selected node. Then you can use the

Layout Now command on the Format menu to align the new node with the existing ones.

To delete a node, you select it and then press DEL or use the Delete command on the Edit menu. If you delete a summary task, the subordinate tasks are also deleted. If you delete a task that has links to other tasks, the relationships are adjusted.

Add a task to the chart

You need to schedule one day to clean up the old office area before the move is complete. Because this task will be easier to accomplish after the old offices are empty, insert a new task after task 31, "Move office furniture/boxes."

1 From the Edit menu, choose Go To.

2 In the ID box, type **31**

3 Choose the OK button.

Task 31 is selected.

4 In an empty area above task 31, drag a rectangle.

A new node appears. The size of the box is automatically formatted the same size as the other boxes. To enter task information, you start typing. The text you enter appears immediately in the entry bar.

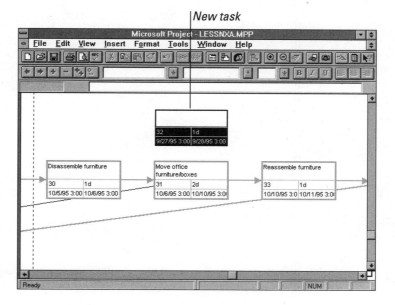

5 Type **Clean old office area**

Because the task has a duration of one day, you don't need to change the default duration.

6   Click the enter button on the entry bar, or press ENTER.

Adding and Deleting Relationships

To create relationships between nodes, you can drag from the predecessor task to the successor task. When you click and drag from *inside* the node, you establish a finish-to-start relationship, with no lag.

To change the relationship type, or add lead or lag time, you double-click the line between the two nodes, and then you enter the new information in the Task Dependency dialog box. You can also delete a dependency in the Task Dependency dialog box.

Assign relationships for the new task

Make "Move office furniture/boxes" the predecessor task to "Clean old office area." "Reassemble furniture" is the successor.

1   Drag the pointer from "Move office furniture/boxes" to "Clean old office area."

A connecting line appears between the two nodes, and the scheduled start and finish dates for "Clean old office area" are now calculated.

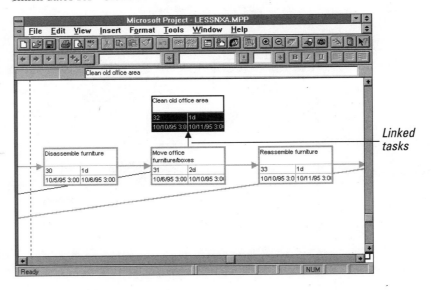

Linked
tasks

2   Click and drag from "Clean old office area" to "Reassemble furniture."

A connecting line appears between the two nodes.

Remove a relationship

Realizing that the "Move office furniture/boxes" task should not be a predecessor for the "Reassemble furniture" task, you can delete the relationship between these two tasks.

1   Double-click the line connecting the two nodes, "Move office furniture/boxes" and "Reassemble furniture."

The Task Dependency dialog box appears.

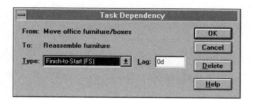

2   In the Task Dependency dialog box, choose the Delete button.

The predecessor relationship is deleted. This part of the PERT Chart looks like the following illustration.

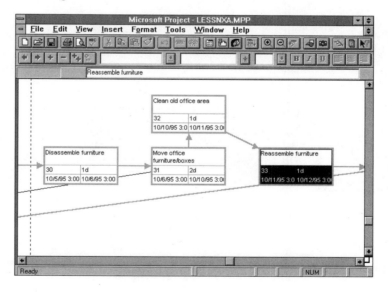

Save the project

Save

▶   On the Standard toolbar, click the Save button. Save the project without a baseline.

Improving the PERT Chart Layout

You can drag a box around a group of nodes to select all of them. To select nodes that are not grouped together, hold down CTRL as you click each one.

By clicking and dragging on a node border, you can place the node where you want it. By holding down SHIFT and then dragging a node, you can move the node and its successors or a summary node and its subordinate tasks. In addition, you can change the fields and border of the nodes in the PERT Chart.

With the Layout Now command on the Format menu, Microsoft Project rearranges the PERT Chart with tasks grouped by outline level.

You can use the Undo Layout command on the Edit menu to restore your previous layout.

Align the new node

To align your new task with others on the critical path, use the Layout Now command. To see the effect of the next steps better, use the Zoom Out command.

Zoom Out

1 On the Standard toolbar, click the Zoom Out button.

2 From the Format menu, choose Layout Now.

   The PERT Chart displays the first task in the project.

3 From the Edit menu, choose Go To.

4 In the ID box, type **32**

5 Choose the OK button.

   Task 32 in the PERT Chart looks like the following illustration.

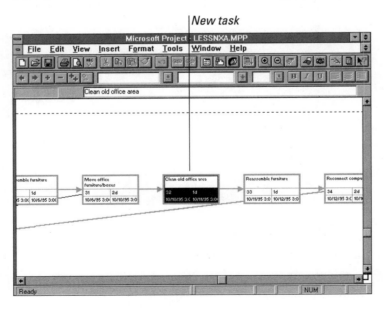

Change the layout options

Use the Layout command on the Format menu to change the appearance of the dependency lines from straight to right-angle.

1   From the Format menu, choose Layout.

The Layout dialog box looks like the following illustration.

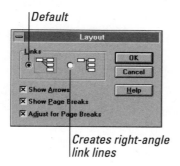

Default

Creates right-angle link lines

2   Under Links, select the option button on the right, indicating that nodes are to be connected with right-angle lines.

3   Choose the OK button.

4   From the View menu, choose Zoom.

5   Select Entire Project.

6   Choose the OK button.

Note the right-angle lines connecting the summary tasks to the noncritical tasks. Your project looks like the following illustration.

Right-angle link lines

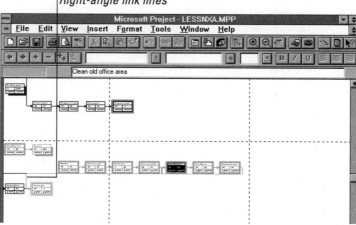

Save

Save the project

▶ On the Standard toolbar, click the Save button. Save the project without a baseline.

Change a field displayed in the nodes

In the Box Styles dialog box, you can change the fields displayed in nodes. In addition to changing any of the five fields displayed, you can change the node size, use gridlines, or display cross marks to indicate progress.

Replace the Scheduled Finish date field with a field to display resource initials. Changes you make affect all nodes in the PERT Chart.

1 On the Standard toolbar, click the Zoom In button three times.

Zoom In

Double-clicking a blank area of the PERT Chart is the same as choosing Box Styles from the Format menu.

2 Double-click a blank area of the PERT Chart.

The Box Styles dialog box appears.

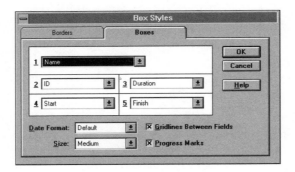

3 Click the down arrow in the box labeled "<u>5</u> Finish" to display the list of field choices.

4 Select Resource Initials from the list.

5 Choose the OK button.

When you add resources to the project and assign them to tasks, the resource name will appear in the lower-right part of the node.

Note   To make the nodes appear smaller, you can also change the number of fields displayed in the nodes. For example, if you do not need to see the start and finish dates for each task, specify that no information appear in the bottom two fields. In addition, you can specify the Smallest (ID only) option in the Size list to display very small node boxes, so that you can see more tasks at once.

Assigning Resources in a PERT Chart

After adding the resource initials field to the fields displayed in nodes, you can assign resources to tasks directly on the PERT Chart. You simply edit the Resource Initials field in the node for the task to which you want a resource assigned.

Assign a resource to a task in the PERT Chart

Because you are going to be involved in selecting the new site, assign yourself as operations manager to this task.

1   From the Edit menu, choose Go To.

2   In the ID box, type **1**

3   Choose the OK button.

4   Click in the lower-right field of task 2.

5   Type **opm**

6   Click the enter button on the entry bar, or press ENTER.

 — *New field*

Using the Task PERT Chart

The Task PERT Chart is a version of the PERT Chart that shows the immediate predecessors and successors of the selected task. The Task PERT Chart displays relationship types, such as finish-to-start (FS) and lead or lag time, next to the connecting lines. By viewing the PERT Chart and the Task PERT Chart together, you can see the project as a whole, as well as the relationships to the selected task. The Task PERT Chart can be especially useful when used with another task view, such as the Task Form.

View task relationships in detail

The Task PERT Chart makes it easy to view all the relationships to a single task and identify relationship types. You can combine the PERT Chart and Task PERT Chart views and note the relationships on the Task PERT Chart in the bottom window when you select different tasks. By increasing the magnification of the PERT Chart in the top view, you can get the big picture and examine details at the same time.

1   Double-click the splitter in the lower-right corner of the view.

The Task Form view appears in the lower half of the view.

2   Click in the Task Form view to make it active.

3 From the View menu, choose More Views.

4 Double-click Task PERT.

In the bottom view, the Task PERT Chart displays the task selected in the PERT Chart, with predecessors to the left and successors to the right.

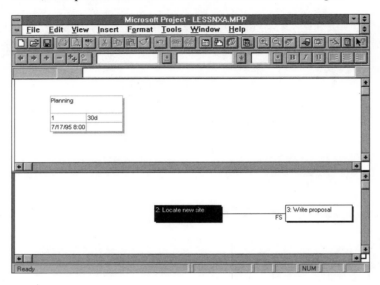

5 Click in the top view to make it active.

Zoom Out

6 On the Standard toolbar, click the Zoom Out button three times.

7 Select different tasks in the PERT Chart, such as task 36, "Move complete."

Observe how the Task PERT Chart changes as you select different tasks.

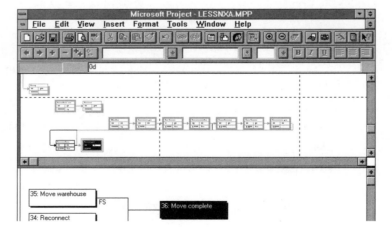

8 Double-click the splitter in the lower-right corner of the top view to return to a full screen view of the PERT Chart.

Save

Save the project

▶ On the Standard toolbar, click the Save button. Save the project without a baseline.

One Step Further

A presentation-quality PERT Chart can help you "sell" your project proposal ideas to others. Adjust the text and borders of the nodes to see how you can improve the look of your PERT Chart.

Format text in nodes

1 From the Format menu, choose Text Styles.

2 In the Item To Change box, select Critical Milestone.

This changes only text in milestones on the critical path.

3 In the Font Style list box, select Bold Italic.

4 Choose the OK button.

Zoom In

5 On the Standard toolbar, click the Zoom In button three times.

Examine the formatting in the critical milestone tasks.

Adjust borders

1 Double-click an empty area of the PERT Chart to open the Box Styles dialog box.

2 Click the Borders tab to make it active.

3 In the Item To Change list box, be sure Critical is selected.

4 In the Style list box, click the down arrow, and then select Marquee.

5 In the Color list box, click the down arrow, and then select any color you want.

6 Choose the OK button.

If You Want to Quit Microsoft Project for Now

1 From the File menu, choose Exit.

2 Choose the Yes button if you see the message box asking whether you want to save your work. Be sure to save without a baseline.

Lesson Summary

To	Do this
View a PERT Chart of the project	From the View menu, choose the PERT Chart command.
Add a task on the PERT Chart	Drag a rectangle in the location where you want the new node to be. Type the text for the node, and then press ENTER.
Assign relationships to tasks on the PERT Chart	Click and drag from inside the predecessor task to the successor task to establish a finish-to-start relationship. You can also double-click a line between two nodes to display the Task Dependency box.
Remove a relationship	Double-click the line connecting the two nodes.
Change the layout of the PERT Chart	From the Format menu, choose the Layout Now command to have Microsoft Project arrange the node by summary and subordinate tasks. Use the Layout command on the Format menu to change the appearance of the connecting lines.
Change the fields in the PERT Chart	Double-click a blank area of the PERT Chart to display the Box Styles dialog box. In the bottom right, click the down arrow to display the list of field choices. Select a field, and then click OK.
Use the PERT Chart to assign resources to tasks	Create a Resource Name or Resource Initials field in the Box Styles dialog box. Then select the field and type in a resource.
Display task predecessors and successors	On the View menu, from the More Views dialog box, choose the Task PERT Chart command.

For more information on	See in *Microsoft Project User's Guide*
PERT Chart	Chapter 9, "Working with Views"
Task PERT Chart	Chapter 9, "Working with Views"

For online information about	From the Help menu, choose Search and then type
Working with the PERT Chart	PERT Chart command
Changing the layout and format of the PERT Chart	PERT boxes: fields PERT boxes: formatting

Using Data From Other Applications

Sometimes information you would like to use in your project is located in another application, such as Microsoft Word or Microsoft Excel. This appendix provides an overview of the different ways in which you can incorporate data from other Windows applications into your project file. In addition to the cutting and pasting techniques you might already know about, you will learn how to use the *OLE* (*Object Linking and Embedding*) features in Microsoft Project to insert data from other applications.

You will learn how to:

- Copy text from the Clipboard into a project file.
- Embed information from another application.
- Link data between applications.

Estimated lesson time: 30 minutes

Start Microsoft Project

If you see the Welcome dialog box, click the Close button. If you see the Tip Of The Day dialog box, read the tip, and then click OK.

If you closed Microsoft Project in the last lesson, you need to restart the application before you can continue.

▶ Double-click the Microsoft Project icon.

Note To complete the activities in this lesson, you will need Word 6 for Windows installed on your computer.

Pasting Text from the Clipboard

One of the easiest ways to include information from another application is to copy text to the Clipboard and paste it into the project file. When you paste text in a project file, Microsoft Project automatically inserts the text as a task (or tasks) and assigns a one-day duration to each task.

For example, while working in Word 6 on a "to do" list in a memo, you realize that you need to include this list of tasks in a project file for an upcoming project. By copying the list of tasks and pasting it in a project file, you can quickly enter the tasks into Microsoft Project without retyping them.

You can use the Copy and Paste commands on the Edit menu, or the Copy and Paste buttons on the Standard toolbar, to copy and paste text from other applications.

Open a Word 6 practice file

Use the practice document file called XB1LESSN.DOC to complete this exercise.

1 Open the Word 6 application.

2 From the File menu, choose Open.

3 In the Directories box, double-click the home directory for Microsoft Project 4, and then double-click PRACTICE.

4 In the File Name box, double-click XB1LESSN.DOC.

Copy text to the Clipboard

1 Select the lines that begin with "Distribute announcements with boxes" and end with "Make coffee."

2 On the Standard toolbar, click the Copy button.

Copy

3 From the File menu, choose Exit.

You can return to this document later. For now, leave the Word 6 application.

4 If you see a message asking whether you want to save any changes to the document, click the No button.

Paste the contents of the Clipboard

When you use the Paste command, Microsoft Project identifies the contents of the Clipboard as text, and inserts the text as tasks in the Gantt table.

Paste

▶ In Microsoft Project, on the Standard toolbar, click the Paste button.

The list of tasks from the memo are inserted as tasks in the Gantt table. Initially, the tasks are not linked and are scheduled to begin on today's date. They each have a one day duration. You can now work with these tasks in the same way you work with other tasks you enter directly into Microsoft Project.

Using Paste Special

The Paste Special command uses a feature that allows you to share information between applications, called *Object Linking and Embedding (OLE)*. If you have copied part of a document onto the Clipboard, and you want to include it in a project file as an object in the chart area of the view (not as text in the task list), you can use the Paste Special command. By using this command, you can insert data that you can later edit with the *source application* (the application in which the data was originally created). By double-clicking the information you insert, you can open the source application and edit what you've inserted. With Paste Special, you can select from the following source types.

Note The source application must be able to support OLE.

- The *application source* option, such as a Word document or Excel spreadsheet, inserts the contents of the Clipboard as an object of the source application type. This option is only available if the original application is still open.

  Objects inserted in Microsoft Project appear in the chart area of the view.

- The *picture* option inserts the contents of the Clipboard as a Paintbrush object in the chart area of the view.

- The *text data* option inserts the contents of the Clipboard as text. Text inserted in a Gantt Chart is inserted in the task list. If you choose the Paste option (rather than Paste Link), you will not be able to edit the inserted data in its source application by double-clicking. Using the Text Data source type and the Paste option has the same effect as choosing the Paste command on the Edit menu or clicking the Paste button.

With the Paste Link option, the contents of the Clipboard are inserted with the source type you specify. If the information in the source file changes, the information you inserted in Microsoft Project is automatically updated to reflect this change. This is called *linking*.

For example, while working on a memo created in Word 6, you create a table of preliminary high and low estimates of costs for catering the moving party. You would like to place this table in your project file. Because the information is likely to change as you receive new bids, you want the latest figures to be reflected in your project file. In addition, you do not want to insert the table as a task, but as an object in the chart area of the view. With the Paste Link option, you can specify that you want to insert the data on the Clipboard as an object.

Note   With the Paste option, the contents of the Clipboard are inserted without linking. This is called *embedding*.

Open a Word 6 practice file

You can use the practice document file called XB2LESSN.DOC to paste link a Word object into a project file.

1   Open the Word 6 application.

2   From the File menu, choose Open.

3   In the Directories box, double-click the home directory for Microsoft Project 4, and then double-click PRACTICE.

4   In the File Name box, double-click XB2LESSN.DOC.

Copy text to the Clipboard

1   Place the insertion point anywhere inside the table at the end of the document.

2   From the Table menu, choose Select Table.

Copy

3 On the Standard toolbar, click the Copy button.

4 Click the Minimize button to minimize the Word application.

The source application must remain open to specify this source application type when you use the Paste Special command in the next step.

Paste and link the contents of the Clipboard

1 Return to Microsoft Project.

2 In Microsoft Project, from the Edit menu choose Paste Special.

The Paste Special dialog box appears. In this dialog box, you can specify the source type and whether or not you want to link to the source application.

Embed Clipboard contents

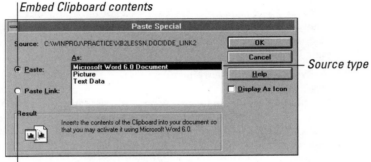

— *Source type*

Link Clipboard contents

3 Click the Paste Link option button.

This option creates a link to the source application, so that your project file is updated whenever the data in the original source file changes.

4 Be sure the Microsoft Word 6 document is selected.

5 Choose the OK button.

The table is inserted in the chart area of the view. The project window looks like the following illustration.

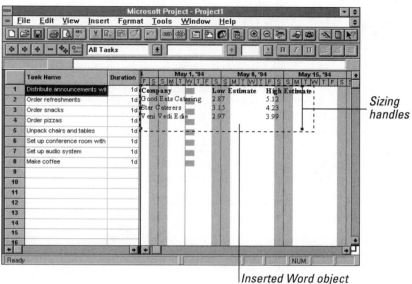

Sizing handles

Inserted Word object

6 Drag the Word object downward and to the right, taking care not to drag a sizing handle, so that the table appears in the lower-right corner of the view.

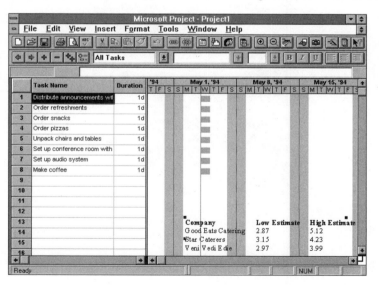

Inserting Files as Objects

When the information you want to include in a project file is not on the Clipboard, you can use the Insert Object command on the Insert menu. With this command, you can create a new object in any application (that supports OLE) installed on your computer, or you can insert an existing file into your project. When you insert an existing file, the entire file is inserted as an object of the source application. You also have the option to link the object to the source file or you can simply embed the file without creating a link to it.

For example, another Word 6 document contains a graphic that you want to use as a logo on the Gantt Chart. With the Insert Object command, you can insert this logo without opening the other document first.

Tip   If you wish to insert only part of a very large file, consider placing the data you wish to insert on the Clipboard, and then use the Paste Special command.

Insert an existing file

Use the practice document file called XB3LESSN.DOC to embed a Word object into a project file.

1   From the Insert menu, choose Object.

The Insert Object dialog box appears. Depending on the applications installed on your computer, the list of applications you see might be different.

Creates a new object

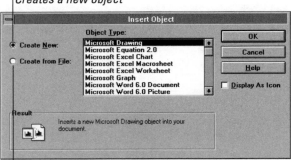

Creates an object from an existing file

2   Click the Create From File option button.

The dialog box looks like the following illustration.

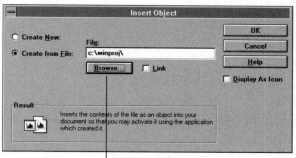

*Displays Open dialog box
to locate and select file*

3 Click the Browse button.

The Browse dialog box appears.

4 In the Directories box, double-click PRACTICE.

5 In the File Name box, double-click XB3LESSN.DOC.

The file name appears in the Insert Object dialog box.

6 Choose the OK button.

Because you did not choose the Link check box, your object is embedded in the
project file. The project file looks like the following illustration.

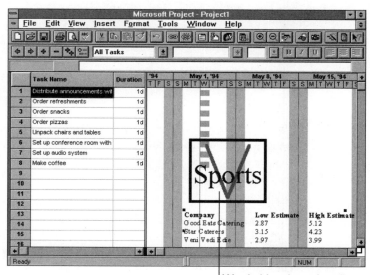

Word object in project file

7 Drag the Word object upward and to the right, taking care not to drag a sizing handle, so that the graphic appears in the upper-right corner of the view.

Edit the object

Edit the object in the source application.

1 Double-click the graphic object.

The Word 6 application window appears, containing the original graphic.

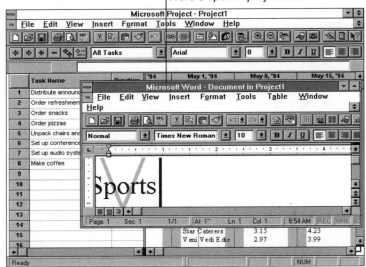

Word 6 open in project file

2 In the graphic, double-click the text "Sports."

You might need to scroll to the the entire graphic.

Italic

3 On the Formatting toolbar, click the Italic button.

4 From the Word application File menu, choose Close And Return To Project.

5 Click the Yes button, if you see a message asking whether you want to save any changes to the document.

You return to Microsoft Project.

6 On the Standard toolbar, click the Save button to save your project file without a baseline.

Save

7 In the Save As dialog box, double-click the PRACTICE directory and name the project file LESSNXB.MPP.

Working With Databases

If project information is stored in a Microsoft Access database file, you can open the file from within Microsoft Project. The Multiple Projects submenu (on the Tools menu) contains the Open From Database and the Save To Database commands. Both of these commands use the Microsoft Access file extension .MBD as the default in their respective dialog boxes. For additional information, see the database topics in online Help.

Quit Microsoft Project for Now

▶ From the File menu, choose Exit.

Be sure to exit the Word application if it is still open.

Lesson Summary

To	Do this
Paste text from the Clipboard (insert tasks in Gantt Chart view)	With selected text on the Clipboard, choose Paste from the Edit menu.
Choose a source type to paste from the Clipboard	With selected text on the Clipboard, choose Paste Special from the Edit menu. Choose the source type, and then click OK.
Link data on the Clipboard to a source file	With selected text on the Clipboard, choose Paste Special from the Edit menu. Click the Paste Link option button, and then choose the source type. Then click OK.
Insert a new object	From the Insert menu, choose Object. Be sure the Create New option button is selected. Select the source application type, and then click OK to create a new object.
Insert an existing file as an object	From the Insert menu, choose Object. Click the Create From File option button. Click the Browse button to locate and select the file. Click OK.
Insert an existing file as an object that is linked to a source file	From the Insert menu, choose Object. Click the Create From File option button. Click the Browse button to locate and select the file. Click the Link check box, and then click OK.

For more information on	See in *Microsoft Project User's Guide*
Copying information from other applications	Chapter 14, "Copying and Moving Information "
Linking project information to other applications	Chapter 15, "Linking and Embedding Objects"

For online information about	From the <u>H</u>elp menu, choose <u>S</u>earch and then type
OLE	OLE
Embedding	embedding
Linking	linking
Databases	database

Using Sample Templates

There are eight sample templates included with Microsoft Project. These templates contain standard tasks and custom features designed to facilitate managing a specific kind of project for a variety of industries. You can use a template as a starting point for creating and organizing your projects. Simply select the template that most closely matches the kind of project you are starting. After you open any of the templates, you create a copy of the template, so you can customize it and create a project file to suit your needs without affecting the original template. This appendix provides a brief description of all the sample templates.

You can use the TemplateWizard to customize templates. For information, open TMPLTWIZ.WRI in your Microsoft Project home directory with the Write program in the Accessories group in Microsoft Windows.

The sample templates are stored in the LIBRARY subdirectory of your Microsoft Project home directory.

Template name	Description
AUDIT.MPT	Contains standard tasks performed for a financial audit. The plan includes the following top-level tasks: Audit Planning, Preliminary Analysis, Audit Activities, Reviews, and Statement Preparation. The Audit table helps you enter and compare budgeted work and the prior year's hours.
EVENTPLN.MPT	Contains the plan for a special event, such as company party, announcement, or wedding. The plan includes the following top-level tasks: Pre-Planning, Event Preparation, and Event Wrap-Up.
LANINST.MPT	Contains the steps for installing a Local Area Network. This template includes a set of Cue Cards describing each phase of the plan. The Cue Cards provide general suggestions for customizing the plan for your own projects. The Cue Cards open automatically when you open this template. Minimize the Cue Cards if you don't want to see them right away. These Cue Cards are located in LANINST.HLP if you need to access them again.
LANSUB.MPT	The subproject for task 2, "Project Start-up" in LANINST.MPT. It includes a more detailed list of the tasks involved for that phase of installing a LAN.
MKTPLAN.MPT	Provides an outline of steps for a marketing project. The plan includes the following top-level tasks: conducting a marketing survey, drafting the marketing plan, and preparing the advertising campaign.

Template name	Description
ROLLOUT.MPT	Contains a plan for rolling out software products for an organization. The plan outlines the steps for an MIS department to perform the following top-level tasks: evaluating and testing new software, installing and supporting the new software, and training users.
ROLLUP.MPT	Contains a specially formatted template that displays subtask dates in the Gantt bars of the summary tasks.
SOFTDEV.MPT	Contains a plan for developing software. The plan includes details for the following top-level tasks: Requirement Planning, Preliminary Design, Detailed Design, Programming and Testing, Integration Testing, System Testing, Installation, and Operations and Maintenance. This template also includes a set of Cue Cards that describes each phase of the project. The Cue Cards provide general suggestions for customizing the plan for your own projects. The Cue Cards open automatically when you open this template. Minimize the Cue Cards if you don't want to see them right away. These Cue Cards are located in SOFTDEV.HLP if you need to access them again.

Open a sample template

1 Open Microsoft Project.

2 From the File menu, choose Open.

If Cue Cards appear, you can minimize them to see more of your project. If you close them, you cannot access them again unless you reopen the template.

3 In the Directories list, double-click LIBRARY.

The LIBRARY subdirectory is located in your Microsoft Project directory.

4 From the File Name list, double-click the template you want to use.

5 From the File menu, choose Save.

By default, Microsoft Project saves your project file with the name of the template and the file extension .MPP. You can specify a new name for your project file or you can select Template for the Save File As Type list to create a new template based on the template that is currently open.

Glossary

accrual method A process that determines whether the cost for a resource is incurred at the start or end of a task, or whether the cost is prorated during the task.

actual data A term that refers to either the project dates or the project costs for tasks that have begun based on data you provide.

baseline plan The original project plan you set after establishing the basics of the plan. You measure the project's progress against the baseline.

calendars The specifications of the days and hours that resources—people and equipment—are available to work. The base calendar applies to all the resources in the project. Resource calendars apply to specific resources.

collapsing In an outlined project, the process of hiding a subtask under a *summary task* so that only the summary task appears.

combination view A view in which one view appears in the top part of the window and another view appears in the bottom part of the window. The view in the bottom part displays detailed information for the task or resource you select in the top part.

consolidation A feature with which you can combine information from multiple projects.

constraints Schedule restrictions placed on individual tasks that affect task start and finish dates.

cost accrual The designation for how costs are assigned to a task. Costs can accrue at the start of the task or when the task finishes. They can also be prorated, accruing costs as work progresses.

critical path The sequence of *critical tasks* in a project.

Critical Path Method (CPM) The process for determining the start and finish dates for individual tasks, creating a *critical path* for the project.

critical tasks Tasks that, if delayed, would result in the delay of the project. Similarly, if the duration of one or more critical tasks is reduced, the project finishes early. Critical tasks are on the *critical path*.

date line A dashed vertical line in the Gantt Chart representing either the current date according to your computer's system clock, or the current date entered on the Project tab of the Summary Info dialog box.

demoting In an outlined project, the process of indenting a task to show a hierarchical relationship to the task above in the task list.

divider In a chart view, the vertical bar separating the table area from the graphic area of the view. By dragging the divider, you can adjust the size of each part of the view.

duration The amount of time required to complete a task. A duration can be measured in working time (nonworking time is not included) or in elapsed time (includes working and nonworking time).

entry bar The area below the toolbar in which the information you type appears. When you press the enter button in the bar the information in the entry bar is entered into the project. Pressing the cancel button in the entry bar leaves the project unchanged. When the information you can enter is limited to specific options, you can click the down arrow in the entry bar to select from a list of options.

expanding In an outlined project, the process that makes visible all the detail tasks below a *summary task*.

field An area in a table or form in which specific information about an individual task or resource is entered and displayed. For example, in a sheet view, the fields are aligned in columns with the field name displayed at the top of the column.

filter A tool that searches through your project to find tasks or resources that match the criteria you set. The tasks or resources that match your criteria are listed or highlighted, so you can focus on the specific information.

fixed costs Costs that remain constant no matter how long the task requires.

fixed-duration scheduling A type of scheduling in which a specific task duration is independent of resource work. With fixed-duration scheduling, the number of resources has no effect on how long a task takes.

footer Text that appears at the bottom of every printed page of a view or report.

Gantt Chart A graphical representation of the project schedule, containing Gantt bars that represent tasks. The length of a bar corresponds to the task duration.

global template A file that contains the default and customized features you can use in Microsoft Project including views, tables, reports, filters, toolbars, menus, and macros. It also contains the settings specified with the Options command. The global template in Microsoft Project is called GLOBAL.MPT.

header Text that appears at the top of every printed page of a view or report.

lag time The amount of delay between the completion of one task and the start of its successor.

lead time The amount of overlap between the completion of one task and the start of its successor.

legend A graphical representation of the meaning of the symbols and patterns used in a printed view.

leveling The process of resolving overallocated resource conflicts. Automatic leveling introduces delays between tasks to prevent overallocation. *See also* resource leveling.

linking The process by which a task sequence is established. The line that links the Gantt bars of linked tasks is called the link line.

milestone A task that represents the completion of a major achievement, phase, or measurable goal. A milestone has a duration of zero (0d).

organizer A tabbed dialog box you use to copy and delete custom features to other project files, such as views, tables, reports, calendars, forms, and collections of macros.

outline A format option in the Gantt Chart view in which a hierarchical structure is established for the project. In an outlined project, detail tasks (*subtasks*) are indented under higher-level, general tasks (*summary tasks*).

overallocation The result of assigning more tasks to a resource than can be accomplished in the working time available. Peak usage of the resource exceeds the maximum number of units of the resource.

PERT chart A graphical representation of the relationships between tasks in which tasks are represented as boxes containing task information.

plan data A term that refers to either the project dates or the project costs based on the original plan before the project schedule is in effect.

predecessor A task that must precede another task.

promoting In an outlined project, the process that moves a detail task to a higher level by outdenting it.

recurring task A task that occurs at regular intervals in a project, such as a weekly meeting or a monthly inspection.

report A formatted collection of information organized to provide project data related to a specific area of concern in the project. Report types include Overview, Current Activity, Cost, Assignment, and Workload. You can also design custom reports to display the information you want.

resource-driven scheduling A type of scheduling in which the duration, start dates, and finish dates of a task are determined by the number and allocation of resources.

resources The people, groups of people, material, equipment, or facilities required to complete a task. The names of all the resources used in a project are stored in the *resource pool.*

resource leveling The process of resolving resource conflicts by ensuring that peak usage of a resource never exceeds the maximum available amount of that resource.

scheduled data A term that refers to either the project dates or the project costs for future tasks, based on data provided by the user after the project schedule is in effect.

subproject A project linked to another project by a common task. With subprojects, you can break up a large project file into smaller, more manageable project files.

subtasks A detail task that is subordinate to a *summary task.*

successor A task that follows another task.

summary tasks General headings with subordinate tasks (*subtasks*) indented below them. Summary tasks provide an outline structure that identifies the project's major phases. Each level of indenting represents an additional level of detail for the task.

tasks The steps in a project.

template A Microsoft Project file format upon which you can base future projects. Standard task and resource information, as well customized settings and formatting in the template, are included in any project file that is based on the template.

timescale The units of time that represent the displayed project schedule. The timescale contains two units of measurement: the *major* timescale and the *minor* timescale. The major and minor timescales are paired in combinations, such as Months over Weeks, Weeks over Days, and Days over Hours.

unit A single resource assigned to a task.

variable costs Costs that increase as the task progresses.

view Any of the various presentation formats that are used to enter and display project information. In combination views, the top part of the screen contains one view, while the bottom part of the screen contains another.

wizards Intelligent online assistants that monitor the selections you make as you work with Microsoft Project. Wizards provide useful tips, suggestions, or prompts related to your current activity.

workspace A set of project files (and their views and settings) that can be opened all at one time.

Index

W

Weekly To-do List report, 180–82
what-if scenarios, 103–4
Windows. *See* Microsoft Windows
windows. *See also* views
 closing, xxv
 moving, xxiv
 open, 154–55
 resizing, xxiv
 splitting, xxiv
wizards, xxxiii, 308
Word for Windows. *See* Microsoft Word
workdays, changing, 92–93
working hours
 changing, 94–95
 displaying totals, 107
 increasing to shorten critical path, 232–33
Workload report category, 178
workspace
 creating, 156–57
 defined, 308
 opening, 163
 saving, 156–57
Work table
 applying to Gantt Chart view, 107
 applying to Task Sheet view, 195–96, 223

Z

Zoom command, 287
Zoom In button, 143, 149, 288
Zoom Out button, 61, 149, 286

Running Microsoft® Software
With Bestselling Books

Running Word 6 for Windows™
Russell Borland

Master the power and features of Microsoft Word for Windows—
version 6.0—with this updated edition of the bestselling guide for
intermediate to advanced users. This example-rich guide contains scores of
insights and power tips not found in the documentation and includes
in-depth, accessible coverage on Word's powerful new features.

832 pages, softcover $29.95 ($39.95 Canada)   ISBN 1-55615-574-3

Running Microsoft® Excel 5 for Windows™
The Cobb Group with Mark Dodge,
Chris Kinata, and Craig Stinson

Here's the most comprehensive and accessible book for all
levels of spreadsheet users. It includes hundreds of tips and practical
shortcuts for using the powerful new features of Microsoft Excel 5
for Windows. In addition to the step-by-step tutorials, straightforward
examples, and expert advice, this updated edition features a new
and improved format designed to help you find answers faster!

1184 pages, softcover $29.95 ($39.95 Canada)   ISBN 1-55615-585-9

Running Microsoft Access® 2
for Windows™
John L. Viescas

Here is the best source of information on Microsoft Access for
all levels. Packed with winning tips, notes, and strategies, this complete
and thorough tutorial runs you through all the ins and outs of data access,
the program's powerful tools, and its robust development environment.
The bound-in disk includes a fully functional database that illustrates
the examples in the book, as well as additional sample databases
that show you efficient table designs for common applications.

944 pages, softcover with one 3.5-inch disk
$39.95 ($53.95 Canada)   ISBN 1-55615-592-1

MicrosoftPress

Train Yourself
With *Step by Step* books from Microsoft Press

The *Step by Step* books are the perfect self-paced training solution for Microsoft Office users. Each book comes with a disk that contains every example in the book. By using the practice files and following instructions in the book, you can "learn by doing," which means you can start applying what you've learned to business situations right away. Build the computer skills you need with the *Step by Step* books from Microsoft Press.

Microsoft® Excel 5 for Windows™
Step by Step
Catapult, Inc.
368 pages, softcover with one 3.5-inch disk
$29.95 ($39.95 Canada)   ISBN 1-55615-587-5

Microsoft Access® 2 for Windows™
Step by Step
Catapult, Inc.
344 pages, softcover with one 3.5-inch disk
$29.95 ($39.95 Canada)   ISBN 1-55615-593-X

Microsoft® PowerPoint® 4 for Windows™
Step by Step, 2nd ed.
Perspection, Inc.
350 pages, softcover with one 3.5-inch disk
$29.95 ($39.95 Canada)   ISBN 1-55615-622-7

Microsoft® Word 6 for Windows™
Step by Step
Catapult, Inc.
336 pages, softcover with one 3.5-inch disk
$29.95 ($39.95 Canada)   ISBN 1-55615-576-X

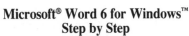
MicrosoftPress

The Step by Step Companion Disk

The enclosed 3.5-inch disk contains timesaving, ready-to-use practice files that complement the lessons in this book. To use the practice files, you'll need the Microsoft® Windows™ operating system version 3.1 or later, MS-DOS® version 5.0 or later, and Microsoft Project version 4 for Windows.

Each *Step by Step* lesson is closely integrated with the practice files on the disk. Before you begin the *Step by Step* lessons, we highly recommend that you read the "Getting Ready" section of the book and install the practice files on your hard disk. As you work through each lesson, be sure to follow the instructions for renaming the practice files so that you can go through a lesson more than once if you need to.

Please take a few moments to browse the License Agreement on the previous page before using the enclosed disk.